Safeguarding Children with the Children Act 1989

Studies in Evaluating the Children Act 1989

Series editors:
Dr Carolyn Davies, Prof. Jane Aldgate

STUDIES IN EVALUATING THE CHILDREN ACT 1989

Safeguarding Children
with the Children Act 1989

Marian Brandon
June Thoburn
Ann Lewis
Ann Way

School of Social Work, University of East Anglia

London: The Stationery Office

First published 1999

ISBN 0 11 322174 6

Published by The Stationery Office and available from:

The Publications Centre
(mail, telephone and fax orders only)
PO Box 276, London SW8 5DT
Telephone 0870 600 5522
Fax orders 0870 600 5533

The Stationery Office Bookshops
123 Kingsway, London WC2B 6PQ
0171 242 6393 Fax 0171 242 6394
68–69 Bull Street, Birmingham B4 6AD
0121 236 9696 Fax 0121 236 9699
33 Wine Street, Bristol BS1 2BQ
0117 926 4306 Fax 0117 929 4515
9–21 Princess Street, Manchester M60 8AS
0161 834 7201 Fax 0161 833 0634
16 Arthur Street, Belfast BT1 4GD
01232 238451 Fax 01232 235401
The Stationery Office Oriel Bookshop
18-19 High Street, Cardiff CF1 2BZ
01222 395548 Fax 01222 384347
71 Lothian Road, Edinburgh EH3 9AZ
0131 228 4181 Fax 0131 622 7017

The Stationery Office's Accredited Agents
(see Yellow Pages)

and through good booksellers

Printed in the United Kingdom for The Stationery Office
J82400 6/99 C12 431208 19585

Contents

Figures and tables

Figures

Tables

Foreword

The Children Act 1989 was implemented on 14 October 1991. At its launch the then Lord Chancellor, Lord Mackay, described the Act as 'the most radical legislative reform to children's services this century'. Shortly after the launch the Department of Health put together a strategy to monitor and evaluate the initial impact of the Act. Taking a tripartite approach, this drew on evidence from statistical returns, inspections and research to develop a rounded appreciation of early implementation. The subsequent strategy plan was published and circulated to relevant bodies, including social services and the major voluntary agencies, in 1993. This plan formed the backcloth for a programme of research studies commissioned by the Department of Health to explore early evaluation in more depth. It is these studies, some 20 in all, which form this new series.

The programme studies investigate the implementation of key changes introduced by the Act and evaluate the facilitators and inhibitors to the meeting of key objectives. A longer-term goal of the programme is to review the aims of the Act in the light of implementation with a view to reconsideration or amendment should this be felt necessary. Finally, a more general and important scientific aim is to consider how far change could be achieved successfully by changing the law.

There are several principles underlying the Children Act 1989 that permeate the research studies. An important strand of the Act is to bring together private and public law so that the needs of all children whose welfare is at risk might be approached in the same way. This philosophy is underpinned by the principle of promoting children's welfare. There should be recognition of children's time-scales and, in court cases, children's welfare should be paramount. To aid this paramountcy principle there should be a welfare checklist and delays in court hearings should be avoided.

The promotion of children's welfare takes a child development focus, urging local authorities to take a holistic and corporate approach to providing services. Departments such as health, education, housing, police, social services and recreation should work together to respond to children's needs. Children, the Act argues, are best looked after within their families wherever possible and, where not, the continuing support of parents and wider kin should be facilitated by avoiding compulsory proceedings whenever possible. Parents should be partners in any intervention process, and children's views should be sought and listened to in any decision-making affecting their lives. To promote continuity for children looked after, contact with families should be encouraged and children's religion, culture, ethnicity and language should be preserved.

Local authorities have a duty to move from services to prevent care to a broader remit of providing family support, which could include planned periods away from home. However, family support services should not be universal but target those most in need. The introduction of Children's Services Plans in 1996 has made the idea of corporate responsibility a more tangible reality and seeks to help local authorities look at how they may use scarce resources cost-effectively.

The themes of the Children Act have relevance for the millennium. The concern with combating social exclusion is echoed through several of the studies, especially those on family support and young people looked after by local authorities. The value of early intervention is also a theme in the studies on family centres, day care and services for children defined as 'in need' under the Act. Further, the research on the implementation of the Looking After Children Schedules emphasises the importance to children in foster and residential care of attaining good outcomes in education. Lastly, attending to the health of parents and their children is another strand in both the family support and 'children looked after' studies.

To accompany the 20 individual studies in the research programme the Department of Health has commissioned an overview of the findings, to be published by The Stationery Office in the style of similar previous publications from HMSO: *Social Work Decisions in Child Care 1985*; *Patterns and Outcomes in Child Care 1991*; *Child Protection: Messages from Research 1996*; and *Focus on Teenagers 1997*.

The editors would like to express their appreciation to the members of the research community; professionals from different disciplines, and service users, among others, who have contributed so willingly and generously to the successful completion of the research studies and to the construction of the overview. Without their help, none of the research would have been written or disseminated.

Carolyn Davies
Jane Aldgate

Acknowledgements

This report could not have been written if the parents, children, social workers, other professional workers, social service administrators and managers had not been so generous with their time. We are grateful to them for their patience in helping us to understand the meaning of 'significant harm' and make sense of the way in which the changes brought about by the Children Act 1989 were being implemented.

The research was commissioned and funded by the Department of Health and we thank especially Dr Carolyn Davies of the Research and Development Division for steering us through from the proposal stage to its completion. She chaired the advisory group whose members we also thank for their time, advice and probing questions. They were Rosemary Arkley, Jenny Gray and Kathleen Taylor of the Department of Health; and academic and professional colleagues: Prof. Jane Aldgate, Jane Gibbons, Joan Hunt, Dr Rosalyn Proops, and Prof. Jane Tunstill. They have all, in different ways, made a contribution to this report, but the faults and omissions are ours and the opinions expressed are not necessarily those of the Department of Health.

In Norwich, colleagues and students at the University of East Anglia have provided encouragement and helpful suggestions, and members of the Norfolk Families in Care Group have helped us to pilot the research instruments and information for families. Jacquie White's patient advice and practical help with data analysis has been, as ever, invaluable. Important team members during the interview phase of the research were Val Lewars and Harvinder Gataora who helped us to understand some of the issues around cultural difference and racism. It is to Harvinder that we owe the fact that a South-Asian perspective is well represented in our research. We also thank Betty Rathbone, formerly of the Bethel Child and Family Centre for helping with the interpretation of the data that emerged from the observation and play sessions with the younger children.

Once more we express our gratitude to Anne Borrett and Heather Cutting for creating order out of our disordered disks and jottings. Dan Edwards and Mark Barton typed in the data and we thank them for their accuracy and good humour. Finally, our thanks go to our families for their patience and encouragement.

Marian Brandon
June Thoburn
Ann Lewis
Ann Way

University of East Anglia

1 The concept of significant harm

In his autobiography, the children's writer Roald Dahl describes a visit to the doctor, when he was 8 years old (Dahl 1984, p. 70). He was asked to open his mouth and, with a few deft flicks of a blade, his adenoids were removed without anaesthetic:

> Out of my mouth into the basin came tumbling a whole mass of flesh and blood. I was too shocked and outraged to do anything but yelp. I was horrified by the huge red lumps that had fallen out of my mouth into the white basin and my first thought was that the doctor had cut out the whole of the middle of my head.

Not only had Dahl's mother requested this operation, she also made the boy walk home afterwards: 'No trolley-car or taxi. We walked the full half-hour journey back to my grandparents' house.' (p. 70)

Mrs Dahl, a loving mother, was acting as a reasonable parent would be expected to behave in Norway in 1924. The event could, however, have caused lasting harm to Dahl's emotional development (not to mention the risks of physical harm from infection) and, importantly, he could have lost trust in his mother. He learned to fear doctors but lasting harm did not apparently arise from this operation: Dahl did not sustain an infection and there were other occasions when his mother, if not the doctors, was able to win back his trust. More harm seemed to ensue from the repeated beatings throughout his school career. At boarding school there was no loving family to console him or explain the strange rituals that accompanied the beatings. For another child from a less caring or hostile family, or even a sibling of Dahl's with a different temperament, the effects of this brutal operation might have been a degree of long-term emotional damage. Dahl himself does not emerge unscathed from childhood. Arguably, his writing does reflect a world in which children are troubled and struggle to overcome the harm inflicted on them by parents and other adults. Yet the events surrounding the incident at the doctor's would not, at the time, have been understood as acts of abuse or maltreatment. The operation and the brusqueness with which it was performed were intended to do the young boy good. The illustration demonstrates that what is acceptable behaviour towards children, by parents and others, is socially defined, historically located, and changeable.

The context of decisions about significant harm

Since the term 'significant harm' first appeared in discussion papers leading to the Children Act 1989 its meaning has been much debated by academics and practitioners working in the family justice field. The move from using the term 'abuse' (the maltreatment of a child by parents or others) to the term 'harm' (the impact the maltreatment has on a child) appears, at first sight, to require a consideration of the extent to which the abusive behaviour in the given circumstances actually harms, or can be shown to be highly likely to harm, the child. However, Section 31(9) of the Act defines harm as 'ill-treatment' as well as 'impairment of health or development'. The link between ill-treatment and harm is found in Volume 1 of the *Regulations and Guidance* (Department of Health (DoH) 1991a). Since the implementation of the Act in October 1991, the meaning of significant harm has been further interpreted by the courts.

Lynch (1992) has drawn attention to the changes in what might be called the language of child care practice over recent years, which reflect a change in emphasis: for example, from child welfare to child protection; from prevention to detection; from suspicion to investigation and enquiry; and from professional judgement to 'have I followed the procedures?'

Cooper (1993, p. 1) demonstrates how Gil's broad definition of child abuse constructed in 1979, like the Children Act 1989, mentions the term 'significant harm' and also anticipates the terms 'future' or 'likely' significant harm:

> Child abuse is a significant harm done or anticipated to a child as a result
> of human action. That action may be intentional or reckless and inflicted
> by individuals, groups, agencies or the state.

Bentovim's description of the concept (in Adcock and White 1991, p. 29), and more recently the working definition of the National Society for the Prevention of Cruelty to Children (NSPCC) commission of inquiry into the prevention of child abuse (Creighton 1995), are similarly broad and include societal fault as well as parental failure. Significant harm can be thought of as:

> a compilation of significant events, both acute and long-standing, which
> interact with the child's ongoing development, and interrupt, alter, or impair
> physical and psychological development. Being the victim of significant harm

is likely to have a profound effect on a child's view of themself [sic] as a person, and on their future lives. Significant harm represents a major symptom of failure of adaptation by parents to their role, and involves both the family and society.

Legal interpretation of terms

The term 'significant harm' appears in Parts IV and V of the Act as the first of the threshold criteria for making a Care or Supervision Order – the threshold for emergency intervention. Section 31(a) in Part IV requires that the child must be 'suffering' or 'likely to suffer' significant harm. Section 31(b) links such harm to deficits in parental care or control.

If both of the threshold criteria are met and the court is satisfied there is no better way of safeguarding and promoting the child's welfare, a finding of significant harm or its likelihood can, as Hoggett (1993, p. 180) notes:

> form the first link in the chain of reasoning which can lead to a Care or Supervision Order to give longer-term protection to the child.

In this way the threshold criteria also act as the test that has to be overcome to allow compulsory measures of care, and indeed state intervention in family life. As Masson (1994, p. 171) claims:

> The balance between the family and the state depends largely on the interpretation of the significant harm test.

The term 'harm'

Harm, meaning 'ill-treatment or the impairment of health or development' is further defined by Section 31(9):

> 'Development' means physical, intellectual, emotional, social or behavioural development; 'health' means physical or mental health; and 'ill-treatment' includes sexual abuse and forms of ill-treatment which are not physical.

Freeman (1992, p. 105) claims that ill-treatment could be said to include emotional abuse but points out that neglect is absent from this list and is not specifically mentioned in Section 31. He suggests:

> It would surely now be regarded either as 'ill-treatment' or the impairment of health or development.

Masson and Morris (1992) warn that lasting emotional damage, in the absence of impairment to health and development, may be hard to prove. They claim it is likely that there will be increased emphasis on medical and psychological evidence to establish significant harm, particularly the emotional damage that may follow from abuse.

The case of Re H (White 1996) emphasises the problems for the local authority of establishing the threshold conditions in cases of sexual abuse, where there is little evidence beyond that offered by the child. In Re H, the child's evidence was rejected by criminal proceedings and the stepfather found not guilty of sexually abusing the girl over a period of years. The standard of proof required in care proceedings is the balance of probability, which in sexual abuse cases is a difficult test to argue. In Re H, Lord Nicholls held that the more serious the allegation, the less likely it was that the event had occurred and, hence, the stronger should be the evidence needed for the court to conclude that the allegation was established.

In terms of 'likely harm', the House of Lords (White 1996, p. 52) took the view that the word 'likely' was being used in the sense of:

> a real possibility that cannot be sensibly ignored having regard to the nature and gravity of the feared harm in the particular case, rather than in the sense of more likely than not.

In deciding that the threshold had been crossed it was noted that a broad range of facts could be taken into account. Lord Nicholls determined that the threshold for a Care Order was that the child is suffering significant harm or that there is a real possibility that he or she will do so. This threshold was comparatively low but did require proof of the relevant facts. It was open to the court to conclude that there was a real possibility of harm in the future, although harm in the past had not been established.

A likely consequence of this ruling is that local authorities will have to be more meticulous in finding corroborative evidence to bring care proceedings. This may mean a further proliferation of expert reports.

The case of Nottinghamshire County Council and P (Current Law Yearbook 1993, pp. 851–2) raises further issues about gaps in protective provision offered by the Act. In this case it was found that the courts were powerless to intervene if a local authority refused to initiate care proceedings.

The term 'significant'

Before the implementation of the Children Act, the *Review of Child Care Law* (DoH 1985) offered some explanation of the meaning of significant harm and emphasised the importance of substantial deficit:

> Having set an acceptable standard of upbringing for the child, it should
> be necessary to show some substantial deficit in that standard. Minor
> shortcomings in the health and care provided or minor deficits in physical,
> psychological or social developments should not give rise to any compulsory
> intervention unless they are having, or are likely to have, serious and lasting
> effects upon the child. (para 15.15)

'Significant', however, is not defined in the Act. Volume 1 of the *Guidance* quotes the dictionary definition of 'considerable, noteworthy or important' (DoH 1991a, para. 3(9)). Freeman (1992) maintains this is a lesser standard than either 'serious' or 'severe'. Where the harm is 'ill-treatment', significant is not defined:

> Ill-treatment is sufficient proof of harm in itself and it is not necessary to show
> that impairment of health or development has followed, or is likely to follow.
> (Vol. 1, para. 3.19)

Yet the same paragraph goes on to say that significance can exist in 'the seriousness of the harm or in the implications of it' (Vol. 1, para 3.19). Masson and Morris (1992) interpret this statement as meaning that ill-treatment may be significant because of:

♦ its seriousness, for example a fractured skull;

♦ the effects upon the child, for example an eye injury for a partially sighted child; or

♦ the nature of the incident, for example throwing a baby (who would be more vulnerable than an older child) even if no injury occurred.

They also claim that reliance may be placed on the likelihood of further significant injuries when there has been a series of apparently insignificant ones. Freeman (1992, p. 103) uses the example of corporal punishment:

> Too many of the notorious child-death cases are exercises of discipline which
> have gone badly wrong. Parents who use physical punishment excessively
> should be sounding warning bells to those engaged in the protection of
> children.

Since we know, however, that large numbers of children are physically chastised by their parents even in the 1990s (Smith et al. in Dartington Social Research Unit 1995), discriminating between 'normal', if undesirable, behaviour, and the build up of behaviour that is excessive or could become 'significant' is no easy task.

The particular child

Studies on developmental outcomes for children who have experienced abuse (Dartington Social Research Unit 1995; Gibbons et al. 1995b) broadly indicate styles of parenting that are harmful to children:

> Physical abuse was, in some cases, an important 'marker' for continuing adverse conditions, including most importantly a harshly punitive, less reliable and less warmly involved style of parenting . . . A physical assault (even if serious), in the absence of serious family problems and a coercive style of parenting, is less likely to have long-term consequences. (Gibbons et al. 1995b, p. 175)

Within these broad indicators there is also evidence that individual children will respond differently to similar events and lifestyles. What is significantly harmful to one child may not damage another. With this in mind, the Act requires the harm a child might be suffering to be compared to that of a similar child:

> Where the question of whether the harm suffered by a child is significant turns on the child's health and development, his health or development shall be compared to that which could be reasonably expected of a similar child. (Section 31(10))

Masson and Morris (1992) and Barton and Douglas (1995) agree that the Act is closest to defining significant harm in this subsection. Constructing a hypothetical 'similar child' provides some point of comparison. Where possible, like should be compared with like, thus the development of a child with a known disability, should not be compared with that of a child without a similar disability. Barton and Douglas (1995, p. 317) argue that there are problems in determining the extent to which this hypothetical child could be wrought: 'Does one have to control for every variable?' Freeman (1992, p. 103) argues:

> it is necessary to look at *this* child in the context of *this* home: abuse in one context is not necessarily abuse in another.

He is not advocating unquestioning cultural relativism but acknowledges the importance of culture in understanding what might be harmful to children, and what might not:

> But what is 'significant' must depend in part upon what is expected and different cultures have different expectations of acceptable child-rearing behaviour. (p. 103)

Parenting

When adjudicating on significant or likely significant harm, a court must be satisfied that the cause of the harm is linked to deficits in parental care or control.

Reasonable parenting must be matched to the needs of the particular child. Some children will be harder to parent than others. Children with chronic illnesses or disabilities may require a higher standard of parental care and vigilance. Children with emotional and behavioural difficulties will provide challenges to parents, irrespective of the cause of the problems. Volume 1 of the *Guidance* (DoH 1991a) makes clear that the local authority has a responsibility to offer assistance under Part III and Schedule 2 'which would be likely to improve the situation sufficiently' (para. 3.11) to help parents become 'reasonable'.

The Dartington Social Research Unit (1995) emphasised that a style of parenting 'low on warmth and high on criticism' is likely to be harmful to children. Rutter and his colleagues (1990b, p. 151) detail the types of parenting, which have a high risk of promoting mental ill health in childhood or adulthood, that could be said to be likely to lead to significant harm. These include changing and inconsistent care-giving, with mothers and fathers moving in and out of a child's life; family discord and quarrelling; and hostility and blame directed at the child.

The capacity of parents to provide adequate parenting may be closely tied to their own experiences and preoccupations. Bowlby (1988, p. 48) described parents of difficult, unhappy or anxious children as those who were:

> Insensitive to their children's signals, perhaps because they are preoccupied and worried about other things, who ignore their children, or interfere with them in an arbitrary way, or simply reject them.

Waterhouse et al. (1993) produced evidence to suggest that lack of discipline and control, as well as too much of it, is significantly harmful to children. The research of Gibbons et al. (1995a) identified 'vulnerability indicators' for children included on Child Protection Registers. For these children a parent figure was found to have at least two of the following factors: an involvement in substance abuse, a criminal record, mental illness, or violence to or from a partner. Parental sensitivity to an individual child will influence the kind of relationship a parent and child establish (Brandon and Lewis 1996). In the poor psycho-social environments described by Gibbons et al. (1995a) and Rutter et al. (1990b) it is obviously harder for adults to be successful parents.

The timing of significant harm: the child, the family and the state

Case law has clarified the debate about the timing of significant harm. Legal commentators (Masson 1994; Hayes 1995) have called into question the extent to which the courts have used their role. Hayes suggests (p. 887) the House of Lords ruling in the case of Re M:

> has shifted the emphasis of the provisions in the Children Act 1989 away from their orientation in favour of assisting families and towards the authorisation of state intervention in family life.

During the data collection period of this study, the case of Re M was being heard, first by Justice Bracewell, then by the Court of Appeal and finally the House of Lords. The matter under consideration was whether baby M, who was 4 months old when he witnessed his father brutally murder his mother, should be made the subject of a Care Order and placed for adoption (the choice of the father and guardian ad litem) or live with his three half-siblings and his mother's cousin, Mrs W, under a Residence Order (the local authority's choice).

The outcome was that the baby remained with his relatives on a Care Order, and many of the judgements relate to the unusual circumstances of the particular case. The principles arising from the judgements, however, concern the timing of significant harm and the role of the courts in the 'social engineering' of family life, where relatives are offering to care for a child.

The decision made by the House of Lords in this case was that the relevant date for the timing of significant harm was the point at which the local authority initiated procedures for protection. The child protection legislation in the Children Act 1989, intended to provide a proper balance between the family and the state, also ensures that the family is free from unwarranted intervention (Thoburn 1991a; Masson 1994). Critics of the Re M ruling claim that the courts overstepped their role by intruding into family life. Hayes (1995, p. 884) says this is an issue of fundamental principle for the role of courts:

> It is one thing for a court to give a reluctant authority powers which it does not wish to have, which is what happens when a Care Order is made against a local authority's wishes; it is quite another thing for the court to direct the authority to exercise those powers in a manner which is contrary to the authority's view of the child's best interests.

The critics argue that there was dubious reasoning in the House of Lords ruling to confirm the Care Order on grounds of possible long-term difficulties, or to help Mrs W to obtain assistance from the local authority. The purpose of a Care Order, argues Hayes, is to give parental responsibility to the local authority, not to monitor progress (for which a Supervision Order could be used) nor to gain access to resources. There are clearly parallels here with the way the Child Protection Register appears to be inappropriately used to secure scarce resources (Dartington Social Research Unit 1995).

The implication of the final Re M ruling, according to Masson (1994), is that no special status is awarded to family arrangements and professional assessment will be favoured, with the courts readily recognising the benefits of a Care Order. This is likely to undermine parental responsibility for family carers like Mrs W who will be obliged to turn to the local authority when parental decisions need to be made.

Hayes' views (1995, p. 887) are that the House of Lords came to the right decision on the interpretation of the language of the threshold test, but failed to provide guidance to the courts on approaching the welfare principle and the welfare checklist where a capable relative is offering to care for the child. Because baby M was to continue living with a family member, the courts:

> failed to grasp the nettle of identifying when it is proper for a court to attempt to maximise a child's chances of obtaining the best possible upbringing, even though this leads to the severance of his links with his family.

'In need' or in need of protection?

As well as commenting on the interpretation of the threshold conditions in practice and in the courts, academic writers have expressed a range of opinions about the relationship between child protection work (as regulated by the procedures in *Working Together under the Children Act 1989* (DoH 1991b) and Parts IV and V of the Act) and the family support work required by Part III of the Act. It is in this area that the earliest research findings about the working of the Act appeared (Aldgate and Tunstill 1994; Giller 1993; Thorpe 1994; Colton et al. 1995). The debate was joined by those in central government departments and local authorities responsible for steering the changes into practice. Even before the date of implementation a 'Dear Director' letter was dispatched from the Social Services Inspectorate (SSI) when it became known that some local authorities intended to deal with resource constraints by limiting family support services to child protection cases. This was incorporated into Volume 2 of the *Guidance* (DoH 1991a, p. 5):

> The definition of 'need' in the Act is deliberately wide to reinforce the emphasis on preventive support and services to families. It has three categories: a reasonable standard of health or development; significant impairment of health or development; and disablement. It would not be acceptable for an authority to exclude any of these three – for example, by confining services to children at risk of significant harm which attracts the duty to investigate under Section 47.

A powerful argument was made by the Audit Commission (1994) and by senior figures at the Department of Health (Rose 1994; Hunter Johnson 1995) that family support and child protection enquiries should be seen as essential parts of a unified child and family service. Several of the researchers whose studies contributed to the Dartington *Child Protection* review (1995) addressed the issue of the appropriate threshold in child protection procedures (Cleaver and Freeman 1995; Gibbons et al. 1995a; Farmer and Owen 1995; Thoburn et al. 1995).

A fundamental principle of the Act is that the primary responsibility for bringing up children rests with their parents. Legal commentators such as Masson and Morris (1992) and Hayes (1995) underline the Act's premise that the state should only intervene compulsorily in very restricted circumstances. Along with Gibbons et al. (1995b), they conclude the state should be ready to help parents discharge their responsibility towards their children through family support provision. Gibbons and her colleagues (1995b, p. 177) spell out the implications for social work:

> Social workers will have to carry out better assessments, and be able to demonstrate convincingly that compulsory intervention in family life is likely to produce benefits for the child.

Several of the writers already cited, including the authors of the Audit Commission report (1994) have explored the overlaps between the 'significant harm' threshold for court intervention and 'significant impairment' – the threshold for the provision of services to a child 'in need'. This leaves the way open in a wide range of cases for professional discretion to be exercised as to whether a court application or family support under the Section 17 provisions should be the way forward.

The concept of need is an important component of welfare legislation, extending before and beyond the 1989 Act. However, the boundaries of need are unclear. The Act states that children in need are those unlikely to achieve or maintain a 'reasonable standard' of health or development unless services are provided. The Audit Commission (1994, p. 5) points out that 'reasonable standard' is not defined 'and neither are the indicators which would suggest such a standard is not being met'.

The Children Act Advisory Committee *Annual Report* (1994) puts the onus on health and local authorities to define 'what they mean by needs', but Parton (1995a, p. 67) comments that this report underlines the centrality of need without any discussion of poverty and deprivation:

> Surely any notion of need has to be located in the wider social, economic and political analysis of the changing circumstances of children and families in this country. The poorest families in Britain have suffered a cut in their real income between 1979 and 1990 of 14 per cent, whereas the average family had an increase of 36 per cent.

The role of law in establishing and meeting need has been described by some as that of a residual, minimal response (Braye and Preston-Shoot 1994, Fox Harding 1991). As Braye and Preston-Shoot point out, the duty to provide information about services is set against the poor performance of local authorities in delivering services to meet identified need. This is well illustrated by the research of Aldgate and Tunstill (1994). The Audit Commission (1994) quoting this research, reports that across a range of 60 local authorities, highest priority in defining need was given to children already being looked after, or to child protection work, whilst other categories received scant attention.

In summary, official *Guidance* and those who have provided commentaries on the Act are in agreement that the aim should be to meet the protection *and* welfare needs of the child, bearing in mind that this will usually be from within the family of origin. The Audit Commission (1994, p. 7) makes clear that:

services should only be offered where there is a likelihood of beneficial outcomes for the child and family.

This would seem to be as relevant to children at risk of maltreatment as to children whose health or development is likely to be significantly impaired for reasons other than maltreatment. For the purposes of considering the best route to provide help for a child in need of protection, it would appear that a child identified as at risk of maltreatment should have access to services for children 'in need' and that services, including those more narrowly defined to protective services, should only be provided if they are likely to be of benefit to the child. A major focus of this study is the effectiveness of support and protective services to a cohort of children newly identified as suffering or likely to suffer significant harm.

The new language of 'reasonable standard of health or development' and its translation into service provision decisions is likely to increase the extent of *need* irrespective of what caused that need. This is occurring at the same time as the language of prioritisation focuses attention on child protection in a climate of cutbacks in resources and a withdrawal from service provision.

James' 1994 study of 30 case reviews carried out under Section 8 of *Working Together* (DoH, 1991b) (notifications of child deaths or incidents of serious harm) identifies amendments that could be made. His language is of 'investigation' not 'enquiry' (see Rose 1994) and there is an absence of the 'lighter less bureaucratic touch' spoken of in the reports of the 1994 and 1995 Sieff conferences (Sieff Foundation 1994; 1995). James' recommendations (1994, para. 4.1) include tighter, more stringent procedures, for example to investigate suspicions of abuse promptly and rigorously:

> On receipt of a referral, the child should be seen on the same day by staff from one of the statutory agencies. It is not acceptable to arrange this through a third party (health visitor, midwife etc.), although their professional contribution may be essential.

Parton (1995b, p. 10) comments that these recommendations do not square with the Audit Commission Report (1994):

> What is apparent is that very different priorities and recommendations for change arise when the starting point is the individual case that has gone wrong.

This explains the difference between James' recommendations and those of writers who mainly studied cohorts of 'run of the mill' child-abuse referrals which, to use Gibbons' analogy of trawling for fish (Gibbons et al. 1995a, p. 32), will include 'a large number of minnows which have later to be discarded . . . as well as the marketable fish'.

There will be an inevitable tension if need and harm are polarised that cannot be resolved unless there is a constructive bringing together of the two parts of the Act. As Rose (1994, p. 7) suggests:

> We should be promoting one integrated approach to the local authority duties under Part III and Part IV of the Act. The aim should be to integrate family support services both practically and conceptually more with child protection, and thereby release more resources from investigation and assessment into family support and treatment services.

It was against this background of debate and of earlier research findings, reported in *Child Protection: Messages from Research* (Dartington Social Research Unit 1995), that we undertook our study of safeguarding children with the implementation of the Children Act 1989.

The research project described in this book was commissioned shortly after the implementation of the Children Act 1989, when concerns were also beginning to be expressed that the requirement in the Act to attempt to work in partnership with family members, especially parents who might have been implicated in the maltreatment, might be placing some children at increased risk of significant harm:

> It has been reported to the Committee that some local authorities may feel inhibited from applying for Care Orders (and some courts from granting such orders) if the possibility of working co-operatively in partnership with the family has not been exhausted (Children Act Advisory Committee 1994, p. 33).

In view of the concern that children may be 'slipping through the net', to use Gibbons' analogy (Gibbons et al. 1995a), we set out to identify a cohort of children who were already suffering significant harm, or where there was clear evidence that they were likely to do so unless protective action was taken. The research aims were to:

♦   reach conclusions about the place of the formal child protection system in helping such children by scrutinising these cases, and then looking forward to see whether effective protective action was taken;

♦   consider the thresholds for action in cases of 'need' and 'risk of maltreatment' which had led to the children in our sample being identified as requiring protective intervention; and

♦　　draw conclusions about whether the protection offered was appropriate.

We aimed to examine, to return to the 'net' analogy, whether the Children Act Section 17 net, intended to gather families in for the receipt of family support services, had, as earlier researchers had postulated, a mesh which was too wide so that many families in need slipped through, thus allowing problems to escalate. At the other end of the spectrum, we examined cases for evidence as to whether the net of the formal child protection system was fine enough to pick up the cases of children who needed its formal intervention, but to leave the other families with children 'in need' free to benefit on a voluntary basis from family support services.

We return in Chapter 10 to the issues and questions highlighted in this introduction and summarise what our detailed study of practice in four authorities, three years after the implementation of the Children Act, can contribute to these essential debates.

2 The study in outline

This chapter describes the four areas in which the study was carried out and the research methods used to select and gather information about the children and their families. A profile of the children and their families is offered in terms of age, ethnicity, family composition, material circumstances and problems at the time significant harm was identified. More information about the children is provided in Chapter 5.

The areas in the study

The sample of 105 consecutive cases was followed through for a 12-month period (between 1993 and 1994) after the assessment was made that the children were suffering or likely to suffer significant harm.

Eight area teams from four different local authorities took part in the study. Two of the areas were large rural counties with mixed urban and rural populations, and with pockets of acute material deprivation. They were called, for the purposes of the research, Coastshire and Fieldshire. The other two were inner-city areas, Woodborough and Hillborough, both of which scored highly on all indices of deprivation. The Social Services' offices in Coastshire were situated in a small sea-port and a small overspill town. In Fieldshire they were found in an industrial town and a market town. In Hillborough and Woodborough they were in inner-city locations.

Socio-economic characteristics

In Woodborough more families were likely to be dependent on income support and numbers living in poverty were higher than in the other areas. At the 1991 Census, Woodborough had fewest owner-occupied households, with Hillborough having nearly twice as many as Woodborough. The two rural counties had more home-owners – roughly 68% of total households. On the research visits in the inner-city areas it was clear that the housing stock was poor and run down. Stairs and landings, and indeed some whole estates, were unpleasant, menacing places for several of the families who were interviewed. One mother interviewed felt unable to allow her children to go out to play after school because of her justified fears for the children's safety. She had been trying for two years, without success, to obtain a transfer of her tenancy to a safer area.

Housing was often temporary and many families were anticipating a move. As one social worker commented:

> Permanent housing, now, is complicated. The council get private landlords to offer housing and the council draws up the lease and they meet the Housing Act requirements but you never feel too sure if the landlords will up the rent and the council won't meet it, or if people start work and they won't be able to afford rents. The other concern is that the landlord might go to court for repossession. It might *not* be long-term any more.

The transitory nature of housing provision for families with children exacerbates the difficulties in maintaining links with the extended family and supportive friends, and keeping continuity at school.

Area policies

Children's services plans

Policies in the four areas were determined by children's services plans which were drawn up differently in all four locations. For three local authorities it was their first plan and for the fourth local authority, its second. The three first plans were largely prescriptive documents offering directives about provision of services. The fourth plan was more pro-active and resulted from a wide-ranging consultation process involving many groups in the area.

Interestingly, the definitions of eligibility for services followed different patterns and conveyed varying messages. One plan moved immediately to the identification of children 'in need' and to prevention and assessment, whereas another spoke of 'assessment of good quality with specific objectives, tasks and time limits set', and the general tone implied a more stringent gatekeeping approach. The third prescribed in detail the two groups of children who would be accepted as in need: children to be definitely accepted included all those on the Child Protection Register (CPR); and those to be possibly accepted included children subject to child protection procedures but not registered, and other tightly defined groups. The fourth plan emphasised provisions, which were accessible on a more universalist basis according to the needs of the groups of people for whom the services were set up.

Thereafter the lists and categories of priority were similar, including children being looked after, child protection enquiries, children on the Child Protection Register and children with disabilities. All the sections on child protection were short and factual referring to *Working Together under the Children Act 1989* (DoH 1991b). One local authority anticipated the mood of *Child Protection: Messages from Research* (Dartington Social Research Unit 1995) and the 'refocusing' debate stating explicitly that:

> too many resources have been invested in child protection investigations often to insure against any accusations of any under-reaction by statutory agencies. This has involved formally investigating quite minor allegations where a family support approach may have been more successful both in helping families and, in so doing, protecting children.

Use of the Child Protection Register

The proportion of children in any one authority for whom registration is seen as necessary varies with the characteristics of the children and families who live there, environmental measures, the policies of agencies and the practices of individuals in the different professions. Gibbons et al. (1995a) show the extent of variation. Policies were changing as this study was conducted with each area child protection committee (ACPC) viewing the registers as a barometer of the results of the policies of its member agencies.

Statistical returns for 1993, at the start of our study, show that Fieldshire's rate of registration at 0.31% of the child population under 18, Coastshire's 0.25%, and Woodborough's 0.33% were comparatively low when compared with Hillborough's at 0.73%. (The percentage for England is 0.43%.) Whilst Hillborough was well above the English average, Coastshire, Fieldshire, and Woodborough (with its socially disadvantaged population) were below. This suggests that thresholds for holding an initial child protection conference (ICPC) were much higher in Fieldshire, Coastshire and Woodborough than in Hillborough. County authorities would be expected to have lower rates of conferencing and registration as the numbers of children living in areas of high deprivation are smaller, but it appears that a combination of agency policy and the practice of individual workers is likely to account for the difference between Hillborough and Woodborough.

Hillborough was well aware of its high registration rate, and efforts were being made to reduce the rate while the research was being carried out. Yet it is apparent that Hillborough's use of the Child Protection Register was very different from the other three areas. As a method of managing social work and multi-agency input to families, we discerned that the use of the Child Protection Register ensured that protection plans were carefully monitored. Many of the child protection plans in Hillborough were notable for their thoroughness and detail about the needs of all family members and not merely protection issues. Fewer of the conferenced children were registered than was the case in Woodborough.

There was information, from research interviews with the social workers in Woodborough, that team and office policy was that all children referred for protection services were likely to be in need and that, if at all possible, families should be helped without recourse to the formal child protection systems. The social workers' view of the consequences of social deprivation in relation to child protection is likely to account for a relatively higher threshold of conferencing and thus a higher percentage of conferenced children having their names placed on the Child Protection Register. It may also mean that the clients with whom the social workers were working, under the formal child protection arrangements, had more problems and were harder to engage, since the system tends not to be used with willing clients. This needs to be borne in mind when reading the chapters that follow.

The ethnic groups in the areas

Because of the dearth of views in child-care research of minority ethnic families, three of the areas, Fieldshire, Hillborough and Woodborough, were selected for the research partly because they were known to have diverse populations that were likely to bring forward a good sample of families of minority ethnic origin, including refugee families.

Since around 30% of the children under the age of 17 living in the Fieldshire area from which our sample was drawn, were of South-Asian descent, we can reliably report that children from this group were under-represented amongst the children identified in that area as suffering or likely to suffer significant harm. However, in both Hillborough and Woodborough, families of ethnic minority origin were over-represented in the research study. The percentage of the under-17 population in Woodborough who are of minority ethnic origin is around 47% but the percentage in our sample was 75%. In Hillborough the percentages were 32% in the general population and 64% of the children in our sample. (The statistics did not allow us to identify whether this over-representation referred to some but not all ethnic groups.)

Selecting the children for study

The research sample included all of the 151 children newly identified, by the eight area teams studied, as suffering, or likely to suffer, significant harm in the areas during an eight-month period between 1993 and 1994. The children were considered for possible inclusion in the study in the following ways:

◆ Child protection advisers or team managers informed the researchers about children in their area newly identified as suffering or likely to suffer significant harm. To make sure all potential children were included, area managers were asked whether there were any other children where significant harm or its likelihood were identified but a child protection conference had not been held.

◆ A template, based on the wording of Section 31 of the Children Act 1989, was used by the researcher in consultation with the social worker who knew the case best. This most often followed attendance at an initial or a 'repeat incident' child protection conference (researchers attended 108 out of 147 conferences) to ensure consistency in the interpretation of the definition of significant harm across the areas studied (see Appendix 1).

◆ With preliminary details gathered, each case was discussed by two of the researchers before being included in the sample. A total of 151 cases were considered for inclusion in the study as cases of *possible* significant harm (see Figure 2.1).

Figure 2.1 *Children considered for inclusion in the study*[1]

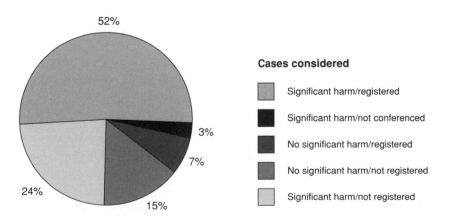

[1] n=151 children considered as cases of *possible* significant harm

- In four cases there was clear evidence of significant harm even though the children were *not* considered by a child protection conference. These families received protective and support services under the provisions of Part III of the Act and were included in the study.

- In 79 cases the child's name was placed on the Register and the research team was in agreement with the conference conclusion that the child was suffering significant harm or was likely to do so without the provision of protective services. These cases were included in the study.

- In 22 cases the research team concluded that the child was suffering or was likely to suffer significant harm but the conference had decided that child protection registration was not appropriate, mainly because it was considered unnecessary or likely to be unhelpful. In one or two cases conferences appeared to underestimate the harm to the child. All 22 of these cases were included in the study.

- In ten cases there was disagreement between the research team and professionals. Although the child was registered, the researchers did not see clear evidence of actual or likely significant harm using the agreed researcher protocol based on the wording of the Children Act. Checks at the end of the year revealed that each of these children's names had been removed from the Register and that in no case had a child been re-referred because of suspicion of maltreatment. These cases were not included in the study.

- Thirty-six of the cases that were conferenced were not considered to be cases of significant harm either by the conference or the researchers, and the children's names were not added to the Register. These were not included in the study.

As shown by Figure 2.2, the largest proportion of families in the sample lived in Hillborough and the smallest group in Woodborough.

Parents were asked, either by the researcher at the conference, or by a letter sent to them separately, whether they would be willing to help with the research.

In total, 105 children were identified (53 boys and 52 two girls). This sample was subdivided into an intensive sample of 51 children, and a background sample of 54 children. The parents of the children in the intensive study had

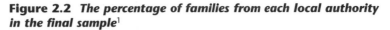

Figure 2.2 *The percentage of families from each local authority in the final sample*[1]

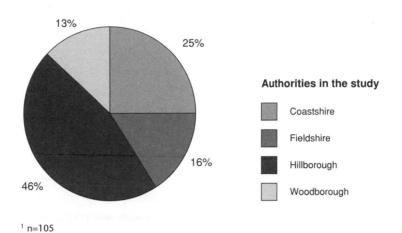

[1] n=105

agreed to play a full part in the research study and they and their child, and relevant professionals, were interviewed shortly after the identification of harm, and one year later. For the background sample of the remaining 54 cases, less detailed, anonymous data were drawn from the records, interviews with the social workers, and attendance at some of the conferences.

Where more than one child in a family was considered to be suffering or likely to suffer significant harm, the youngest child, who would normally be most vulnerable to serious consequences in terms of health and development, was identified as the *index child* to be studied. In 38% of cases, two or more children in the family were identified as suffering significant harm and the youngest child was chosen for the study. In the majority of cases (62%) either only one child was identified, or it was clear that one child was suffering more harm than others in the family.

The methods used

Once the sample had been identified, interviews were conducted with the professionals who had been most influential in the decision about the extent of harm to the child; there were interviews with the parents of the 51 children in the intensive sample; and play-based interviews or observations were carried out with the children. At Stage 2, 12 months after the initial incident or cause for concern, parents, children and social workers were interviewed again. Protocols were developed for researcher ratings of several variables and outcome measures, which were based on the data collected from the different sources (see Appendix 2).

At Stage 2, files of the 105 children were scrutinised. As well as noting any changes in the children and families over a 12-month period, information was collected about the assessment process and the different ways in which the cases proceeded through the system. Notes were made about the way in which decisions were formed as to whether the child was suffering or likely to suffer significant harm, and detailed information gathered on the nature of the services provided before and after the identification of harm. (Appendix 4 gives further details of the standardised tests and other research instruments used with the children.)

The qualitative data were analysed using the personal computer (PC) version of the 'Statistical Package for the Social Sciences' (SPSS) program. Themes and issues emerged from the data and from the interviews, allowing comparisons to be made with earlier studies and conclusions to be reached about the nature of practice and ways in which the service might be improved.

The children and families in the study

In Chapter 10 it can be seen that the outcomes for the 105 children and their families were mixed and that, in many ways, one year is too short a time-span to be able to say with any clarity that children have been safeguarded from harm or serious impairment of their development. What we hope to make apparent, however, is that the outcome for children suffering or likely to suffer significant harm will be influenced by a number of factors. The first factors to be considered are the *profile* and experiences of the child, up to and at the time harm was acknowledged; and the profile and experiences of the child's family. The second factor is the filtering and assessment *process,* during which decisions are made and help or treatment is secured for the child and the child's family. The third influential component is the services themselves – the *output* from Social Services and other agencies concerned with the health, welfare and development of children. The characteristics of the children and families, the process and the output all contribute to the interim *outcome* for the child and his or her family that forms the latter part of this book.

Profile of the children

As shown by Figure 2.3, almost half of the children (46%) were less than 5 years of age, with 17% unborn or under 12 months of age at the time of entering the study. Almost 30% were aged 5–11 years and the remaining quarter were adolescents of 12 years or over. The age of the children in the cohort is to some extent a factor in the decision to choose the youngest child as the index child.

Figure 2.3 *The children's ages at the start of the study*[1]

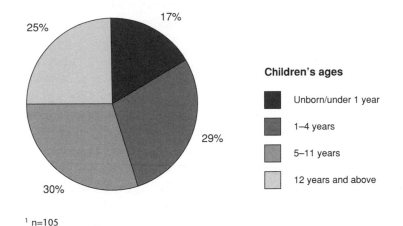

25%

17%

29%

30%

Children's ages

■ Unborn/under 1 year

■ 1–4 years

■ 5–11 years

□ 12 years and above

[1] n=105

At the time of entering the study, the majority of the children had emotional and behavioural difficulties or disabilities which preceded, but were exacerbated by, the maltreatment (see Table 2.1).

Table 2.1 *Difficulties and special needs of the children at Stage 1 (n=105)*

Difficulty/disability	% of children[1]
Physical disability	13
Blind or partially sighted	2
Hearing or speech disability	11
Moderate learning disability	19
Severe learning disability	1
Behavioural problems	33
Other problems including emotional difficulties	39
Child beyond control of parent to some extent	20
First language not English	9

[1] Does not add up to 100% as some children had more than one of these difficulties: 66% had at least one of these disabilities

Indeed, almost two-thirds of the children could be described as difficult to parent because of their special characteristics. The children's special needs required visits to hospital, special units, special schools, as well as particularly skilled parenting. Some children and parents were already receiving additional help, but most were not – a point to which we shall return.

The extent of family problems, poverty and adversity, provides an important backdrop to understanding the deficits in well-being for these children, and the harm they were suffering

Family composition

Table 2.2 shows that almost half (47%) of the children were living in single-parent families headed, in all but four cases, by the mother. A third were living with both parents and 16% of the children were with a parent and a stepparent. The remaining 8% were living with carers.

In half of the cases where the child was living with both parents, the parents were not married. Forty-four of the fathers had parental responsibility and 43 did not. Separations between parents and partners characterised many of these families during the year of the study. There were disputes about residence or contact (or earlier custody disputes) in 16 cases. These disputes in themselves were often a source of harm to the child.

Table 2.2 *Family composition at Stage 1*

Child living with	No.	%
Both parents	34	32
Mother only	45	43
Father only	4	4
Mother and male partner	14	13
Father and female partner	3	3
Adoptive parents	1	1
Other carers	3	3
Mother and relatives	1	1
Total	105	100

Ethnicity

Table 2.3 details the ethnic origin of the children and shows that 59 children (56%) were of white British ethnic origin, both parents of 29 children were from a racial or cultural background other than white British (28%) and that 17 children (16%) were of mixed ethnicity. The issue of ethnicity is explored further in the next section. For most (91%) the first language was English, but nine of the children were more comfortable using a language other than English.

Table 2.3 *Ethnic origin of the index children*

Ethnic origin	No.	%
White British	59	56
African–Caribbean	15	14
African	2	2
Indian	2	2
Pakistani	4	4
European/other (e.g. Turkish)	5	5
Child of travelling family	1	1
Black child of mixed parentage	11	10
Child of other mixed racial or cultural origin	6	6
Total	105	100

Case studies

From the backgrounds described, the following four case studies provide individual profiles of children from each of the age ranges shown in Figure 2.3.

● ●

JUSTINE

Justine was registered at a pre-birth conference in the category of likely neglect, and was born prematurely by emergency Caesarian section after her mother had fallen down the stairs. At birth Justine was below the third centile in weight and was placed in special care for a week. These factors did not augur well for this baby, who was not at all easy to parent in her early weeks. Justine's mother had been in care since she was ten and Justine was her mother's second child. The first child had been made the subject of a Care Order and had been placed with maternal grandparents.

TOMMY

Both the parents of 3-year-old Tommy had learning difficulties. The family was homeless and Tommy lived with his parents in a hostel during the major part of the study. Tommy was prone to infection which prompted weight loss. He appeared to be failing to thrive and was under-stimulated. One particular incident also occurred where his mother had been seen by a member of the public to pinch Tommy's face. Both parents were said to be devoted to Tommy and shared his care equally. Tommy was aggressive to other children in the nursery he attended. Almost all the children in this nursery, which was located in an area of high deprivation, displayed difficult behaviour and had poor speech.

MARY

Mary had come to England three years earlier from an African war zone as a refugee with her father, her stepmother, two brothers and two half-brothers when she was 6. Two of her brothers and a stepsister had been left in the country of origin, as had Mary's mother, and their fate was a constant source of extreme worry for the whole family. Two children had been born in England. This was a 'mine, yours and ours' situation that was extremely complex emotionally, and marital stresses exacerbated Mary's difficult behaviour. Now aged 9, Mary had not had the help she needed to recover from the losses and trauma of her early life. She was devoted to her father but resentful of her stepmother, and she was not displeased when the stepmother was rehoused following a violent assault on her by the father. However, Mary missed, and worried about, her young siblings. Her father was torn between his love for his older children, especially Mary whose problems he only partially understood, and his love and sense of duty to his wife and the younger children. Language problems complicated the situation further. It had initially been assumed that his wife was the main carer but it soon became clear that the children preferred to be with their father and that the strategy of encouraging the wife to take out an injunction against him was unhelpful. Both parents acknowledged that they needed help but the child protection process appeared to them to be totally irrelevant to the multiple practical and emotional needs of themselves and their children.

CHELSEA

Chelsea was the oldest child, at 15, in a family of six children with three different fathers. Her mother's third partner was in prison as an illegal immigrant and he was deported during the period of the research study. Chelsea had mild learning difficulties and was at a special school. In the past all the children's names had been placed on the Child Protection Register under the category of neglect. Chelsea had suffered serious burns in a fire when her mother had left the children alone. She sought affection, which made her vulnerable. She became pregnant by a young neighbour who had been intimidating and molesting her for a number of months. She terminated the pregnancy. It was this situation that prompted the initial child protection conference.

Well-being

In the light of the information about the 105 children, the well-being of over half of them (56%) was rated as 'poor' at the time of identification of significant harm. Figure 2.4 shows that the children with poor well-being tended to be older (two-thirds of these children with 'poor' well-being were in the 5–18 age range). Less than one in ten could be described as of 'average' well-being and these children were all under 5. Only one child's well-being was good and this child was under five. (The rating for 'average' was based on an average for children living in similar circumstances to those in which most of the sample children lived.) A more detailed picture of the children is given in Chapter 5.

Figure 2.4 *The children's ages and well-being at Stage 1*[1]

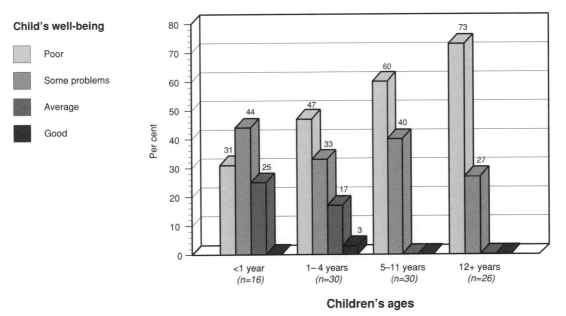

[1] n=102; missing data=3; x^2:17.208 df:6 p<.01

Profile of the parents

Fathers or father-figures

We considered it important to interview as many of the fathers or male carers as possible, because of the criticism that fathers are too readily left out of both social work practice and research. Nineteen fathers or mothers' male partners were interviewed in the course of the intensive sample study of 51 children, and there was brief contact or a partial interview with another five.

In 11 cases there was either no father in the household or the other father was at work, in prison (two cases) or kept out of the way of the researcher. Thus, just over half of the men who were in a caring role at the start of the study were interviewed.

Mothers and mother-figures

As shown in Table 2.2, 43% of the children's mothers were caring for their children alone. At the time of the harm to the child the majority of the mothers were in receipt of state benefits, with only 18 holding employment of some kind. The picture remained more or less the same throughout the study for both mothers and fathers.

Most of the families lived in council accommodation. Eight mothers and nine fathers were owner-occupiers. Seven mothers lived in lodgings, a hostel, mobile homes or homeless families' accommodation. There were no major differences by Stage 2 of the study.

Other characteristics of the parents

We compared, in detail, the cohort of 105 of families in this study (1993–94) with the cohort in the *Paternalism or Partnership?* study of 1990–91 (Thoburn et al. 1995) which considered 220 cases discussed at initial child protection conferences, 60% of which did not result in registration. In most respects a similar pattern is apparent, of families suffering multiple deprivation and with high incidences of marital discord, physical and mental illness and addiction problems.

However, in our present study, where all the children were suffering or likely to suffer significant harm, there were some interesting differences. At the time that the harm was identified, 43% were living in a household headed by a mother living alone, compared with 30% in the *Paternalism or Partnership?* study.

The main carer (usually the mother) also tended to be older in this sample with only a quarter being less than 25 years old, compared with 36% in the *Paternalism or Partnership?* sample. Table 2.4 shows other similarities and differences. Interestingly, although more families in the significant harm cohort are described as of upper- or middle-class background, significantly more of them are dependent on state benefits and fewer are living in owner-occupied homes. Equal numbers appear to have mental health problems, but there is a higher incidence of both violent domestic conflict and of substance abuse in the significant harm cohort.

Table 2.4 *Family and parental characteristics*

Characteristic	% of 220 cases (1990–91 study)	% of 105 cases (1993–94 study)
Mother aged <25	36	26
Lone-parent household	29	47
Described as upper- or middle-class	14	25
Dependent on state benefits	50	82
Owner-occupier	17	8

Twenty of the mothers were known to have been looked after by the local authority in their childhood, 20 were known or suspected as having been physically abused, and 15 sexually abused as children. This information was rarely available for the fathers.

Five of the fathers and at least one mother were known to be 'Schedule 1' offenders, either because of physical or sexual offences against children. Information collected from files or from interviews suggested that 33 mothers and 22 fathers displayed immaturity of personality. Thirty-four mothers and 47 fathers were either alleged or known to have engaged in violent behaviour in the past, and five mothers and 20 fathers had convictions for offences involving violence. Given all the disadvantages and problems described, it was hardly surprising that the well-being of 98% of the main parents was rated by the researchers as poor or giving cause for concern at the time of the child protection procedures.

Family problems

A summary of the specific problems experienced by parents or carers in the year before the initial child protection conference is found in Table 2.5. When compared with the specific problems experienced in the year since the initial child protection conference, it becomes clear that by far the greatest problem for the families was financial in both years. In the year before the conference, nearly half of the families experienced marital conflict. A high incidence of domestic violence was also found by Farmer and Owen (1995) in their study of registered cases undertaken just before the implementation of the Children Act 1989 and in a study of cases of neglect and emotional abuse (Gibbons et al. 1995a). Approximately a third of the families had experienced divorce or separation, drug or alcohol addiction, had moved house or experienced a number of other problems.

Parents' health

A further source of information was the standardised Rutter 'malaise' inventory which asked families about their own health and sense of well-being (Rutter et al. 1981). This scale was completed by 26 of the main parents during the first stage of interviewing at Stage 1 and over three-quarters had a score which suggested that they may be clinically depressed.

Categorising family problems

We used the typology identified by Cleaver and Freeman (1995) to give a more global picture of the sorts of families whose children are identified by the statutory services as suffering or likely to suffer significant harm (see Appendix 2).

Table 2.5 *The families' difficulties and problems*

Difficulty/problem	In year before Stage 1		In year after Stage 1	
	No.	%	No.	%
Serious physical illness	17	17	14	14
Mental illness	20	20	24	25
Hospital admission	22	22	26	27
Death	9	9	5	5
Divorce or separation	34	34	20	21
Family member moved out of family home	48	48	43	44
Birth of a child	—	—	21	21
Unemployment	29	29	24	26
Moved house	35	35	40	41
Financial	77	77	76	80
Accident	7	7	3	3
Onset of disability or terminal illness	—	—	1	1
Miscarriage/termination of pregnancy	6	6	2	2
Drug or alcohol addiction	31	31	26	28
Marital/partner violence	47	47	31	32
Other problems	37	37	21	33

The definitions of 'multiple problem' and 'infiltrating perpetrator' are self-evident. Cleaver and Freeman (1995) define 'single issue' families as those which come to the attention of the agencies because of a particular suspicion such as intra-familial sexual abuse or physical abuse by a parent against a particular child within the household. We also included in this category cases where there was serious marital conflict but in other respects the child was adequately cared for. Cleaver and Freeman (1995, p. 52) describe acutely distressed families (refugee families tended to be in this group) as those where:

problems accumulate, but are dealt with until one overwhelming incident precipitates child abuse. Such families tend to be composed of single or poorly supported immature parents or others who are physically ill or disabled. The child abuse usually takes the form of physical aggression or neglect when parents cease to be able to cope

We found that all except three of the families could be fitted easily into one of these four categories (see Figure 2.5). Table 2.6 compares our 'significant harm' study population with the Cleaver and Freeman (1995) study of all families where abuse of any type was suspected. The proportions for the two studies are similar except that there are more acutely distressed families in our cohort.

Figure 2.5 Types of family[1]

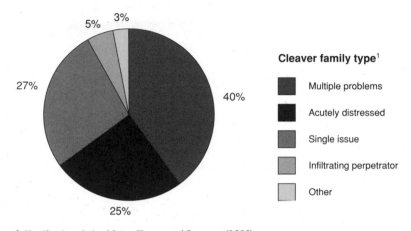

[1] Classification derived from Cleaver and Freeman (1995)

[2] n=104; missing data=1

Table 2.6 Types of family in two studies

	Cleaver and Freeman (1995) study (n=83)	Significant Harm study (n=105)
	%	%
Multiple problem	43	40
Acutely distressed	13	25
Single issue	21	27
Infiltrating perpetrator	9	5
Other	—	3
Total	100	100

Children of minority ethnic origin were less likely to be members of families with multiple problems of long duration. Those with both parents of minority ethnic origin were more likely to be in the 'acutely distressed' group, and children of mixed ethnic origin were more likely to be in the groups of families where a specific issue had resulted in maltreatment or the child's needs remained unmet (see Figure 2.6).

Figure 2.6 *Ethnicity of the children and types of family*[1]

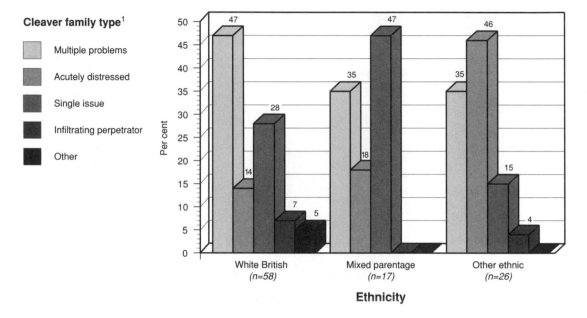

[1] Classification derived from Cleaver and Freeman (1995)

[2] n=101; missing data=4; x^2:14.027 df:6 p<.05

Despite all the difficulties of parents and children, most of the parents were committed to the welfare of their children and there was evidence that, over the years, they had sought help for their own and their children's problems and been met with very different responses. There were only 15 cases where there was no evidence that a parent was committed to the child's welfare although the problems of many parents and children made it very difficult for them to consistently demonstrate their commitment by competent parenting.

Summary

The study was drawn from eight area teams from four separate local authorities which we named Coastshire, Fieldshire, Woodborough and Hillborough. The population studied lived in a mix of rural, urban and inner-city areas. Three out of the four areas included families of minority ethnic origin, including refugee families.

Although Coastshire and Fieldshire had similar populations and similar registration rates, Hillborough and Woodborough had very different registration rates. There were also differences in the authorities' policies and in the way they constructed their children's services plans and child protection procedures.

The sample comprised 105 children, newly identified as suffering or likely to suffer significant harm when matched against a template based on the wording of Section 31 of the Children Act 1989. Most cases, but not all, had been identified for inclusion following a child protection conference. The selection criteria for the research appeared robust. Although the research team were mostly in agreement with professionals, in ten cases there was disagreement. Although the child's name was placed on the CPR, the research team thought the child was *not* suffering significant harm and did not include the child in the research. One year later all these children's names had been removed from the Register and no child had been re-referred because of maltreatment.

The sample of 105 was sub-divided into two groups: the *intensive sample* of 51 children where parents, children and relevant professionals were interviewed at the time of harm and one year later; and the remaining 54 cases which made up the *background sample* which provided less detailed, anonymous data from records and interviews with social workers. The progress of all 105 children was tracked throughout the year of the study.

Around 46% of the children were aged under 5, 30% were aged 5–11 years, and the remaining 25% were adolescents of 12 and over. This sample reflected a mix of ethnic groups so that only 59% of the children were white British, 28% of the children had two parents of minority ethnic origin, and 16% were of mixed-race parentage. Two-thirds of the children were described as difficult to parent because of special characteristics. The older children, in particular, were found to have poor well-being at the time of identification of harm.

The parents in this study suffered material and social hardship and an array of problems and difficulties. Most of the families were living on state benefits, many in poor-quality housing, and 43% of families were headed by lone mothers. Almost a third of the families had problems with addiction, and one in five had experienced mental illness. In almost half of the families there was, or had been, domestic violence and in some of the others there was, or had been, serious marital conflict. The majority of families had many unmet needs at the time when increased concern for the children's well-being led to their inclusion in the research sample.

Using Cleaver and Freeman's (1995) classification of family types, we found that 40% of families had multiple problems of long standing. In our study, however, there was a higher incidence than in earlier studies of cases with either an accumulation of crises or life-limiting events, or a single incident with major repercussions for family stability. These tipped normally coping families into situations where the child suffered, or was highly likely to suffer, significant harm.

3

The safeguarding process in the 105 cases

In this chapter we focus on the thresholds over which the 105 families moved in relation to the harm to the child, the close link between need and harm, the way the families viewed what happened to them, and the extent of their involvement in the procedures as required by the Children Act and its *Guidance*. Figure 3.1 shows the process in diagrammatic form. Case studies illustrate how the process had an impact on particular families. The views of the children are reported in Chapters 5 and 6.

The first and second thresholds: referrals, strategy meetings and Section 47 enquiries

Table 3.1 records the involvement with Social Services. It shows that, of the 105 families in our study, 80 children and/or their sibling(s) had previously sought help from or been referred to a social services department. The action taken by the social services department is described within the table.

In each of the four research areas a referral to Social Services that suggested child maltreatment led to consultation between the team or practice manager and the social worker, to determine the nature of the case.

Telephone checks would usually be made with other professionals and the keeper of the Child Protection Register before a decision was made about whether to hold a strategy discussion or meeting as described in *Working Together* (DoH, 1991b) as the first stage of the formal child protection process. There was information available from 98 of the 105 cases about strategy meetings. There was no formally designated strategy meeting or discussion in 35 cases. In 31 cases there was a meeting, and in 32 cases, a discussion with other members of the investigating team, usually over the telephone.

There was less information about whether family members took part in the strategy meetings or discussions, but of the 50 cases where the information was available, only three mothers, three fathers and one child attended a strategy meeting. This comes as no surprise since a strategy meeting should

Figure 3.1 *The safeguarding process*

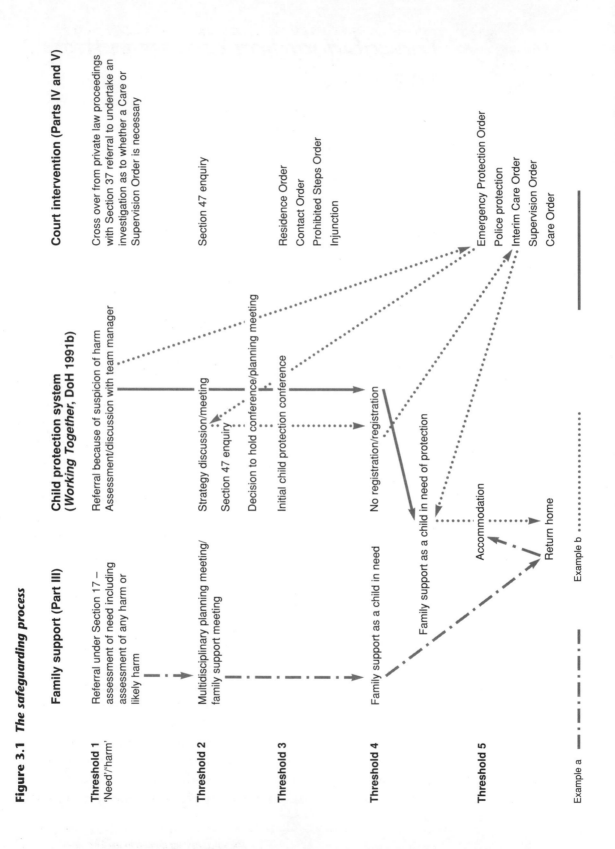

Family support (Part III)

Court intervention (Parts IV and V)

Child protection system
(*Working Together*, DoH 1991b)

Threshold 1
'Need'/'harm'

Referral under Section 17 –
assessment of need including
assessment of any harm or
likely harm

Referral because of suspicion of harm
Assessment/discussion with team manager

Cross over from private law proceedings
with Section 37 referral to undertake an
investigation as to whether a Care or
Supervision Order is necessary

Threshold 2

Multidisciplinary planning meeting/
family support meeting

Strategy discussion/meeting

Section 47 enquiry

Section 47 enquiry

Decision to hold conference/planning meeting

Threshold 3

Initial child protection conference

Residence Order
Contact Order
Prohibited Steps Order
Injunction

Threshold 4

Family support as a child in need

No registration/registration

Family support as a child in need of protection

Threshold 5

Accommodation

Return home

Emergency Protection Order
Police protection
Interim Care Order
Supervision Order
Care Order

Example a — · — · — · —

Example b · · · · · · · · · · · ·

Table 3.1 *Previous abuse/protection status of the families (n=105)*

Abuse/child protection status	%[1]
Not previously known to Social Services	24
Previous concern, not investigated as child protection	39
Previous child protection investigation, not registered	18
Other children previously on Register	23
Index child previously on Register	16
Other children on Register at time of incident	3
Index child already on Register at time of incident	3
Previous care proceedings on other child(ren)	14
Previous care proceedings on index child	5
Previous Care Order on other child(ren)	11
Previous Care Order on index child	3
Previous Place of Safety Order/Emergency Protection Order on other child(ren)	8
Previous Place of Safety Order/Emergency Protection Order on index child	7

[1] Does not add up to 100% since some children were in more than one category

confine itself to practical arrangements about the enquiries and should *not* become involved in a detailed debate about the nature of the alleged abuse. However, it became clear that some area teams use the term 'strategy meeting' to describe both case discussions on whether there *should* be an enquiry under child protection procedures and the discussions about the *mechanics* of the enquiry. Other area teams used the term 'strategy meeting' to describe a meeting of professionals that fell somewhere between a planning meeting, without the parents being present, and a strategy discussion. At such a meeting the 'evidence' on maltreatment would be sifted and a decision might be taken to make no further enquiries; to continue making enquiries outside the formal child protection system; or to initiate a full child-abuse investigation. This was explained by one team leader as a way of avoiding unnecessary distress to the family if a full investigation was not initiated. However, if a child protection conference was called subsequently, reference had to be made to this meeting, and almost inevitably this led to conflict with the parents and the accusation that 'it was all fixed before we even got here'.

Immediate emergency action might have to be taken at this early stage; alternatively it might have been taken first by the police, and a strategy or planning meeting would follow (see Figure 3.2). Emergency protection was used in 15% of cases at Stage 1 (six Emergency Protection Orders and ten children taken into police protection). Relatives were used as protection at the early stage in 12% of cases. (Further details about emergency action are found in Chapter 8.) In three cases the alleged abuser was provided with, or was helped to find, accommodation to prevent the removal of the child. In the majority of cases accommodation for the alleged abuser was not needed; in four cases, it was not wanted; in one case, it was wanted but not offered; and in another case, it was offered but not taken up.

Figure 3.2 *The use of emergency protection procedures*[1]

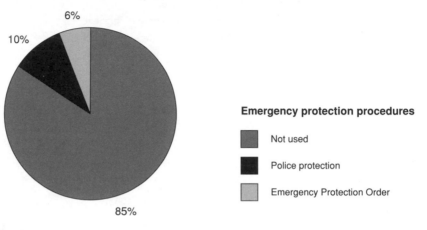

Emergency protection procedures

- Not used
- Police protection
- Emergency Protection Order

6%

10%

85%

[1] n=105

In the 80 cases already known to Social Services (some still receiving a service and some which had been closed after earlier intervention) a new incident or new set of circumstances might precipitate formal child protection procedures. The family would then be informed that a child protection conference was to be held. In one office, however, regular planning meetings were held for cases already allocated to a social worker to which parents were invited and at which most of the agencies would be represented as at a child protection conference. The decision as to whether or not to hold a formal child protection conference would be taken at that planning meeting in the presence of the parents. One problem with this system was that two meetings covering the same ground might take place within a day or two involving most of the same people. Balanced against this was the advantage that, more often than not, it was agreed that a protection plan could be put in place without the need for a formal conference. If it was concluded that a move into an enquiry under Section 47 was needed, the parents were fully informed about what would happen.

Working in partnership with parents

Of the 40 parents who expressed an opinion about this stage of the process, ten considered the service at the time of investigation to be fairly or very satisfactory, while 30 were not very satisfied or unsatisfied. Thirty-one children were medically examined: 25 of these children were accompanied to the medical by a parent or relative.

A researcher rating on the involvement of parents at the investigation stage showed that approximately one-fifth were thought to have participated or be partners; two-fifths to have been fully informed or to have had some information; one-fifth to have been manipulated or placated and one-fifth not to have been involved at all. This compares, interestingly, with the 1990–91 study by Thoburn et al. (1995) where, of the 220 families whose cases were considered at child protection conferences (40% of which did not result in registration), only 11% were thought to have participated or been partners at the investigation stage, 82% to have had some or full information or to have been informed and consulted to some extent but only 5% to have been manipulated or placated, and 2% where the involvement was totally lacking. There are contrasts between the studies at each end of the partnership ladder, with far more families in this study being placed in the manipulated/placated/totally lacking categories (37%) than in 1990–91 (7%), and far more in the participation/partnership categories (20% as compared with 11%). At the top end of the continuum this may be attributed to improvements in policy and practice skills following the requirement in the Children Act 1989 to seek to work in partnership. At the other end of the scale the lack of involvement may in part result from the fact that all the children in this present study were suffering or likely to suffer significant harm, whereas this was not the case with a significant minority of those about whom conferences were held in the 1990–91 study.

The following quotation from a mother illustrates the effect on parents when they are informed about alleged incidents if due thought has not been given to the manner in which the information is presented:

> I didn't know about it until I had a phone call a week later from the manageress [of the residential home where respite care was arranged for her 12-year-old son] asking me if I'd like to come in for a cup of coffee – and that's how it was – informal. 'I'll come and pick you up if you like', and all the way in the car she didn't say a word. I sat in the lounge and then the social worker and the police walked in and said 'Mrs W?', and I said 'Yes', and they said 'We're from Child Protection'. Can you imagine how I felt?– Gulp! I felt like I'd been punched into the ground, you know. Just suddenly like that. The way it was done, it was appalling.

Working with professionals

Close working contact with the police was a feature in six of the offices, and of the 59 cases where there were formal enquiries about the alleged abuse, 50% were by social workers and police together, 27% by one or two social workers, and 15% by the police alone. (Insufficient information was available to the researchers in 8% of cases.) When it was necessary to inform parents that a specific allegation had been made (in 55 cases), 38% were told by social workers and police together, 40% by one or two social workers, and 11% by the police alone. (This information was not available in 11% of cases.) A Child Assessment Order (CAO) was considered in one of the 105 cases, but not used.

None of the study areas operated a protocol, used in some authorities, about which sorts of enquiries will be handled separately and which by the police and social workers jointly.

The third threshold: child protection conferences

An initial or incident child protection conference was held at some stage in the year after concerns were identified in 101 of the 105 cases. From the evidence available, in 53% of the cases the social work manager was the person whose opinion was most influential in deciding that a conference should be held, followed by the conference chairperson in 25% of the cases. Perhaps surprisingly, social workers were considered to be most influential in only 5% of cases.

In all but one case, parents were invited to most or all of the initial child protection conferences, demonstrating a substantial change in practice after the implementation of the Children Act 1989, which was in line with its partnership philosophy. In 77% of cases a parent attended the conference (42%, mothers on their own; 9%, fathers on their own; and 26% both parents). In most cases they attended the whole conference, though in one authority it was normal practice for professionals to meet briefly before the family members were invited in. There were only 22 'supporters' (mostly grandparents) who attended conferences but they were generally greatly valued:

> I didn't agree with some of the things they were saying. I wanted to say something but I didn't know half the people that were there. I just felt odd with them all looking at me and asking questions. I was glad my mum was there, really. I wouldn't have gone if she hadn't been there.

Seventy-two children were too young to attend the conferences but only three of 33 children aged 10 or over (an 11-year-old, one 14-year-old and two 15-year-olds) attended for most or all of the time. Interpreters attended in six of the seven cases where interpretation was needed. We discuss some of the difficulties of using interpreters in Chapter 6.

The researchers were able to observe the way in which the conferences were handled and how parents were involved. The welcomes were carried out seriously and with respect, and preparation and briefing time was given to family members by all the chairpersons. It was an opportunity to convey to parents the idea that the chairperson was acting independently and would help them to put their views across. Most of the chairpersons were able to meet the parents in the room where the conference would be held, so that they were already present before the professionals arrived, but in another area the professionals gathered early in the conference room whereas parents waited in a room outside, to be spoken to by the chairperson before being invited in. Such arrangements are known to be daunting for parents (Thoburn et al. 1995):

> I was shocked at the amount of people there. I thought it would be about four or five. But it was very fair. I thought everyone said what they wanted to say and I was given a chance to say what I wanted to. It was a help, my solicitor being there. It gave him an insight into what was going on, and he gave me moral support.

> I was shitting myself. I didn't know what to expect. It was murder for a few days beforehand. I was really frightened. And then we got there and I was alright. I thought, 'This is my son you're talking about, this is my family'; and I managed to hold myself together a bit.

From observation of the conferences, the research team concluded that parents were more likely to be involved in the information-giving parts of the conference than in the decision-making process:

> I don't agree with the way they talk around you. They invite you to come and then they don't take any notice of what you've got to say. They've already made the decision when they ask you what you think. They don't include you in the plan either, really, do they?

Involving parents as partners in the protection process is difficult, and, as we concluded from the *Paternalism or Partnership?* study, not always appropriate in the early stages of child protection work (Thoburn et al. 1995). There were instances where parents were overawed by the occasion, or became angry, or were unable to deal with the setting, or felt that what was said was inaccurate, and became upset. The skills of the people chairing the conferences were stretched to the limit.

The language of abuse and neglect tended to prevail within the conferences so that discussion of the harm to the child was not often overtly focused upon, despite the fairly routine reading out by the chairperson of the *Working Together* (DoH, 1991b) definition of 'signification harm' as a requirement for registration. There were many examples of competent chairing, where explanations were given to parents, where they were asked for their views and for information which enabled them to participate as much as possible, given the restrictions of the occasion. However, in the 81 cases where it was possible to rate whether parents agreed with all or the main decisions, only 47% appeared to do so. Despite the best efforts of the chairperson, a substantial majority of those who attended did not feel that their views and needs were seriously considered. A grandparent said:

> I'm not going to say nothing at the next conference. It's just a mockery –
> a load of people gathered in a room wasting their time. Some of the things
> they said were true. I thought that everyone there would help her [their
> daughter, mother of the children] as well, but it was a waste of time.
> Nothing's been done.

If a strategy meeting, involving discussion of key issues, had been held, to which they had not been invited, families were likely to be resentful when they learnt of this. It did sometimes appear to the researchers that in some cases professionals present were indeed 'going through the motions' for the sake of the family, and had arrived at the conference to defend positions already reached at the previous meeting:

> I felt that it was all discussed behind my back, and I felt when I asked
> questions I was fobbed off. They said 'We don't think so and so.' But who
> are they anyway?

> The information and evidence at the conference was twisted. Stuart [aged 2]
> is delayed but it was because he'd been left a lot because of my ex-husband
> and because I was pregnant. I really don't think they listened to a word I said.
> They made a big thing about his weight and I blew up! I totally blew up!
> They said that his weight dropped, but with Stuart you can take ages building
> up weight and then the next day – whoosh, it's gone down again. Even the
> foster carer said that.

The fourth threshold: registration and the child protection plan

Figure 3.3 shows that the names of 76 children were placed on the Child Protection Register at the initial conference. Twenty-one children were not registered and a decision on the remaining four was deferred: two of these were subsequently registered, as were two of the original 21 who were not registered. At the majority of conferences parents were not asked as a matter of course to give their views on registration. Sometimes they were able to give their views because a parent objected to the decision or, by contrast, because they approved of it. In one area, it was explained that parents could listen to the discussion about registration but were not allowed to contribute to it. At nearly all of the other conferences the decision was taken as if the parents were not present at all. In contrast, one chairperson routinely turned to the parents and asked their views about whether registration would have a positive or negative impact on the child and the family. Nowhere was a question routinely sought, or information given, about the child's wishes in respect of registration, and the minutes rarely gave information about the child's views on whether he or she would find registration helpful.

Figure 3.3 *Registration status of the index children*[1]

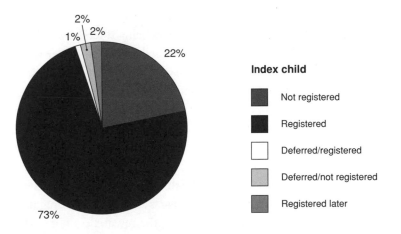

[1] n=104; no later information for one case

The conference chairperson was the most important professional in the decision about registration in 55 out of 97 cases where the information was available. A combination of professionals influenced 30 cases. As already noted, parents had little influence and most were well aware of this:

I didn't agree with that. I didn't like what they were doing for my name to go on the Register. But I didn't know quite what to do about it. I've never been in that position before. The lady who was saying about putting their names on the Register, I don't agree with that. I just wish their names weren't on there 'cos I haven't done anything – no harm to them or anything. They just put them on there probably for lack of responsibility. I know I can't get up in the mornings, but I suppose everyone has that problem sometimes.

I said I didn't mind if Elijah went on the Register because I thought if anything happened to Elijah it would be down to them then, but on the other hand, I've never hurt my baby.

We don't want his name on the Register at all. We were told his name would be put on the Register and we were asked about it at the meeting, and we said we didn't want it. But we hope it will change in three months' time.

Child protection plans

Whether or not a child's name was placed on the Register, all conferences agreed the outline of a child protection plan, and usually there was some attention to meeting some of the needs of the child and other family members. In devising protection plans it would seem desirable to consult parents about what would be helpful to them, and indeed, this has been argued to be one of the main reasons for inviting parents to conferences. However, there were no instances of parents being directly asked what they would like to see in the plan, as opposed to being asked whether they agreed with the ideas of professionals. In some cases it appeared that consultation with parents about the plan likely to be put forward had been part of the social work service leading up to the conference. These plans were then presented to the conference by the social worker, with the parents generally signalling agreement.

The plans varied from a very general list to a highly detailed plan for each child in the family which included health checks and developmental assessment. In most cases an assessment of parenting ability, usually the mother's, was included. In one area, the researchers noted that detailed support plans were made to help families when the decision was taken *not* to register the child. The researchers concluded that in 55 cases the social workers themselves were the most influential people in deciding what form the social work service would take, and in 27 cases the team managers were most influential. This number was reversed when deciding what resources should be provided, with team managers or senior social workers being most influential in 46 cases, and key social workers in 31 cases. Parents figured low on both lists, with only one or two being observed to have a significant impact on these decisions.

Of the 61 families where there was enough information to gauge the parents' experience of attendance at the initial conference, 28% of parents did not attend; 36% attended and were glad they went; 12% wished they hadn't gone; and 24% attended and were neutral or mixed about it.

The fifth threshold: care proceedings and placement

Out-of-home placements and court action are discussed in more detail in Chapters 7 and 8. In summary, most of the children lived for most of the year with at least one parent. This applied especially to those children whose parents were both of minority ethnic origin. For those who lived mainly away from home, there is a trend (which does not reach statistical significance) for children of minority ethnic origin to have their major placement with relatives.

Emergency procedures were used in 16 cases at the early stage (and in four other cases later on in the year). In nine cases legal proceedings had already commenced, and in 17 cases care proceedings were recommended as part of the protection plan. Residence Orders were advised in three cases and Contact Orders in one case. During the year following the initial child protection conference, 28 orders were used which involved removing the child from home. By the end of the year, 21 children had been the subjects of care proceedings.

After the conference: implementing protection plans and providing services

As a result of the recommendations of the initial child protection conference there was no action or further help in two cases and assessment only in seven cases. The service was provided mainly by several workers or other social services staff in 36 cases; multi-agency help was provided in 52 cases; and other help, usually practical but of a definite and positive nature, in three cases. Chapter 6 describes in more detail the help and resources which were offered.

During the year the protection plans should have been put into action. Where the child remained at home, as did the majority, the plans should have helped families to protect their children. Whilst there were examples of families who greatly valued the help that was offered, others felt they had no choice in the matter or did not perceive it as helpful. These two mothers demonstrate the range:

> I'm saying I got conned. They said if I went for treatment I'd get him back and then when we went back to court they wanted all the reports, so to me it was all one big con. They waited till I was in hospital before I got the truth. I feel cheated. I feel as though I'm serving a prison sentence for a murder I didn't commit.

> They took her into care because they were a little bit concerned because I had a lot of problems of my own. They took her for seven or eight weeks and it did give me a break. She came back and I was still a bit wary about things, but I wanted her back, you know, to be a family. I know it's hard but you do love them all.

Of the 91 families to whom services were provided, there was some evidence that a choice of help was offered to three-quarters of them whilst the remaining quarter did not appear to have any choice at all. There seemed to be little opportunity for parents to influence the choice of social worker, less than one in five being able to express a preference. This was an issue particularly for families from minority ethnic groups, or whose first language was not English. We return to this issue in Chapter 6.

Turning to the parents' perspective, just over half of the families interviewed said that they received help following the case conference. More than a quarter of parents said that they did not want help, whilst one in five wanted help but did not receive it. Although this mother did not seek help for herself, her need for assistance was clear and she reluctantly accepted that her child's health and development would be monitored:

> I'm not given any help. They just come to check on the baby. No, I don't want any help. From my previous experience when you ask for help it's like you're incompetent and it goes bad against you. So you'd be a bit wary before you asked for anything. I wouldn't ask for anything. It's important to carry out [the recommendations] about the drugs, but at the end of the day it's not what I think. It's what they think. They're running my life for me. That's how it is and that's how it feels.

Of the 40 parents and relatives we spoke to, over half were at least fairly satisfied with all or some of the help, but one in five were dissatisfied, and five family members were positively angry about what had happened. This grandmother spoke for her daughter:

> One thing that would be helpful to our daughter would be that all these lies – they're gonna do this and they're gonna do that – if they put something into action it would be better. I mean, they've got all the right people, all trained staff and all that, but where are they? They train monkeys better. I've seen a better bloody response in bloody monkeys. They said things like, if we put her on the Register we'll give her more help and we can get taxis here and there, but I mean what help is taxis – spending money what we haven't got on things like that? Why not spend it on something better? Why don't they save it up and pay the bills? It's just a farce, innit?!

An overview of the process

In analysing the views of parents and relatives about the degree to which they were involved in child protection intervention, it was clear that most found the process painful and difficult. For some, it was an incomprehensible and even destructive intrusion into their lives; for others, the experience was supportive and it helped them to turn a corner at a difficult time. What seemed a reasonable arrangement to social workers might not be perceived as such by the families. Again, we stress that in all of the cases in the sample there was clear evidence that a child was suffering or highly likely to suffer significant harm, and in all but a tiny minority this initial evidence was confirmed as further information came to light. Social workers are caught in a number of dilemmas in child protection work. They must act in the best interest of the child while trying to understand and provide support to the parents. They must offer what is possible, on restricted budgets and with scarce resources. They may build up a trusting relationship, often only to find that seeking a court order is inevitable, and then stand accused of betraying parents. Throughout they must respond in a calm and fair way to parents and children who might be emotionally volatile and sometimes violent, and whose circumstances and stresses are ever-changing.

Case studies

The following three case studies give examples of the complexity of the process and the variations within it:

ERIC

Eric's family had struggled for ten years on their own trying to bring him up while he suffered from a particular syndrome which left him unable to integrate his thoughts. He was in need of constant reassurance from any nearby adult about what was happening to him at that moment. He had learning difficulties, speech and language difficulties, and a hearing impairment. Although he was a child with special needs from the start of his life, the family only received help in the previous two years, after his mother had suffered four minor strokes, in part due to the strain under which the family had to operate.

Eric was 12 at the time of the research study. There were two older brothers who had recently left home to live independently and a younger sister still at home. Eric's father had unexpectedly been made redundant. The family had been put in touch with a community psychiatric nurse two years previously, who advised them about the benefits, and the care they were entitled to, and the family's GP wrote to the social services department requesting respite care.

Clearly, Eric was a child in need, even before the Children Act 1989 definition became operative. The system, which was meant to support him and his family, had not identified him until his mother became ill. Basic assistance, including advice on welfare benefits, special holiday play schemes and respite care, had never been offered in time. A diagnosis of his unusual condition had not been made early enough, so his parents did not know how to handle him and how best to meet his needs.

A thorough and comprehensive assessment by a number of different professionals, co-ordinated by a specialist voluntary agency just prior to the research study, concluded that Eric should be in a special boarding school. His parents described the assessment as 'an eye-opener':

> What impressed us most was that three specialists spent time on him, and they met and put it together, and they actually told us what it was like to parent Eric. It was the first time in 12 years that anyone had told us what it was like to live with him.

Although Eric's parents had a recommendation for a boarding school, neither Social Services nor Education separately or jointly took responsibility to place him. Meanwhile Eric reached puberty, grew physically, and wanted more freedom, which led him into risky situations and made him very vulnerable.

It was recognised that the residential unit was not an ideal set
and that he did not like going there, nevertheless his attendance at n
ued, together with a monthly weekend stay with a volunteer family, which
enjoyed. It was at the residential unit that an allegation was made that he had
sexually abused a younger female resident. He had been left unsupervised
with her and he regarded her as his friend. His father's view was that the two
young people had been 'experimenting'. The implication of the police questioning was that, because Eric had simulated sexual intercourse with the girl,
he must have been sexually abused at home. His parents were so shocked that
they felt they must discover who might have been abusing him, as they were
certain that it had not happened at home, so they agreed to a video interview.
Viewing the video tape confirmed their view that the police and social worker
had already made up their minds that he had been abused at home. They
thought that during the video interview 'they were putting words into his
mouth' and that the professionals did not understand his condition. Eric
became even more disorientated. He was unable to distinguish what was
appropriate behaviour in *any* situation, quite apart from a sexual one.

An initial child protection conference was held but Eric's name was not
placed on the Register. The key workers who found Eric and the girl together
were not present at the conference and most of the other professionals did not
know him. Eric's newly allocated social worker was not able to be present
either. Eric's father said:

> My daughter's headmistress was at the conference and when I took Sally to
> school I stopped kissing her because I thought she might think 'What's going
> on here?' It all felt underhand – all cloak and dagger, as though they might be
> watching us.

The system went from bad to worse in terms of offering help to Eric and his
family. The lack of a proper diagnosis, the inappropriate placement with staff
who did not supervise him carefully enough, the lack of plans for the special
boarding school because the money could not be found, and the initial child
protection conference all increased, rather than decreased, Eric's parents' anxieties and thus Eric's own confusion. The parents were assisted, by a
voluntary agency, which provides support to parents or children with learning disabilities, to make a formal complaint.

● ●

WILLIAM

William was 2 years old at the time of the initial child protection conference.
William's mother, Liz, told the researcher that William's conception had been

a mistake, and that during the year in which he was born she had sought psychiatric help because of her suicidal thoughts. Liz and her husband split up after his birth. William went on to develop asthma and was admitted to hospital on a number of occasions. Liz described herself as 'going downhill', and frequently talked of having him adopted. William's father's contact with the family was erratic, and he would talk of returning to the family home to help out, but never did. This added to Liz's distress. The only member of the extended family who offered support was Liz's mother, but she was confined to a wheelchair and therefore limited in what she could do.

The social services department were alerted when the oldest child in the family, 6-year-old Darren, did not attend school because he was caring for William and his sister, Donna (aged 3), who was developmentally delayed. A social worker was allocated, and three weeks before the initial child protection conference William was accommodated at Liz's request. The hospital had described him as 'unkempt' and the foster carer found him 'filthy', not toilet-trained and unable to eat socially. There was an allegation that Liz was drinking heavily. The chairperson at the conference said in her opening remarks:

> This is not a single incident – or a series of incidents but a concern for the quality of life and care that has led to a growing cause for concern for these children.

● ●

A referral had already been made to the social services department for family support and this had been offered in the form of foster care for William. All the ingredients of a possible breakdown in family functioning were present – mental ill-health; developmental delay in one child, chronic illness in another; unsatisfactory marital separation; and a child drawn into the parental role of caring for siblings. The support system hardly had time to operate before child protection procedures were introduced and an allegation of neglect of all three children was made.

One of the reasons for holding the conference was because the social worker had found it difficult to gain Liz's co-operation, although Liz herself was aware that she was 'going through a bad patch' and in need of help. (Indeed, she told the researchers that she liked her social worker and found her helpful.) At the conference, the protection plan outlined a whole range of services which were to support her, but this made Liz think that 'everyone was ganging up on me'. She knew that she had many problems to face and that she was depressed. The medication she was on had made her sleepy and unable to cope with all three children. A year later, there had been an application for a Care Order on all the children, which resulted in a Supervision Order on one of them and no orders on the others, except that increased contact for the grandmother was secured by a Section 8 Contact Order. William spent three months in foster care; there were family sessions at the child and family psychiatric unit; second-hand furniture was provided; advice for Liz came from the drug dependency unit; and William had three sessions a week at nursery school when he returned home. At Stage 2 the picture emerged of a family able to function again, but still requiring a great deal of help. This was in part a result of the intervention, but also because of the arrival of a new and more supportive partner for Liz.

The use of the formal child protection procedures had succeeded in raising the urgency of the situation in the minds of the family, as well as the professional network. The court had provided the authority to ensure that the older child attended school. Although William was undoubtedly a child suffering significant harm before the initial child protection conference, and the intervention was a success in preventing his deterioration, it was at the expense of the mother's trust in the system. Liz told the researcher at the Stage 2 interview:

> The social workers should trust the parents really. . . . They take it the wrong way, I think, and they put a bad view on me 'cos I've had problems in the past. They shouldn't look at it that way, should they? They should help you. It's been hard to trust anyone really [since the first research interview]. You get lack of trust. They know I wouldn't do nothing to the kids. I'm not that sort of person. You just feel you're being spied on all the time, and that's not really nice.

● ●

DELROY

Delroy, aged 13, came from a large extended family of African–Caribbean descent. He was the youngest of five children. His mother had a learning disability which meant that whilst she managed to care for the children when they were younger (with the support of their father), later, when she was separated and the children became adolescents, she could not control them and they were cared for by their grandmother.

This arrangement was altered when their mother met another partner. Delroy and his next eldest brother moved back into their mother's flat. Soon, however, the situation deteriorated rapidly. There was no heating in the flat, no hot water, windows and doors were broken. The boys began to offend and roam the streets and quickly accumulated a string of offences. The social services department became involved and provided practical and material help to improve the home conditions, but subsequently another older brother moved in and the situation became worse again.

The social worker was alarmed by the dangerous position Delroy and his brother were in, both environmentally at home and by their offending on the streets. The brothers assumed a defiant posture and were determined that 'no-one will put us in care'. Eventually the social worker persuaded them that they should be accommodated with a foster carer. (All of this work was carried out by a worker committed to preventive child care, using Section 17 money and guidance.) However the boys so disliked the foster arrangement that they returned of their own accord to their grandmother, with a request that they should be allowed to remain with her. The extended family met and decided that one brother should return to his boarding school and live with his grandmother at weekends and holidays, and that Delroy should live with his older sister's family. At this point it was decided to call a child protection conference to see if the boys were in need of protection.

● ●

This was a highly dangerous situation for adolescent boys to be in because of their possible drift into crime, not to mention the possibility of exploitation and physical or sexual assault. Delroy had already been identified for the research study as a child likely to suffer significant harm, before child protection procedures were invoked, because of what was happening to him and the fact that he had been out of school for a year. The social worker had worked for a long time with the family, knew the boys well, and had their trust. When the conference took place all the family attended, including Delroy and his brother. A serious discussion took place about whether their names should be placed on the Child Protection Register. The family was very much part of that discussion, especially the boys, who participated in a mature and sensible way. They were not registered.

A year later, Delroy was living with his sister and her family: well fed, well dressed and well cared for; supported to a certain extent by Section 17 money. He was attending school regularly, although not yet attaining his potential and tending to fight to settle disagreements with peers; in contact with all the members of his family, including his father; proud of his football prowess and devoted to his local first-division football team.

The strong extended family, the trusted social worker and the involvement of all in the decisions about Delroy resulted in a 'success', so that he was not considered to be suffering significant harm at the end of the study. There were, however, remaining problems that might easily escalate unless they were managed carefully by the professionals and his school, in particular. The question of case closure had become an issue, with pressure on the social worker to close, even though he felt it important to continue. He considered Delroy still to be vulnerable. (Delroy's exit from child protection procedures was not an issue because Delroy was not registered.) To the researchers and the family members there appeared good reasons why social work support should continue. These included the continuing need, at times, for financial support; the fine balance of Delroy's schooling; the influence on Delroy from his brothers, who sailed close to the wind with regards to offending; and the importance of the social worker holding so much professional knowledge about the family on which to base decisions, should the need arise.

Investigation or enquiry?

These cases reinforce the advice in the Audit Commission report (1994) and the Department of Health *Guidance* on Parts III and IV of the Children Act (DoH 1991a), that Sections 17 and 47 should be used in parallel to help vulnerable children and their families. In all these cases the needs of children and parents were inextricably linked with the circumstances leading to mal-treatment.

In this chapter we have referred to one of the key principles in the Act: the requirement of Social Services to attempt to work in partnership with parents and children. There was evidence of procedures being used that facilitated partnership-based practice but, in these difficult and complex cases, much to show how hard it is to achieve this aim. In each case in our sample the child's welfare and protection was the paramount consideration and attempts to work in partnership were quickly abandoned or 'put on the back burner' when formal protection procedures were found to be necessary.

In the chapters that follow we look further at this principle, as well as the 'no order' principle, and the encouragement to make greater use of the help of relatives and to involve non-resident parents.

Summary

The five thresholds in the child protection procedures examined in this chap-ter are: referrals, strategy meetings and Section 47 enquiries; child protection conferences; registration and the child protection plan; and care proceedings placement. Information provided includes who attended the meetings, who influenced the decision-making, the office culture in relation to the conduct of initial child protection conferences and registration, and the provision of services. The opinions of parents, about what they found helpful or unhelpful, are reported.

There were widespread differences between the area teams about the early approaches to allegations, strategy meetings and enquiries. Some offices moved quickly to formalise enquiries into investigations involving the police; some used strategy discussions or meetings to assess the allegations; and others involved parents and professionals in planning meetings to make the decision as to whether a child protection conference should be convened. The decision to hold a conference was most influenced by social work managers. The participation of parents consisted mostly in information-giving rather than decision-making. The position was similar regarding the decision to place the child's name on the Child Protection Register, with little involvement of the parents or children in the decision. The research team concluded that just over half of the 105 cases probably did not need to be registered (just under half of those actually registered).

Help and resources were offered to the vast majority of families, some of it welcomed by family members and some not. Detailed protection and support plans were usually made, irrespective of whether a decision was taken to place the child's name on the Child Protection Register.

The chapter concludes with case studies, giving examples of how the child protection process affected the lives of three families.

4 *The nature of the maltreatment*

The type and severity of maltreatment and the resultant harm to the child are examined in this chapter. How professionals categorise the harm is considered and the extent to which the Children Act language of 'harm', rather than the earlier language of 'abuse', is used. Case examples are provided to demonstrate the different categories of harm and maltreatment. The chapter concludes with a detailed critical examination of 24 particularly high-risk cases, where there was an element of danger to life or limb or serious risk of sexual assault by a parent or parent-figure still in contact with the child.

Type of maltreatment

The research team placed the harm to the 105 children in one of 15 categories (see Table 4.1). This is a fuller list than the categories of registration used by *Working Together* (DoH 1991b). The categorisation of types of maltreatment for the 105 cases results from a detailed examination of data from several sources and can be compared with the categories of registration used by the conferences in respect of the 78 children who were registered (see Table 4.2).

The most frequent type of maltreatment was neglect, often alongside physical, emotional or sexual abuse. There were 46 children in the categories which included neglect. The element of neglect is not surprising in relation to the social circumstances of the families, explained in Chapter 2, but it should be remembered that there are many more families also suffering from poverty and poor housing in the general population, whose children are not thought to be neglected and who do not come to the attention of the agencies.

Cases were allocated to the 'emotional cruelty' category if there was evidence of specific non-physical acts of cruelty (which could be acts of commission or deliberate omission). Emotional neglect does not necessarily relate to social problems although its impact is likely to be exacerbated by them. The aetiology of emotional neglect is complex (Garbarino 1986; O'Hagan 1993; Stevenson 1996). It rests in the subtle interplay between parent and child which may have been influenced by the parents' temperamental history; by the birth of the child; by the child's temperament and any disabilities; and by

Table 4.1 *Types of maltreatment*

	No.
Physical and emotional neglect	15
Emotional neglect	15
Physical neglect	14
Sexual abuse	14
Physical abuse	12
Combination neglect	11
Excessive punishment	7
Neglect and sexual abuse	4
Emotional cruelty	3
Physical and sexual abuse	2
Emotional cruelty and sexual abuse	1
Emotional cruelty and neglect	1
Physical and sexual abuse and neglect	1
Combination cruelty	1
Persistent punishment	1
Total	**102**[1]

[1] Insufficiently detailed information on three cases

the pattern of relationships between parents (or parents and partners). A multitude of strands contributes to reinforcing the development of a secure or insecure emotional attachment (Howe et al. 1999). Most important, in establishing secure attachments for children is the parents' own sense of self-worth and felt security. Many of the parents lacked a sense of self-worth and the child-rearing pattern of 'low on warmth, high on criticism' (Dartington Social Research Unit 1995) had become established with its known consequences of serious harm to the child.

The *Working Together* (DoH 1991b) categories of registration tended to be poor indicators of the harm likely to be experienced by the child. A continuing use of the word 'abuse' in the majority of cases did not assist the parents or workers to focus on the effects on the child of parental behaviour since the type of actual or likely future harm was often different from the type of incident that led to the conference or planning meeting. The 'last straw' was often laid on the fragile foundations of months or even years of 'shaky' parenting and relationship problems (Dartington Social Research Unit 1995). The significance of the high-criticism, low-worth environments in which many of these children lived was often not recognised by the conferences. In such cases the protection plans concentrated on preventing the recurrence of

Table 4.2 *Categories of registration cases considered at conferences (n=101)*[1]

Category	No.	% of those registered
Neglect	24	30
Physical	22	28
Sexual	13	16
Emotional	7	9
Neglect and emotional	5	6
Physical and emotional	3	4
Neglect and physical	2	3
Neglect and sexual	2	3
Physical and sexual	1	1
Total	79	100
Not registered	22	22

an often rather minor incident and ignored the massive burdens under which many of the parents and children were struggling.

The severity of the maltreatment in our 1993–94 study is shown in Table 4.3 and comparison is made with a study of 220 cases that reached a child protection conference prior to the Children Act (Thoburn et al. 1995). Similar

Table 4.3 *Severity of maltreatment*

Type of maltreatment	% in 1990–91 study[1] (n=220)	% in 1993–94 study (n=105)
Death[2]	0.5	4
Serious physical injury	2	2
Moderate physical injury	6	2
Persistent or deliberate serious chastisement	1	1
Severe neglect	1	8
Penetrative sexual assault with violence	4	4
Penetrative sexual assault without violence	4	4
Life-threatening failure to thrive	—	1
Other serious maltreatment	12	13
None of the above	60	62
Total	100	100

[1] Thoburn et al. 1995

[2] In two cases involving a death, this was of a previous child; in one of these cases there was a pre-birth conference

numbers came into the less serious 'none of these' category, but there were more cases in the severe neglect group in the present study. Although 65 cases did not fall into any of the 'severe' categories, there is no intention of minimising the impact of this maltreatment on the children. The context of the family circumstances and relationships contribute to or mitigate against the degree of harm suffered. As *Child Protection: Messages from Research* (Dartington Social Research Unit 1995) has noted, a one-off episode of abusive behaviour in the context of a generally caring family will be less harmful than a succession of apparently less serious punishments in a less caring household.

Identity of the alleged abuser

The term 'alleged abuser' covers a broad range of activity: from negligent care or supervision, to loss of control on one occasion; from persistent hostility to the child over a long period of time, to intentional intimidation or violence. In 12 cases the person responsible for the abuse was convicted for this offence. Over half of the alleged abusers were mothers or stepmothers (54%), whilst a quarter were fathers and stepfathers or other male carers (see Table 4.4). Given that the major carer in two-parent families is usually the mother and that, at the time of the harm, there were 45 lone mothers, this is not surprising.

Figure 4.1 shows the seriousness of the maltreatment and whether the child was living with the person believed to be responsible. It indicates that this was less likely to be the case if the maltreatment was rated as 'serious'.

Table 4.4 *Person believed responsible for maltreatment*

	% in 1990–91 study[1] (n=220)	% in 1993–94 study (n=105)
Mother	30	53
Father	30	17
Stepmother	1	1
Stepfather	11	4
Other male carer	2	4
Male and female parents/carers jointly	14	9
Male friend/relative	3	5
Stranger to family	2	1
Combination of circumstances/not clear	7	7
Total	100	100

[1] Thoburn et al. 1995

Figure 4.1 *Children living with the alleged abuser, and severity of maltreatment*[1]

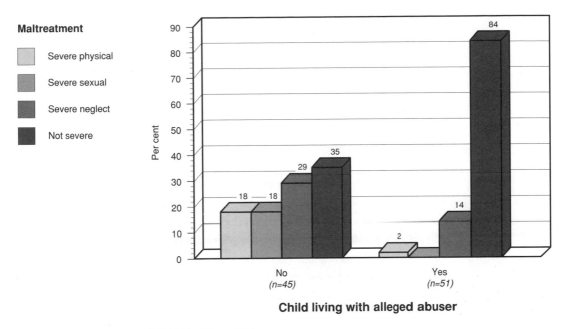

¹ x^2:27.33 df:3 p<.0001

Responsibility for the abuse

Fifty-two mothers and 18 fathers accepted partial or total responsibility for harming their child; 6 mothers and 12 fathers denied any responsibility; and 27 mothers and 37 fathers were not implicated in the maltreatment. These figures suggest that the basis for co-operative working was potentially present at the start of child protection procedures in that the majority of parents accepted that something that could be harmful to their child had occurred.

Turning to the extent of agreement between the social worker and the parents about the seriousness of the maltreatment, 66 parents agreed or partially agreed with the social worker about whether maltreatment had occurred and its seriousness; 83 agreed or partially agreed with the social worker about who was responsible for the maltreatment; and 61 parents agreed with the social worker that they themselves were at least partially responsible, again suggesting that in most of the cases there was a basis for working in partnership.

At the time of the second research interview (Stage 2), parents were asked to look back to the time of the original conference and to answer questions about ill-treatment and harm that the child might have been suffering.

One in five said their child was definitely not suffering significant harm, and one parent said she didn't know. Two said 'no', but they thought their child was always difficult or at a difficult stage and therefore suffering harm in some way; a quarter said 'yes – a little', and then modified their replies with comments such as 'well – not *harm*'; but almost half of the parents interviewed said that their child had been suffering significant harm.

The willingness of almost half of the parents to acknowledge that what was happening to their child at the time of the initial child protection conference was harmful suggested that the word 'harm' had more meaning for the parent as a description of what had occurred, and was more 'acceptable' to them, than 'abuse'. (Cleaver and Freeman (1995) found similarly.)

For social workers to know that the majority of parents can recognise, or be helped to acknowledge, their responsibility for the harm to the child, should enable them to take a less bureaucratic, distancing approach to families. A more 'play-fair' and 'participatory' approach would enhance the possibility of working in partnership to improve the well-being of all the members of the family (Howe 1992).

Examples of maltreatment and harm to the children

The following case studies provide examples of how the different types of harm to the children could be linked to the Children Act 1989 threshold of 'significant harm'. Overlaps between categories are demonstrated:

● ●

ILL-TREATMENT

Sarah (aged 2) was ill-treated by her mother who was arrested for assault. In the conference it was alleged that her mother had punched and kicked her when she asked for food, slapped her across the head, pulled and shaken her, and shouted and sworn at her. The mother admitted to bruising her on the thigh but denied the other allegations. At the first interview the researcher recorded that Sarah's mother's only interaction with her for over an hour was to tell her many times in an irritated tone to go and wipe her nose. On a second occasion, while waiting to see Sarah's father, the researcher recorded that she was smacked twice in an hour by her mother. The likely future harm for Sarah was possibly physical but almost certainly emotional, unless substantial improvements could be made in the parenting she was receiving.

IMPAIRMENT OF HEALTH

Melanie (aged 11) came from a family where the children were kept isolated from their peers. Their father saw all outside contact as intrusive. He had video cameras fixed outside the house with monitors in every room to check whoever came to the door. He did not allow the three younger siblings to attend school for six months because he complained that the school for children with special educational needs was not meeting their needs for a good education. The children were described at the initial child protection conference as 'living in a siege with videos'. During the year following the conference, the professionals tried to undertake an assessment of the family under the terms of an Interim Care Order. Melanie's weight fell and rose alarmingly on a number of occasions. The doctors described these rapid changes in her body weight as likely to be damaging to her internal organs. The isolation from normal social intercourse was impairing her mental health, too.

IMPAIRMENT OF DEVELOPMENT

Seven-year-old Rowan was referred to the formal child protection system by his mother because of his sexualised behaviour, both before and after an incident when he found pornographic magazines while he was playing with his friends. He re-enacted the contents with his siblings at home. His mother told the researcher that Rowan had always been interested in sex, and she described occasions when he kept 'coming up to me and touching my breasts. I didn't know how to handle it. It may be more difficult for me because of my past' [of being sexually abused]. She said he had been in care 'loads of times when I couldn't cope. It was because of his behaviour: he wets a lot and is destructive.' She added that she 'used to be so strict with him when he was little. I used to do outrageous things to him. I used to try to suffocate him on a number of occasions. But we've been settled for three years now and I'd expect him to be improving.'

His teacher described Rowan as having 'global developmental delay and speech problems. He has occasional emotional outbursts, not usually physically aggressive, more angry or upset. He is a lovely little boy needing security and reassurance of his worth, but wanting to please and succeed.' Rowan's emotional development was being impaired as a result of a long history of not having his basic needs met. His mother had been seeking help for many years but had received only episodic help rather than the consistent and reliable relationship-based multidisciplinary service she and Rowan clearly needed.

THE PARTICULAR CHILD

Donovan (aged 11) was regarded as a difficult child by his father since the time of his mother's death four years previously. His father said that he had never cried after the loss of his mother. Donovan had been sexually abused by a stranger two years after his mother's death. He attended a special school for children with learning difficulties but did not like it and often refused to go. 'He has a number of strategies that he employs to get him out of work. He can be demanding and does need lots of adult attention.' Donovan's father allowed him to disappear for hours at a time and, on one occasion, for nearly a week before calling in the police. During the year following the initial child protection conference Donovan was sexually abused again by a stranger while travelling about on trains with another boy during the late evening. Donovan had developed into a very difficult child to parent and to help.

• • •

Lily (aged 5) had come as a refugee to this country with her mother, sister and an older girl of 14 years. When Lily was a baby her father had been shot during the fighting in her home country, as were most of the other members of her family. Her mother had to flee at a moment's notice. Lily and her sister and the older girl were cared for in a mission station until her mother returned and brought them to England. Leaving their country meant losing the familiar place where they had spent most of their short lives and an uncle and aunt who had kept in touch with them. When they arrived in England, the older girl, who was Lily's attachment figure, also split off on her own. As a result of these traumatic experiences Lily became mute. Lily and her sister became the subjects of an initial child protection conference because they had been taken into police protection twice when their mother had left them on their own for long periods.

PARENTAL CARE

A pre-birth conference took place when it was known that the mother of four children, all of whom had been taken into care in the past, was pregnant again. The mother had lived at different times with three different Schedule 1 offenders, and had been unable to protect her children from being physically and sexually abused. Though the children were removed she kept in contact with her oldest daughter. In spite of the separation, the mother collaborated with her then-current partner in writing pornographic letters to her daughter, allowing him, in the words of the psychiatrist involved, 'to groom her'. The father of the expected baby would not give his name to the police and refused to be interviewed by Social Services. The mother's family did not appear adequately concerned about her involvement in what had happened to the other children. In view of this persistent lack of protective responses from the mother and relatives, care proceedings were instituted, the baby was moved at birth and quickly placed for adoption.

Predicting dangerous situations

In view of public and media reactions to the deaths of children, it is not easy for professionals, especially social workers and child protection managers, to disentangle potential danger to the child from potential risk to themselves, their carers and their agencies. Whilst sexual assault by a parent on a child of any age is recognised to be dangerous to the child's emotional health, its discovery is unlikely to arouse the interest of the media in the way that occurs when a child dies as a result of a physical assault or severe neglect.

It is not surprising that the question which causes much anxiety to social workers in child protection work is: 'Does this family contain the potential for inflicting death or life-limiting injury to the child, and how will I know?'

In order to look more closely at what might constitute 'dangerousness' the research team listed the characteristics that have been highlighted in cases of child deaths. All cases with the following characteristics were identified and described in more detail:

♦ the child was under 5 or particularly vulnerable to physical assault because of a disability;

and

♦ the child was being, or there was any risk of his/her being, seriously physically injured or sexually assaulted; or

♦ the child was being neglected and consequently exposed to the risk of serious injury, assault or life-threatening/life-limiting failure to thrive; or

♦ the child's physical health or development was being, or was likely to be, significantly impaired;

or

♦ the child was over 5 and not otherwise especially vulnerable, but there was a high probability of life-threatening injury, impairment of development or sexual assault by a parent or other member of the household.

There were 24 such cases, just under a quarter of the cohort. All but one of these children were under the age of 5. The one older child was a 15-year-old at serious risk of death from an eating disorder, believed to have an emotional cause. Formal child protection procedures were not used in this case, even though the child was recognised as suffering significant harm; nor, in the opinion of the research team, would they have been helpful. Instead, a multidisciplinary approach was taken, with regular meetings between health professionals and social workers to maintain a consistent plan of intervention and monitoring, which involved the parents and the young woman. The remaining 23 cases (48% of the children who were under 5 at the start of the study) are considered as a group in this and subsequent chapters. Seventeen were in the 'background sample' and six were in the 'intensive sample'. The details of these cases are summarised in Table 4.5. Six were unborn at the time of the conference; eight were aged under 1 year; three were aged 1 and two each were in the 2-, 3- and 4-year-old groups.

Table 4.5 *Particularly high-risk cases involving children under 5 (n=23)*

Age of child	Severity of maltreatment (actual or likely)	No. of categories of maltreatment or impairment recorded (actual or likely)	Actual or likely significant harm at Stage 1	Willingness of parent(s) to co-operate with protection plans
Unborn	Penetrative sexual injury	6	Likely	No
	Serious neglect	7	Likely	To some extent
	Serious neglect	4	Actual	To some extent
	Serious neglect	10	Likely	To some extent
	Serious neglect	7	Not clear	To some extent
	Serious neglect	7	Likely	No
<1	Fractured limb	1	Not clear	No
	Serious neglect	9	Likely	To some extent
	Serious physical injury	10	Likely	No
	Not in 'severe' categories	3	Likely	To some extent
	Not in 'severe' categories	—	Likely	No
	Serious neglect	9	Actual	To some extent
	Older sibling died	—	Likely	No
	Fractured limb	10	Actual	No
1	Not in 'severe' categories	—	None	To some extent
	Not in 'severe' categories	—	Likely	No
	Older sibling died	—	None	To some extent
2	Not in 'severe' categories	15	Actual	No
	Not in 'severe' categories	14	Actual	To some extent
3	Not in 'severe' categories	14	Actual	No
	Serious physical injury	5	Likely	Very
4	Penetrative sexual assault	7	Likely	No
	Not in 'severe' categories	8	Actual	To some extent

The type of maltreatment

At the time of the initial conference, two of the children living in dangerous situations were feared to be at risk of death because of the death of a previous child in the family at the hands of a parent. Two children were considered to be at serious risk of physical injury if they remained with parents who had injured a child in the past. Two children had fractured limbs, which were believed to be the result of rough handling rather than deliberate intent to injure, one of these having been caught in the middle of marital violence.

Seven children were included in the category of life-threatening neglect: most being children of mothers who had seriously neglected previous children; though in two cases, concern arose because the mothers had not cared for *themselves* during pregnancy. In those latter cases, there were indications that the mothers were unprepared or unable to accept help in looking after themselves and a young baby.

One child had been sexually abused by an older sibling; another baby was born to a mother who had a history of allowing known sexual offenders to have access to her children, and was alleged to have colluded in the sexual abuse of a previous child who was now in care.

Eight children were included in the category of 'other serious abuse'. In these cases, there was evidence to suggest that they were exposed to persistent maltreatment that could be life-threatening.

To demonstrate the complexity of many of these cases, Table 4.5 also shows the frequency with which there were indications, at the time of the initial conference, of the different types of ill-treatment or impairment of health or development. These included *likely* as well as *actual* significant harm, including physical, sexual, emotional, behavioural and intellectual impairment or ill-treatment. If a child was actually suffering and likely to continue to suffer neglect, for example, this would be recorded twice; but if a child was actually suffering neglect at the time of the conference, but it was clear that this would not happen in the future, it was counted only once.

For the six unborn children and most of the eight who were under 1, the ratings were 'likely', except that two mothers deliberately harmed themselves while pregnant and questions were raised about an intention to harm the unborn child. Additionally, two of the babies aged under 1 year old had suffered physical injuries. The emotional and social development of another was already considered to have been impaired because of the intensity and frequency of violence between his parents, which also placed him in physical danger.

In five cases no specific incidents of actual or likely ill-treatment or impairment were recorded. These included the two children where a previous child in the family had died. One was placed with his mother in a residential setting and his health and development was being very carefully monitored. The other was in the long-term care of his grandmother. One child was listed only once under the category of physical ill-treatment. The parents' explanation, that an injury was the unintended consequence of rough handling by the father, was accepted. His general health and development were good. The remaining 17 children were listed under more than one category of ill-treatment or impairment.

Three of the six children listed under ten or more categories were members of families where violence between the parents was both frequent and extreme. Another child, who was born with a physical disability and had learning difficulties, was physically abused by her mother's boyfriend. The mother of one infant was an in-patient at a long-stay psychiatric hospital.

It was considered that 12 of these 23 children were not actually suffering significant harm but that they would be likely to do so unless protective action was taken. Seven children, all except one of whom were aged 1 or over, were considered to be already suffering significant harm. In two cases the degree of harm or likely harm was still unclear, and in two other cases as further information became available, it was considered that they were neither suffering nor likely to suffer significant harm. They were left in the sample in view of the seriousness of the original concerns and so that we could check whether this assessment had been appropriate.

Parents' willingness to co-operate with protection plans

At Stage 1, 11 of the parents of these 23 children were rated as 'not at all co-operative', 11 were rated as 'co-operative to some extent', and in only one case were the parents rated as 'very willing to co-operate'. This suggests that parents' unwillingness to engage with the workers, in ensuring that protection plans were effective, was an important factor to be considered in the early weeks. This situation could lead to the isolation of families, where doors would be shut on the professionals attempting to help, assess and monitor, with the consequent heightening of danger to the child. In such circumstances it is not surprising that all 23 cases were reviewed at a child protection conference and that the names of all except five were entered on the Child

Protection Register. In only one of these 18 registered cases did the researchers consider that registration was either unhelpful or unnecessary:

● ●

A pre-birth conference on a child, whose mother was detained under the provisions of mental health legislation in a psychiatric hospital, was attended by the grandparents but not the mother. The mother's illness had started in adolescence, but in the very recent past a change of medication had enabled her to care better for herself within the hospital. It would have been possible to work on a voluntary basis with the extended family on the issues of care and placement but it became clear shortly after the birth that the mother would be unable to parent her child. The baby could have been accommodated without registering the child. (The grandparents were extremely distressed by the registration.) The baby was placed for adoption with the agreement of the grandparents. The mother's consent was likely to be dispensed with.

This case was one of a small number where a parent was in need of protection herself, due to disability or being still under the age of 18. In none of these cases was the Official Solicitor brought in to ensure that the interests of the vulnerable parents were safeguarded.

● ●

The subsequent handling of these cases and the interim outcomes for the 24 children living in potentially dangerous situations are described in later chapters.

The interplay between unmet needs and harm resulting from maltreatment

Returning to the total cohort of 105 cases, in order to get a fuller picture of the needs of the children, which a protection plan might be expected to meet if it were to reverse the pattern of maltreatment and prevent future harm, we combined information about the family environment with data about the different aspects of the maltreatment. A 'need/risk of harm' grid was developed from Hardiker's work (Hardiker et al. 1991), the 'need' axis being based on the wording of Section 17 of the Children Act 1989 and the 'risk of maltreatment' axis bringing in the concepts of maltreatment and parental fault (see Appendix 3).

Table 4.6 shows that 78 of the children were in the 'high need' category in that they had a range of needs that would require concerted multi-agency intervention if significant impairment to health or development was to be prevented. Fifty children were at high risk of significant harm as a result of maltreatment, and 42 children were at high risk of maltreatment and in high need. Nine children were at no risk or low risk of maltreatment but were in high need; only two at high risk and six at medium risk of maltreatment were in the 'low need' group. Even these would be 'children in need', as defined by Section 17(a) of the Children Act 1989, in that they would be unlikely to achieve a reasonable standard of health or development without the provision of services under Part III of the Act.

Table 4.6 demonstrates that in most cases there is an overlap between the needs of children, which arise from environmental, health and relationship problems, and their need for protective and support services as a result of parental maltreatment or neglect.

Table 4.6 Risk of maltreatment, and level of need, at Stage 1 (no. of cases)

Level of need	Risk of Maltreatment				
	None	Low	Medium	High	Total need
None					
Low			6	2	8
Medium		4	9	6	19
High		8	28	42	78
Total risk of maltreatment		12	43	50	105

Summary

The term 'abuse' is unsatisfactory as a way of describing the many different circumstances represented by the families in the study. 'Maltreatment' or 'ill-usage' are terms more applicable to the incidents or situations. The most frequent type of maltreatment was neglect, with 46 of the 105 children allocated to categories that included it.

An analysis of the cases suggests that the emphasis in the Children Act 1989 on the nature of the harm to the child, and on parental willingness to work co-operatively to alleviate the child's distress, might prove more effective in enhancing the well-being of children than a narrower concentration on abusive acts of commission or omission by the parents.

Half of the parents when asked whether they thought that their child had been suffering significant harm at the time of the incident leading to the initial child protection conference said that they thought they had been. The extent of agreement between social workers and families regarding what had happened, and the fact that at least half of the parents accepted full responsibility for what had happened, indicate that the basis for co-operative working was already present in a substantial proportion of the cases. This state of understanding needs to be nurtured rather than challenged by formal child protection procedures.

In 40% of cases, either an element of coercion, through the formal child protection system of the court, was clearly needed, or the nature of the possible harm was so serious that a formal monitoring system was essential.

The cases were scrutinised at the start of the research and allocated to a matrix of 'need' and 'risk of maltreatment'. Forty-two children were thought to be in the 'high need' group and also at high risk of maltreatment. A detailed critical examination is included of 24 cases where there was an element of danger to life or limb, or serious risk of sexual assault by a parent or parent-figure.

5 The children in more detail

We turn now to look more closely at the information, collected from parents, professionals and the young people themselves, about the children's well-being. Most of this detailed information comes from the intensive sample of 51 children, although more limited additional material is available for the 54 children in the background sample. This material, from and about the children, contributed to an understanding of their emotional and behavioural development and their health. The children's overall well-being in the contexts of school and home is then considered. The chapter concludes with a consideration of identity, ethnicity and culture. (The sources of information are described in more detail in Chapter 2 and in Appendix 4.)

In Chapter 2, we describe how, at the time of entering the study, many of the children had emotional and behavioural difficulties or disabilities that preceded, but were exacerbated by, the maltreatment. Indeed, almost two-thirds of the children could be described as 'difficult to parent' because of their special characteristics. The extent of family problems, poverty and adversity has already been outlined and provides an important backdrop to understanding the deficits in parenting and the harm the children are suffering.

Children's well-being is perhaps best demonstrated in their behaviour. How children behave and the pattern of their behaviour with parents, teachers and peers is often a good barometer of problems, or indeed of resilience. A child who gets on well with peers, makes and keeps friends easily and is well-liked by teachers is likely to be able to withstand maltreatment better than a friendless child who is unpopular at school and at home (Howe et al. 1999). The ability to respond well and be well accepted by others most often goes hand in hand with a good relationship at home however. Michael Rutter has written extensively about resilience and the circumstances in which children can recover from developmentally adverse experiences including maltreatment (Rutter et al. 1990a). Resilience stems from a number of factors, from:

♦ personal characteristics, including temperament;

♦ previous experience (for example, parenting);

♦ the way in which the child copes with negative experiences and the chain of events stemming from them;

- subsequent experiences which may be positive and in some way counteract the harm; and

- the way people can cognitively process or think about themselves as individuals (Rutter 1995 in Howe et al. 1999).

Pre-school-age children

At Stage 1, the research provided an overview of the well-being of each of 19 younger children. These young children were usually seen at play at home in the same room as their parent or carer. Some children were seen at play at a day nursery. Researcher ratings were derived from this time spent with the child (which included a play-based interview and a period of observation), interviews with parents, standardised questionnaires and scales, and information from professionals who knew the child, for example health visitors, paediatricians or nursery workers. The advice of a clinical psychologist was available to assist the researchers with the analysis of these data. Three broad categories of well-being were derived – 'poor', 'average' and 'good', – from assessments of the children's fine and gross motor skills and cognitive abilities, communication skills, ability to use play, and their social behaviour.

At the time of coming into the study, there was concern about the fine motor skills and cognitive abilities of four of these 19 pre-school children. Six of them were behind in their gross motor skills and the same number raised concern about their ability to play. Nine children had a delay in their ability to use language. Social behaviour and emotional development was poor for eight children. It is the children with poor social behaviour, who are aggressive and difficult at playgroup, who find themselves victims of social exclusion from an early age. Several of these children were on the threshold of exclusion from community-based playgroups and it tended to be the qualified nursery staff who coped better with their difficult behaviour. Here a nursery worker describes 3-year-old Harvey:

> He is difficult to control. He has behavioural problems and finds it hard to get on with his peers. He can become very difficult and disruptive. Harvey has a defiant nature. He can't concentrate for very long. He destroys things at the nursery – it's very hard to work with him. He's hostile to the other children and not a good mixer. He doesn't want affection and he's hard to get close to. If he could warm to you I'm sure some of his problems would resolve.

Fortunately this child's difficulties were understood at the nursery and this worker was able to find something likeable about Harvey and to stick with him:

. . . he's not a bad kid, you don't feel – thank God he's not coming into the nursery today. We can cope with him. I try to tell his mum to help him, but it doesn't seem to work.

It is easy to see how children like Harvey will be at risk of exclusion from school in a couple of years' time.

Concern was also raised about the appearance and general demeanour of six of these pre-schoolers, and researchers noted that almost a third of these young children looked to be thriving less well than other siblings in the household.

● ●

Two-year-old Zak came into the study because of registration following physical injury to him by his mother. His parents were separated at the time. He was a wanted child who had a normal birth and, on the whole, good subsequent development. During the period of play with the researcher, it was apparent that Zak's relationship with his mother was poor. He rarely made eye contact with her and did not go to her for help or reassurance. She made repeated harsh instructions to him to wipe his nose, which he ignored. His mother offered him no physical contact or comfort and Zak did not seek any. His language was limited to babble and single words. He used play quite imaginatively, and generally followed instructions well. There was no concern about his gross motor skills and his fine motor control was within the average range. Zak's appearance and demeanour did cause concern. Although a large and well-nourished child, Zak appeared pale and pasty with several faded bruises on his face. His reluctant and hesitant demeanour was in stark contrast to his cheery, smiling, baby sister who looked robust and healthy and elicited smiles, cuddles and positive remarks from her mother.

Zak's overall development was said by the health visitor to be 'average' but there was a delay in his speech. His emotional development and the poor relationship with his mother were the prime causes for concern. It was also noted by the health visitor that Zak was hostile and aggressive in his relationships with other children. The overall context of Zak's development was also exacerbated through having lived with severe and repeated violence inflicted by his father on his mother.

● ●

Kovacs and Devlin (1998) remark that each sibling may experience family life differently and that these differences shape the way children conduct their relationships as they develop and make sense of their world. Zak's baby sister might continue to elicit positive responses from her mother, particularly if the violent father stays away from home, or her experience of being parented could become more like her brother's.

A year later, at Stage 2, it was possible for the researchers to see 17 of the 19 pre-school-age children. At this stage some improvements were apparent in that only two children caused concern about their fine motor skills, play and cognitive abilities. Gross motor skills were now a concern for only three of the children. Social behaviour was, however, still a concern for five (almost a third) of the children, including Harvey and Zak (described above). Language was a problem for six of the children (more than one in three) and was usually combined with other problems, as in the case of Tommy:

● ●

Twelve months after the first visit, Tommy was still very slight and tiny for a child of $3^1/_2$. He was seen for the second time by the researcher at his day nursery. Tommy was unwell during the play interview and had just returned to the nursery following one of his regular absences due to illness. He was happy to play with the researcher however, and showed reasonable concentration, using the toys well. Tommy communicated adequately but usually without speech, using three word-phrases like 'going in here'. He asked for his mummy three times. Tommy played more on his own than with the researcher but maintained good eye contact and smiled occasionally. He seemed quite self-contained. The nursery worker commented:

> Although Tommy is globally delayed, his behaviour and social skills have improved since last year. He is less inclined to bite and pinch the person next to him. When he is told off he shakes his head and pulls at his face and gets quite upset. Perhaps this is what his parents do in front of him when they get frustrated with him. He has come on a lot in the last year, particularly in his concentration and speech.

● ●

Given the extent of Tommy's problems at the time of coming into the study, these improvements are heartening.

School-age children

The same sources of information were available for the older children as for the pre-schoolers, with the addition of the Rutter standardised scales (Rutter et al. 1981) for emotional and behavioural development (EBD), which were completed by parents and teachers, and the child depression inventory (CDI) for children over eight (Kovacs and Beck 1977) (see Appendix 4 for details). The research interview combined activities and questionnaires to gauge the child's well-being and ascertain his or her own worries and wishes. There were also questions to elicit the children's views about professional help and services they had received and an opportunity for the children to comment on how things were turning out for them. The interview was still largely play-based for the majority of children, did not include any direct questions about the maltreatment itself and was not problem-focused. The questions and activities were adapted to the maturity of the child or young person, and choices were offered in the way the interview was conducted. Informed consent from all of these children was carefully sought, and confidentiality within limits guaranteed (see Appendix 4 for more details of the interview structure).

● ●

Ten-year-old Verity was in a foster home at the time of the alleged incident of sexual abuse by another foster child in the family, Shane, who was two years older. She was unsure about whether she wanted to participate in the research and deferred her decision until she had spoken to the researcher. Verity needed reassurance that the interview would not include any discussion of the incident with Shane or any other abuse in the past. After a cursory look through the interview materials, Verity decided she would help with the research, and said that she had enjoyed the interview and that the activities and the child depression inventory (CDI) had been 'fun' to complete. Analysis showed that Verity was a troubled child who scored highly on the depression scale. During the interview, she was able to talk about her worries and fears for the future, and made it clear that she did turn to her foster carers, parents and grandparents for support.

● ●

Although the interview with the older children tended to be carried out in private (usually in the kitchen or a spare downstairs room, and occasionally in the child's bedroom), some children wanted to discuss some of the issues raised by the interview with their parent, either at the time or later.

● ●

One thirteen-year-old picked out a reply he had given to the CDI – 'I'm sure that somebody loves me' – and said to his father, 'That's you, isn't it?' By asking this, he showed his insecurity but managed to gain the confirmation from his dad that he wanted and needed. During the research interview a year later, he remembered that he had spent a long time talking with his father after the previous research interview about having his name on the Child Protection Register. He said he had not understood about this before.

● ●

Emotional and behavioural development

When teachers completed the Rutter standardised scale of emotional and behavioural disturbance in respect of the 27 school-age children at the beginning of the research (Stage 1), 40% of children showed no signs of conduct or emotional disorder, 40% showed some sign of disorder, and the remaining 20% had scores which indicated that they may have been seriously disturbed. Since only a small number of Rutter scales were completed by teachers after 12 months (a sign of the enormous pressure schoolteachers were facing as the National Curriculum was being established), there is no Stage 2 information from these scales (Rutter et al. 1981). Parents completed equivalent scales about their child's behaviour and these form the basis of our assessment of the children's well-being one year later. Figure 5.1 shows the parents' and teachers' views of the children's behaviour at the time they came into the study.

Figure 5.1 *Teachers' and parents' opinions about the children's behaviour at Stage 1*[1]

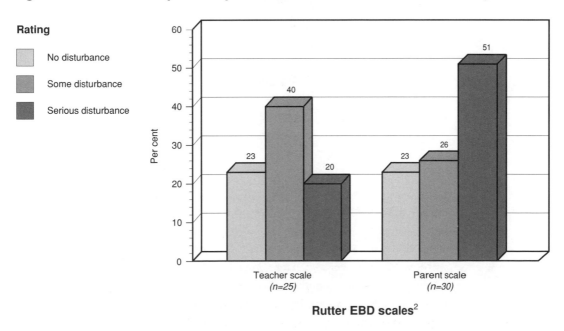

¹ Not statistically significant

² Emotional and behavioural disturbance scales (Rutter et al. 1981)

There was a trend (which did not reach statistical significance) for the parents to be *more* likely than teachers to identify patterns of behaviour in their children that suggested emotional or behavioural disturbance. Their ratings showed a higher level of disturbance at Stage 1, than did those of the teachers, with parents identifying three-quarters of the children showing signs of disturbance.

Figure 5.2 *The children's behaviour as reported by parents at Stages 1 and 2*[1]

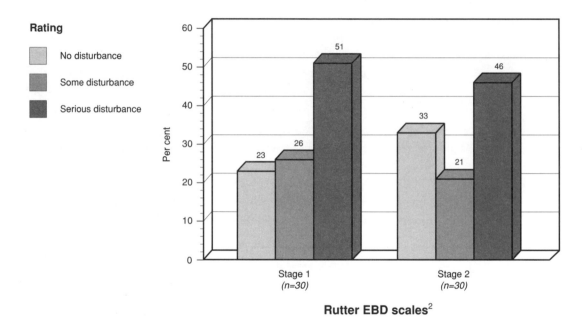

¹ Not statistically significant

² Emotional and behavioural disturbance scales (Rutter et al. 1981)

Figure 5.2 shows that a year later, at Stage 2, when the main parent or carer completed the scale again, improvement in the behaviour of some of the children was acknowledged but two-thirds of the children were still showing signs of disturbance. According to the parent scales, a fifth of the children were worse, just over a quarter showed no change, but over half were somewhat better. At the second stage the improvement in the parent ratings might be accounted for, in part, by the increased number of foster carers who completed these schedules. Carers might have been putting a positive gloss on the child's behaviour and emotional functioning in what was for many the early honeymoon stages of a placement.

Mental health

When children aged over 8 completed the self-report child depression inventory (CDI), at the time harm was identified, 11 children (55%) showed some signs of depression, with seven of them (35%) scoring well above the depression threshold (Kovacs and Beck 1977). A year later (at Stage 2), when the scales were used with 19 children, 11 of them (58%) showed signs of depression, including three (16% of the total) who showed signs of being severely depressed. A quarter of the children had improved over the year, just under a fifth were worse, while over half of them (nine children) remained unchanged.

Figure 5.3 *The children's depression scores[1] at Stages 1 and 2[2]*

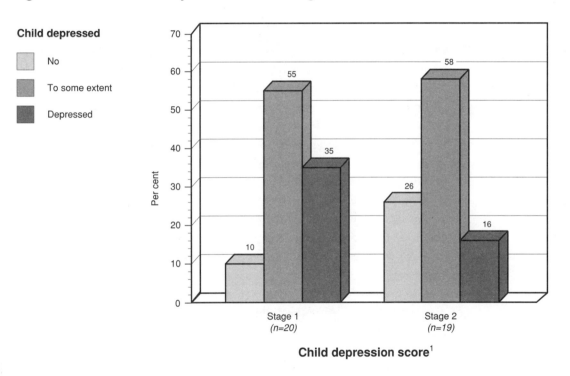

[1] Using the Kovacs and Beck (1977) scale

[2] Not statistically significant

Depression is regarded as a robust symptom of harm across all ages and these figures show a higher proportion of depression than would be expected from children in a community sample (Kendall-Tackett et al. 1993). Although the numbers in our cohort are small, they contribute to a growing body of evidence from studies with larger sample sizes indicating that children who have experienced abuse, and particularly sexual abuse, have depressive symptoms (Sharland et al. 1996; Monck and New 1996).

Post-traumatic stress disorder (PTSD)

Three items were added at the end of the CDI to gauge whether the child might be suffering from post-traumatic stress disorder (see Appendix 4 for further details). Five children at Stage 1 (a quarter) had scores which indicated that this could be so. Twelve months later, at Stage 2, the same five children again gave answers which indicated that the problem was still present.

Emotional development and worrying

The extent of emotional harm to the children is outlined in Chapter 4. The sadness and unhappiness came across clearly in the research interviews. For a quarter of these children the extent of this distress was extreme. In the self-report child depression inventory completed during Stage 1, four children had thoughts about killing themselves, ticking the statement 'I sometimes have thoughts about killing myself, but would not do it.' This increased to seven children at Stage 2. The researcher discussed this response with the young people, some of whom had not mentioned these feelings to anyone else. Six out of the seven young people who had suicidal thoughts were living away from their parents and four of them were looked after by the local authority. The youngest child was 8 and the oldest 16.

It was also apparent that the children worried about aspects of their own and their parents' lives and that this was scarcely diminishing by Stage 2. The teachers reported that the majority of the children 'had many worries' and considered that one in three worried a great deal (see Tables 5.1 and 5.2). The parents or carers were also likely to describe the children as having many worries, with almost half of the children said by parents to be worrying a great deal, although they picked up on this less well than did teachers. A year later, at Stage 2, parents or carers described a third of the children as still having many worries.

Other aspects of the interviews with 26 of the school-age children confirmed the extent of the worrying. Over two-thirds of these children said they had worries during the earlier interviews, though some of the most apparently unhappy children would not admit to having any worries. One child who had denied having any worries at Stage 1, said to the researcher a year later, at Stage 2, when she had moved to live with her father, that things had been 'really quite bad' at the first interview and she hadn't felt able to talk about it. The children were not noticeably less worried by the second year, although many were more settled and the *intensity* of their worries had diminished.

Table 5.1 *Emotional difficulties of the children at Stages 1 and 2*

Rutter scales[1]	Teacher	Parent		Kovacs CDI[2]		
Emotional state	Stage 1 (n=27)	Stage 1 (n=31)	Stage 2 (n=23)	Emotional state	Stage 1 (n=20)	Stage 2 (n=19)
Solitary, often alone	13 (48%)	10 (32%)	5 (25%)	Feel alone	7 (35%)	7 (37%)
Miserable, unhappy, tearful	18 (67%)	12 (39%)	7 (29%)	Sad frequently	10 (50%)	5 (26%)
Unresponsive, apathetic	8 (30%)			Suicidal thoughts	4 (20%)	7 (37%)
Fearful, afraid	17 (63%)	12 (40%)	9 (39%)	Feel like crying many days or everyday	7 (37%)	2 (11%)
Enuretic	—	13 (42%)	4 (17%)			

[1] Rutter et al. 1981

[2] Kovacs and Beck 1977

Table 5.2 *Children's worries*

Rutter scales[1]			Kovacs CDI[2]		Children's interviews	
Teacher	Parent					
Stage 1 (n=27)	Stage 1 (n=31)	Stage 2 (n=23)	Stage 1 (n=20)	Stage 2 (n=19)	Stage 1 (n=26)	Stage 2 (n=23)
22 (82%)	21 (68%)	13 (15%)	7 (35%)	6 (32%)	18 (70%)	17 (66%)

[1] Rutter et al. 1981

[2] Kovacs and Beck 1977

There were some similarities in the sort of worries that the children mentioned but important individual differences. Almost half of the children said they worried about home and their family, and a quarter of children had worries about friendships. In the first interview seven children were worried about the future. By the second interview this had intensified and half of the children were worried about the future: about where they would live, about whether they would get a job when they left school, and so on. The events of the previous year seemed to have had an unsettling effect on many of these young people, heightening a general sense of insecurity. Ten of the 26 children were worried about school, and five said they were worried about bullying. Some children had one big worry, but others could list a catalogue of concerns.

Two children were very worried (in both years) about the person outside the family who had sexually abused them, and one of these girls was extremely anxious, when first interviewed, about going to court to give evidence.

At Stage 1, three-quarters of the children said when completing the child depression inventory that they were worried about aches and pains. (Teachers noted on their Rutter scales that 8 of the 27 children often complained of aches and pains.) At Stage 2, the CDI indicated that two-thirds of the children still worried about aches and pains.

More children, however, were concerned about their parents' health and well-being. A 10-year-old girl in accommodation was worried that her parents would have a car crash and die on their way to see her. Ricci, aged 14, was concerned for his mother's health:

> I don't like it when my mum gets ill – she's had lots of operations. I stayed home to help her.

This sense of premature responsibility and worry for parents (and siblings) was also recognised by professionals and carers:

● ●

> Six-year-old Tanya, who had lived in bed and breakfast accommodation with her mother, was said by her foster mother to be 'like a little adult, and ever so worried about her mum'.

● ● ●

> Shelley (aged 9) was said by her head teacher to be often worried about her younger brother and was found searching for him at school, to check that he was alright.

● ●

Many of these 'parental children,' when asked their 'three wishes', would express concern about their mother. For example, Andrew (a 15-year-old in accommodation) wished that his mum would be alright and that he could live at home. His only worry was whether anything would happen to her, and he was fearful that she might take another overdose. Several children who lived in households where there was violent conflict between parental figures were prematurely competent or 'parental children'. There is more detail about these children later in this chapter and in Brandon and Lewis (1996).

These standardised scales and questionnaires show a bleak picture for almost half of the 51 intensive sample children, who were still showing signs of depression and disturbance at home and at school a year after child protection concerns were raised. This was as likely to be the case for children who were looked after by the local authority as those living at home with parents or relatives.

Behavioural difficulties

One in three of the 105 children in the full sample had behavioural problems, which were graphically described in 3-year-old Harvey's case earlier in the chapter. A considerable amount of detail about these difficulties is available for the intensive sample of 51 children. A summary of behavioural problems is provided in Table 5.3.

Table 5.3 *Behavioural difficulties, using the Rutter scales*[1]

| Behaviour | Parent | | Teacher |
	Stage 1 (n=31)	Stage 2 (n=23)	Stage 1 (n=20)
Resentful or aggressive when corrected	n/a	n/a	12 (46%)
Fights regularly, quarrelsome	19 (62%)	14 (61%)	15 (56%)
Disobedient	20 (65%)	13 (56%)	13 (48%)
Irritable, quick to fly off the handle	20 (66%)	14 (60%)	14 (50%)
Often tells lies	22 (71%)	8 (35%)	13 (48%)
Steals (more than once)	14 (48%)	6 (26%)	8 (30%)
Destructive (property)	16 (51%)	10 (44%)	9 (33%)

[1] Rutter et al. 1981

During Stage 1 parents or carers indicated that almost two-thirds of the children were disobedient. This dropped to just over half by Stage 2. The parents' and teachers' views of the disobedience were largely confirmed by the children themselves. When completing the self-report CDI, at both stages ten out of 19 children said they did not do as they were told and two of these children said they never did what they were told. This was more often said with a sense of upset than triumph; these children did not revel in their difficult behaviour.

The types of difficult behaviour demonstrated by children of all ages confirms that a year after serious concerns came to light, many could still be said to be hard to care for:

Brian, aged 8, was described at the child protection conference as verbally and physically abusive to his mother. His mother also described sexualised behaviour where Brian would stand up at the window displaying his genitalia to passers by. Brian also repeatedly walked along outside window-sills upstairs, threatening to commit suicide, and had been known to lie down in the road waiting to be run over.

● ● ●

Fifteen-year-old Susie was beyond her single mother's control. She was aggressive to her younger sister, but the most serious problems were created by a long-standing eating disorder which was damaging her health and education. Susie was also incontinent.

Health

The file search for the 105 children indicated that 14 children (13%) had a physical disability. Additionally, two children in the total sample had severe sight problems and 12 had a hearing or speech disability. Twenty per cent of the total group were known to have a moderate learning disability, and one child had a severe learning disability.

Information on the 51 intensive sample cases, from a range of sources including *Assessment and Action* schedules from the '*Looking After Children*' materials (DoH 1995a; Ward 1995), provided information about the children's general physical health. For half of this group there were no particular health problems, a third had some problems, and nine of the children (16%) had poor health at Stage 1. This included children with respiratory problems who were living in poor-quality, damp housing. At Stage 2 just under half of the children showed no change, almost a third had improved, and the health of two children (4%) had worsened.

At Stage 1, six of the children in the intensive sample were said by their parent or carer to have a chronic or debilitating illness; at Stage 2, this applied to three children. Tommy exemplifies the problems, but also the improvements, for some of the children with poor health. During the Stage 2 interview the social worker described Tommy (who was 2 at the start of the study):

He's a very frail child in terms of his health but he's robust physically. He looks as though a breath of wind would blow him away – he's very small, slight, thin and pale, with blond hair, pale eyes and no colour in his cheeks. He runs in, falls down, picks himself up, dusts himself down and he's off. So he's a curious contrast. He picks up lots of infections and loses weight [he was thought to be failing to thrive] and he's weighed and measured every fortnight. A clear pattern has emerged that's very reassuring for his parents, where he loses weight rapidly with each bout of illness but picks up again. As he gets older it's getting easier. You can tell from his weight records when he was poorly. He was very prone to infection at the beginning, because of unsuitable housing, but we've done something about that.

At the first stage of the study it was known that a quarter of the 105 children had had a spell in hospital in the previous six months (this included hospitalisation as part of the child protection process). At the second stage only four children (9%) had been in hospital in the previous six months.

Maintaining a healthy diet for their child was said by 19 of 51 parents (39%) to be a problem, and seven of these said the problem was caused by inadequate finance. A fifth of the children had an inadequate diet one year later, and insufficient money was given as the reason in three cases. This improvement is almost entirely accounted for by the number of children at the second stage being looked after by the local authority, where money for food is not a problem. Table 5.4 summarises these data on health alongside data on the other *Looking After Children* dimensions (DoH 1995a; Ward 1995).

The children at school

There was evidence to suggest that, at Stage 1, the educational needs of 45% of the children were being poorly met. A further third had 'some problems'.

At Stage 2 the situation had worsened for a fifth of the children, half still had some problems, but the situation had improved for a third of the group. For two children harm to their education and intellectual development was one of the most significant of their difficulties at the time of entry into the study. For example, 6-year-old Sam had never been to school until he was accommodated at the start of the study.

School, or for the younger children, day care, could be a source of support and a haven. When asked who their best helping person was the answer was 'teacher' for a third of the children interviewed.

Table 5.4 *Children's well-being and progress at Stages 1 and 2[1]*

Rating based on data from all sources	Health	Education	Identity	Family relation-ships	Social relation-ships	Social present-ation	Emotional behavioural develop-ment	Self-care
	%	% aged 4+	% aged 2+	%	% aged 2+	% aged 4+	% aged 2+	% aged 4+
Stage 1								
Poor	16	45	7	33	20	20	47	19
Some problems	35	37	32	44	40	20	40	21
Rarely/minor problems	49	17	61	22	40	59	13	60
Total numbers	*(n=55)*	*(n=40)*	*(n=54)*	*(n=54)*	*(n=55)*	*(n=54)*	*(n=53)*	*(n=43)*
Stage 2								
Poor	6	19	6	12	12	8	22	10
Some problems	31	50	18	34	37	14	48	24
Rarely/minor problems	63	31	75	54	51	78	30	66
Total numbers	*(n=51)*	*(n=36)*	*(n=49)*	*(n=50)*	*(n=51)*	*(n=51)*	*(n=50)*	*(n=38)*
Change between Stages 1 and 2								
Worse	4	19	11	12	10	10	10	8
No change	48	39	39	33	46	30	38	58
Improved	30	33	26	43	32	32	48	18
Already good and still good	18	8	24	12	12	28	4	16
Total numbers	*(n=50)*	*(n=36)*	*(n=46)*	*(n=49)*	*(n=50)*	*(n=50)*	*(n=50)*	*(n=38)*

[1] Using *Looking After Children* dimensions (DoH 1995a; Ward 1995)

One in four of the children had talked to a teacher about the abuse they had experienced. School was also a place where three-quarters (14) of the children interviewed said they 'often had fun'. In the first year only two out of 19 children said that they had no fun at all, and only three said they rarely had fun. By the second stage of the research, 15 out of 18 who responded claimed to have 'lots of fun' and only three 'rarely had fun'. There were no children saying they 'never had fun' at school. This contrasts with less positive views about other aspects of their lives and underlines the importance of school for these children.

Being at school was not without its problems, however. The Rutter scales completed by teachers in the first year indicated that over a third of the

27 children tended to be absent from school for trivial reasons, and seven children truanted to some extent. Parent Rutter scales showed that nine out of 31 children had tears on arrival, or refused to go to school occasionally.

One child's difficulties, however, were not fully taken account of at school:

●●●●●●●●●●●●●●●●●●●●●●●●●●●●●●●●●●

Lauren described how a week before she was due to give evidence in court against the man who had sexually assaulted her, her class teacher discussed court as the place where young people who broke the law were dealt with. Lauren was not an easy child to care for at home, or to teach. Her class teacher said of her:

> She displays bullying behaviour and greatly resents being corrected about it, and then tends to sulk. I think she revels in special attention, so I try to treat her like a normal class member, otherwise I would make a rod for my own back.

●●●●●●●●●●●●●●●●●●●●●●●●●●●●●●●●●●

Her educational attainment was below average in most areas and although her difficulties were in part acknowledged, they were also discounted. Her class teacher commented: 'Undoubtedly a difficult year for Lauren, but this has not affected her work too obviously'. Her headteacher commented: 'She is a capable girl and could do much better if she is prepared to work.'

These unsympathetic attitudes did not help Lauren, who had waited a year to give evidence in court about a man who still terrified her.

Several items in the child depression inventory (CDI) related to school. One question asked: 'Do you have problems with school work?' At Stage 1, well over half of the 19 children who replied said they had difficulties, and 7 of these children regarded doing school work as a big problem. At Stage 2, things had improved, and almost two-thirds of the children said they did not have a problem with school work, although it was still a big problem for three children.

A third of the children who spoke to the researchers had worries about school in general. Fifteen-year-old Joe said:

> I worry about the SATs (standard attainment tests) – all of them. I always try my hardest, but I worry I won't get a good job. At the moment, because of all the bother, people expect less of me – they don't expect me to do good work, so I have to work extra hard.

Bullying at school

Over half of the children in the intensive sample were said by their parent or carers to be bullied at school. Five of the older children themselves mentioned bullying as one of their worries during the first interview, and four at the second. Teacher Rutter scales indicated that almost half of the 27 children were to some extent bullies themselves, although parents and carers were less likely to say this.

The teacher Rutter scales revealed that well over half of the 27 children were not much liked by other children, whereas parents judged a lower proportion (a third) of the children as not much liked by others. Twelve months later, however, parents indicated that the proportion of children disliked by their peers had dropped to a fifth. Being disliked by friends was confirmed by many of the children themselves, in their lists of worries and wishes. For example, one 8-year-old boy worried that no children at school liked him.

Friendship

Information was gathered from a range of sources about friends and friendship. Parents and carers said that most of the children had special friends, but 12 children, one in four, were said not to have any special friends. When the children themselves were asked if they had plenty of friends, four children did not feel they had enough friends. Twelve months later this number had doubled to eight children. Seven children said they had trouble getting on with people. For an important minority this was exacerbated by changes in living arrangements and of school. A quarter of the children had changed schools unexpectedly during the year of the study, which might account for some of the increased difficulties with school work and friends. This change was not a wholly negative experience for all of these children. Two were happier at smaller schools, and one was pleased to move back to a school where she had friends.

Attempts by professionals to learn more about children's worries about school could help to allay many of these fears, and to make school an even more satisfying experience for these children.

The children at home

Family relationships figured prominently in the interviews with the children and parents. Positive family relationships, and particularly secure attachments, can mitigate the harm resulting from an episode of abuse or neglect (Howe 1995; Dartington Social Research Unit 1995). Conversely, difficulties within the family may themselves be a source of harm, particularly if they render parents unresponsive to their children's developing needs. Important variables apparent in this study were the child's relationship with others in the family – particularly the main carer; the impact on the child of any problems in the relationship between the parenting adults (divorce, partner conflict or violence); and separation from important family members.

The child's relationships within the family

Three-year-old Kelly said of her mother's house: 'No one don't love me there.' Family relationships in general were poor for a third of the children (18 out of 51) and produced some problems for half of the children in the intensive sample. By Stage 2, family relationships had improved for 21 children; had worsened for six children; and 18 had experienced no change. Six children's family relationships had remained good.

Information from the adaptations of the *Looking After Children: Assessment and Action Records* (DoH 1995a) used in the research showed that, at the time of coming into the study, parents or carers said that more than one in four of the 49 children did not get on well with them. A year later, this had improved so that less than one in 20 children was described in this way, although it should be noted that at Stage 2, more of these data came from foster carers.

Research interviews with 30 of the school-age children revealed that 16 of them felt closest to their mother. Three children said they were closest to their father and four claimed to be closest to their sibling. Alarmingly, seven children felt close to no one in the family. Fourteen children said they confided their worries to someone in their family, but eight did not. One child said he had no one to confide in.

When asked who kept them safe at home, half of the children said their mother, but a fifth, including some as young as 6, said 'myself'. When completing the child depression inventory, two out of 20 children were not sure whether anybody loved them.

During the first interview three quarters of the children said there were rows and arguments in the family, usually with mothers or with brothers and sisters; less often with fathers. When asked whether they 'got on' with their family, less than half of the children (13) said they did. Over a quarter didn't get on, and the same number got on 'sometimes'.

From the children's responses it would appear that for most, conflict at home was happening around them rather than involving them directly. Since almost half of them were living in families where there was violent conflict between parental figures (and for several of the others there was conflict that stopped short of physical violence), the harm stemming from this should not be underestimated.

A third of the children during the first interview said that they were frightened. Six of the children, like Poppy, were frightened of people outside the family:

Poppy (aged 9) had reported a serious sexual assault by her mother's partner, three months after the event, when the relationship had ended. Because of the delay in reporting, a prosecution was not pursued. Poppy was terrified of this man, who lived in her neighbourhood, and her mother was reluctant to let Poppy play outside. These fears and restrictions persisted for two years. Poppy's mother had difficulties allaying her daughter's fears, feeling she could not keep her safe in that neighbourhood. The relationship between mother and daughter deteriorated after the abuse was disclosed. Although Poppy's mother fully believed her daughter, and supported her, she found Poppy's distress and her ensuing difficulties hard to tolerate, partly because they stirred memories of her own sexual abuse as a child.

Three children said they were frightened of their father. Nathan's father was separated from his mother, but the violence and conflict had not stopped after the separation:

When Nathan (aged 15) was asked what was the best thing that had happened since the recent problems had emerged, he said his mother getting an injunction against his father. The worst thing was the temper he had developed himself, after his dad left home.

One child was frightened of her stepfather and particularly of his drinking. When asked if they had ever been hurt, half the children (15) said yes, a third said no, and the remaining four children declined to answer. Six children who answered this question said they loved the person who had hurt them. They were not asked to say who the person was.

Sofia (aged 16) had her name included on the Child Protection Register following a physical assault by her father, who was trying to prevent her leaving home after a family row about her behaviour. Sofia was clear that it was her father who had hurt her. Sofia and her family had moved to the UK four years previously, and the differences and conflicts between her culture at home and her developing independent ideas were difficult for her:

> Yes, my dad has really hurt and upset me. He believes in different things and I believe in different things – so that's the reason we have arguments. I do love him though.

Harm from divorce and parental conflict

Harm stemming from parental separation (also discussed in Chapters 7 and 8) affected the children's behaviour, friendships and educational achievements:

For Stephen (aged 15) his parents' violent and hostile separation caused him to feel protective of his mother and sister. It also had a detrimental effect on his behaviour at home, where he was aggressive towards his mother, and at school, where he was excluded for assaulting another boy. Stephen made it clear to the researcher that he did not want to see his father or anyone from his father's side of the family. During the Stage 2 interview Stephen said he wasn't very happy about the way things had turned out:

> I would have liked things to be the way they were, with my mum and dad together – but that's all gone now. Things are pretty bad at school. I was doing really well, but these past months or so the work's been slipping, and I'm getting detentions and misbehaving in class. I don't know why. It's my own doing now.

Some of these children found it hard to talk about their difficulties in the first year, when the problems were worse.

By the second year, when 10-year-old Rachel was living with her father following a court order, she felt more able to talk about how her parents' separation had affected her. When asked what was the worst of all the things that had happened, she said her parents' splitting up and 'Living with my dad, then living with Mum, then living with Dad, then Mum, and that. . .' At several points in the interview Rachel said that she wanted her parents to be back together again, and this was one of her final three wishes.

Her worries at this stage were that she might have to leave her dad to go back to live with her mother, that she might lose all her friends, and what would happen if her stepdad got drunk. Rachel was one of the many 'parental children' who were preoccupied about the welfare of their parents and siblings. She was very anxious about her mother, who lived in a violent relationship with her new husband, and needed to see her mother regularly, although she lived 200 miles away.

● ● ●

Hayley, aged 5, was part of the study because of a court order, which ultimately stopped contact with her father because of suspicions of sexual abuse and because of his violent behaviour towards her mother. Hayley's well-being was no better in the second year than in the first. Her parents' separation had been extremely acrimonious and, since contact had been stopped, her father had made threats to the family and forced the family car off the road with Hayley inside. In the researcher interview during Stage 1, Hayley said she could tell any worries to her mother but said she did not have any. In the interview in the second year Hayley was quite agitated. She worried that 'Daddy might kill my Mummy (but don't tell Mummy)'. She was adamant that no one in her family should know about these worries, and she hadn't even told her teacher, who she said she liked and trusted a great deal.

● ●

It seems that Hayley felt unable to burden her frightened mother with her own worries and fears about her father. Like Stephen, Rachel and other children, she was protecting her mother to the best of her ability.

Almost half of the 105 children (47%) had recent experience of violent conflict between parental figures at home. Some of these children's circumstances, and the harm ensuing from them, have already been described. Sleep disturbance was noted for eight of the 28 children in the intensive sample who had experienced parental violence. Temper tantrums, aggression or extreme passivity with sudden outbursts were also frequent for 11 children. A paediatric nurse's comments on a 6-year-old child give the flavour of this type of behaviour:

> I've seen her very upset on the ward – literally running up the curtains – when her father got violent on the ward and had to be asked to leave.

Six of these children, who were aged 8 or over, completed the child depression inventory (CDI): three scored above the threshold for depression. Three children also gave responses to the post-traumatic stress disorder (PTSD) questions, which indicated that there was a possibility they were suffering from this disorder. Some of the older children were hovering on the verges of mental ill health.

Even when the violence had stopped it still seemed to preoccupy many of the children, a conclusion also reached by Cockett and Tripp (1994). The children's subsequent behaviour often earned them labels of disapproval. Several of the children were described by their parents as 'disobedient', 'complaining', 'difficult' or 'always playing up'. The backdrop of violence was ignored by most of the adults (including professionals) when explaining the children's behaviour. The children were labelled, inaccurately, as perverse rather than perceived as struggling to deal with frightening and even terrorising experiences (Brandon and Lewis 1996).

Identity, ethnicity and culture

Many items in the child depression inventory related to self-esteem and provided information about the older children's perceptions of themselves. A third of the 27 children who completed the inventory said they did most things, or everything, wrong, and this was the same at Stages 1 and 2. A quarter of the children said they did not like themselves, and one child said he hated himself. A quarter of the 27 children felt bad things were their fault. At Stage 1, the time of coming into the research, over half of the children did not like the way they looked, and three children thought they looked ugly. Harter (1983) singles out children's views about their appearance as key indicators of self-esteem, with a positive view about how they feel they look linked to higher self-esteem, and vice versa. One year later, at Stage 2, three-quarters of the children felt they looked 'alright', but the same three children from Stage 1 still thought they looked ugly.

The *Assessment and Action* schedules (DoH 1995a; Ward 1995) provided information from parents and carers about racial identity, which added to the more general information already collected. Most of the school-age children of minority ethnic origin were having to live in two cultures, one at home – which might be restrictive and wholly supervised by parents – and one at school – where they attempted to merge into the freer, more adolescent-oriented culture. This was particularly difficult for teenage girls from minority ethnic groups because the difference between, say, a Muslim view of how a teenage girl should behave with boys, is vastly different from the informal, gender-equal back-chatting repartee which occurs in most mixed comprehensive schools in the UK. What is acceptable, and even carries status, within the social setting of school might be deplored at home and cause shame to the family:

●●●●●●●●●●●●●●●●●●●●●●●●●●●●●●●●●●

In one family, the parents regarded the fact that their daughter had truanted from school on one or two occasions to meet her boyfriend as equivalent to compromising her virginity, which in their culture was essential to ensure marriage – their greatest wish for their daughter. Both the girl's father and older brother seriously assaulted her when she was found out. The girl was old enough to press charges in her own right, but she chose not to. Not only was the girl forbidden to see the boy any more, but she had to promise not to trespass against the cultural norm again. She found herself more or less a prisoner at home. She told the researcher that she was working as hard as possible so that she could go to university, away from home, when she was 18.

●●●●●●●●●●●●●●●●●●●●●●●●●●●●●●●●●●

The use of two languages by children, one for home and one for school, did not seem to present problems for the children, provided that they were proficient in both. When their English was poor then there were problems at school, which rippled out into every aspect of their education:

●●●●●●●●●●●●●●●●●●●●●●●●●●●●●●●●●●

One child in the sample had arrived in this country with an African language as her first language and French as her second. She was finding it very difficult to attain to her ability at school because of her lack of skill in the English language. Her ability to learn was also hindered by family troubles and her stepmother's hostility towards her because of her alleged disobedience. Eventually, during the year following the initial child protection conference, the child was placed away from home and an Interim Care Order made.

●●●●●●●●●●●●●●●●●●●●●●●●●●●●●●●●●●

On the whole, the children seemed to manage in the same way that other children have coped in the past within the UK, using a code or dialect at home that may be distinct from the one they adopt at school. Playground language may be similar to home language but classroom language may be different, or both may be dissimilar to home.

Almost two-thirds of the children in the intensive sample had friends from the same ethnic group (24 of 28). Almost a quarter had friends from mixed groups. However, five children who were of minority ethnic origin did not have friends from their own ethnic group.

In answer to the question of whether the child was protected against discrimination, the answer was 'no' for one child. The remainder of responses were split evenly between 'yes' and the unsatisfactory answer of 'to some extent'.

⚫ ⚫

One Asian boy, Ashok (aged 14), was the subject of a child protection conference because of over-chastisement from his father. At the conference details emerged about the repeated racial taunting of this boy by white youths in the neighbourhood. The police officer at the conference felt unable to pursue enquiries about the alleged racial discrimination. Ashok, who had learning disabilities, was particularly vulnerable to attack in the community. He was also worried about bullying at school and being picked on by teachers.

⚫ ⚫

After 12 months, at Stage 2, 18 out of 19 of the intensive sample children who were of minority ethnic origin were having contact with people of the same ethnic group. When parents and carers were asked whether the child was aware of ethnic customs, the answer was 'yes' for 17 of these children and 'no' for two. The family of a Muslim child said that involvement in child protection procedures had made them more conscious than ever of the importance of explaining the values of their culture and religion to their daughter.

Summary

This chapter uses interview data and information from professionals to give additional background on the children, especially the 51 in the small sample. Many of the pre-school children displayed deficits at both stages of the study, particularly in their social behaviour and speech, although there were some improvements at the second stage. The school-age children were assessed by their parents and teachers on standardised scales, as well as by the researchers. The children's emotional and behavioural development were examined in the context of home and school from the information gleaned from research activities with the children. The methods illustrate simultaneously how much valuable information may be gathered from a simple, carefully constructed play interview and conversation based around themes and issues.

Sadly, the chapter overall gives a picture of children struggling to cope. An important minority emerges: children who worry and are alone with their worries, having to rely on themselves for their own protection. The quality of many of the children's relationships appears wanting, with an inability to 'get on' at home having a possible effect on their ability to avoid trouble with their peers. For those children of school age, the school environment often provided a haven where they had fun and where they found a trusted person in their teacher.

The data in this chapter emphasise further the necessity for regular, accessible help for, to use the words of the Children Act 1989, 'the particular child'.

6 The helping services

Patterns of service delivery

This chapter offers an analysis of practice with the children and their families and is influenced by an American study of services intended to prevent the need for children to go into public care or to remain there (Jones 1985). Services are considered along the dimensions of *intensity* and *duration* of intervention. Social work methods are described and we offer an analysis of the extent of negotiation or coercion used with parents, and whether the focus of intervention was on the whole family or the child. The analysis also draws on the work of Fisher et al. (1986), Millham et al. (1986) and Packman et al. (1986) who examined the interactions between legal processes and social work practice, and Hallett (1995) who studied inter-agency co-ordination in child protection. Chapters 7 and 8 provide additional information about out-of-home care and court orders. This chapter also looks at the specific issues which arose for families of minority ethnic origin, particularly where English was not their first language.

Intensity of current service

When patterns of service intensity at Stage 1 were examined, it was apparent that some differences were linked to the age of the child. Cases where little help and few services were offered or provided tended to involve older children. Some parents and some of the teenage children, themselves, spurned offers of help. One young woman, for example, was accommodated at her request, but then rejected further offers of support, left her flat and would not accept continuing social work help. Often the explanation for an apparently inadequate level of service could be found in the unwillingness of the parents or the older children to accept a service, as well as in the inadequacies of the agencies' policies or prioritisation systems.

High-intervention cases

The largest group of families (over half) comprised those who were already in receipt of a high level of services which, for the most part, continued – with appropriate additions after the event that led to heightened concern. This group included the small number of cases dealt with outside the formal child protection system.

Significant harm as a trigger for resources

The second largest group of families (a quarter) found that the increased attentions of child protection professionals gave them access to an increased level of services. For these families, most of whom were already known to the area team social workers but receiving a 'revolving door' type of service, co-ordinated help was not available *until* the incident that prompted the conference galvanised the agencies into action to provide the help that was needed. Whilst a few families had declined previous offers of help, most had been requesting it. They might not, however, have been in agreement with the agencies about the *type* of help that would be most likely to alleviate their distress. These cases fitted into a pattern of waiting until 'need' became 'significant harm' so that a service could be provided:

● ●

Nina's family had been referred to the social services department because of parental stress, related to coping with six small children in a tiny two-bedroom flat. The family was linked to the neighbourhood family centre after a minimal assessment, and attendance at playgroup was encouraged, but Nina rarely attended. The family's needs were not properly assessed or acknowledged until child protection concerns were raised. It was then discovered that Nina's father had an untreated mental illness and that violent conflict between the parents was commonplace. Nina's mother was worn out and had a succession of low-grade illnesses. With treatment and specific help the father's health improved, the extent of the violence decreased, and Nina's mother's well-being and confidence improved. Nina's playgroup place was paid for after the conference and, because the family did not have to pay, she attended regularly. With this concerted, co-ordinated help to all family members the family's functioning improved dramatically and the actual physical harm and risk of future harm to Nina and her siblings subsided.

● ●

Registration and low intervention

In contrast, for one in ten of the 105 cases, a child protection conference and registration did not result in the provision of more services. For two pre-school children the flurry and antagonism of child protection investigation, registration and assessment culminated in little help or support, even though they were both high-risk cases. Resources offered in child protection plans did not materialise. In the meantime, the parents felt powerless to make their own arrangements. As one parent explained:

> I waited so long for the playgroup place that they promised, that I fixed it up myself with my mum. It made me cross really, 'cos I could have done it myself all along but didn't think I should.

Non-registration and low intervention

In a small group of cases, already known to the departments, there was evidence that a child was suffering significant harm but little was done. One grandmother, whose daughter had a drug-addiction problem before the birth of a child with severe physical disabilities, told the researcher:

> Since the first conference, Social Services hasn't offered a thing. No social worker came until today [two months later] and I think it's urgent because my daughter is in need of so much help for herself, and unless she has help the children will be at risk because of her negligence. It's difficult to unravel whether she is as she is because of the worry of the baby, or whether because of the worry about the baby she is taking her amphetamines again and is not herself, or whether she is still addicted to the drugs like she was in the past.

The children in this family were not registered at the initial child protection conference and this may have been one of the reasons for a lack of priority. The family had also moved into temporary accommodation and, in so doing, had moved to a different social services area. This entailed waiting for another social worker to be allocated and the loss of a relationship with the worker who made the assessment.

Services provided during the year following the initial child protection conference

Sections 17 and 18 of the Act, and Schedule 2 Part I, lay out the kinds of support local authorities can provide. These range from 'advice, guidance and counselling'; 'assistance in kind or cash'; 'day care and supervised activity'; and 'accommodation for any child in need' to specific provisions such as laundry services or attendance at a family centre. Information was collected about the services provided after the child protection conference or planning meeting, from the files and from professionals, parents and children. From this material we found that 64% of families were consistently or episodically provided with general family support and guidance; 47% with welfare rights or advocacy; and 65% with cash or material aid. In 60% of cases a supportive relationship was established with the parent, and in 70% of cases with the child.

Involvement with the child was generally high, and services were offered very much with the child in mind. In over a quarter of the 105 cases the help was directed at the child only. With Colton et al. (1995), in their study of children in need, we noted that this focus on the identified child can be to the exclusion of other needy members of the family. Only 14% of siblings, for example, were provided with short-term accommodation or respite care, although it was clear that it could have been helpful to parents and children in several cases where it was not offered.

In a minority of cases services, which were offered previously and rejected, were accepted following the coercion of child protection procedures. However, as Table 6.1 shows, many services had been provided before the incident that triggered inclusion in our sample. The main difference, remarked on by parents and social workers and evidenced in the files, was an increase in the provision of a relationship-based casework service as a context for the provision of practical help, and in some cases, therapy for the parent or child. This was likely to happen irrespective of whether a formal child protection conference was held or the child's name was placed on the Register. One parent commented:

> What was helpful was with the feelings – you can get everything out of your system talking to a social worker. You can have a good cry and go back from day one and get it out and it's good to talk about it.

Table 6.1 shows the services offered in the year following the initial child protection conference. The parents in the intensive sample were asked if they felt supported overall. Sixteen per cent of the parents interviewed felt they were supported, 50% felt they were to some extent, and 35% felt that they were not. In contrast, 61% of the children who were old enough to respond to this question indicated that they felt supported, 22% felt supported to some extent, and 17% did not feel supported at all. The children's far more positive responses compared with the parents' responses suggests that social workers have invested time and energy in their contacts with the children and that the children valued their efforts.

There was not enough information to rate parental satisfaction with the service in a quarter of the cases. In 51% of the cases where there was sufficient

Table 6.1 *Provision of specific services during the year following Stage 1 (n=94–100)*

Service	Not needed	Not wanted	Wanted	Offered, not taken up	Episodically provided	Consistently provided
Day nursery, child-minding, after-school care	63	4	—	3	3	27
Playgroup – fees	86	6	—	—	1	8
Domestic help	98	2	1	—	1	8
Family aid/support worker	78	7	—	3	1	10
Volunteer service	95	3	1	—	1	—
Respite care for any child in the family	91	3	1	—	2	3
Short-term accommodation for any child in the family	76	7	2	1	8	6
Help with accommodation for alleged abuser	91	4	1	1	2	1
Attendance at self-help group encouraged	72	11	1	13	1	2
Parents support/social group	62	9	1	12	6	10
Attendance at family centre	57	11	—	8	7	17
Parenting skills training	52	10	1	7	13	16
Holiday for parents/parents and children	88	4	3	—	4	—
Holiday for child(ren)	90	4	—	—	5	—
Social work relationship and support for index child	37	12	1	2	10	38
Individual therapy for index child	68	5	4	2	13	8
Group to support child	82	6	2	—	4	5
Group therapy for child	92	5	—	—	2	1
Volunteer/befriender for child	92	6	—	—	2	—
Accommodation for index child	56	14	3	—	5	22

information, parents were either satisfied with all the help or with some of it, 14% were satisfied with some but not other aspects of the service, 20% were dissatisfied, and 14% felt angry about it. Thus, a picture emerges of a significant minority of parents left dissatisfied by their contact with child protection and family support services.

Whilst many parents were ambivalent about the service provided by the social worker and other professionals, the great majority of the *children* who were old enough to give their views both wanted the help offered by the social worker and were satisfied with it. The Children Act's principles of the paramountcy of the child's welfare and the importance of children's feelings being taken into account were much in evidence in these cases.

As shown in Chapter 9, most of the parents still had unmet needs at the end of the study. It is likely that in this fact lies the answer to why around half of the parents felt unhelped, dissatisfied and unsupported. In other words, whilst some were dissatisfied by services actually provided, more were *unsatisfied* because needed services did not materialise (a point also made in the study by Thoburn et al. (1999) of family support work):

> I would like answers to our problems. We feel pretty washed out. The systems conspire against us and no one is really interested. They're just there to do a job. Their priority is not to solve the problem.

> They're very efficient at arranging case conferences, planning meetings and reviews, and all and sundry come to these meetings and they all love to sit round a table and come up with ideas, but what happens after that? Bugger all! Absolutely nothing till the next time.

> No, after that conference there was nothing. They said they were going to counsel my daughter but they never did. They didn't counsel me neither. I mean to say I'm a mother and I've been abused, and then I found out my son's been abusing my own child. You can't turn round and have the same perspective that someone else has on it. If it's someone else, you can say 'I'll kill him' but you can't do that when it's your own family. I felt as though I was on my own and I had to get on with it. They never really looked into why he was doing it. That made me angry because they said at the meeting he must have got it from somewhere, pointing at the home-base, and it was actually when he was in care before that it happened. No apologies or nothing like that. They are so quick to blame the parents.

Yet, parental responses were positive sometimes. This mother represents the views of those who considered they had been helped:

> At the time I was glad to have the social worker because otherwise, before she came, I was trying to get back where I used to live myself, but it wasn't getting anywhere. The main thing is looking after the children and I don't find that a problem . . . It was a big intrusion at the time but I don't think it could have been done any differently. The social worker comes and takes Bernadette

[13] out once a week and talks to her [about the sexual abuse], you know, and Bernadette can talk to her. I'm happy about that because my daughter didn't talk to me much about it. No one's interfering in my life. I've just had the social worker to help me.

These quotations disclose the frustration, confusion and hurt, as well as the satisfaction, that was experienced by the parents. They also reveal the ability of parents to know what they wanted from the services, as well as their recognition of subtleties and reasons why they did not get what they thought they needed.

There were more examples of co-ordinated work involving partnerships between field social workers, other professionals and those based in family centres or resource centres than was the case in the earlier studies reported in *Child Protection: Messages from Research* (Dartington Social Research Unit 1995). There were many examples of highly skilled, tenacious and caring practice which gave cause for optimism about the ability of properly trained, resourced and supervised social workers to provide an effective helping and protective service based on well-established casework principles.

In line with studies reported in *Child Protection: Messages from Research*, we found that once a child is identified as having been maltreated by a parent or carer, and continues to be at risk of maltreatment, there is likely to be at least an adequate response in terms of helping the child, though not always other members of the family, if the child is removed from their care.

The child/family focus and the coercion/voluntary dimensions

When studying the services offered to children and families within the intensive sample of 51 cases, four recurring patterns emerge relating to the issues of the predominant focus of the work (whole family or child) and the use of coercion (see Figure 6.1). The family casework 'with negotiation' and 'with coercion' patterns represent practice which focuses on the child and the family jointly. In 'child-focused casework' and 'child rescue', the practice focus is on the identified child (often to the exclusion of the needs of other children in the family). The needs of the parents are secondary or remain unmet.

Forty-four of the intensive sample of 51 could be plotted within the four patterns in Figure 6.1 Twenty-eight children and their families were receiving what could be broadly called family support (in the top half of the diagram – family casework with varying degrees of negotiation and coercion). Sixteen children were receiving help with a minimum of support to their families (child-focused casework and child rescue). Ten of the 12 children in the more coercive 'child rescue' quadrant were on a legal order.

Figure 6.1 *Patterns of help (intensive sample of 51 cases[1])*

	Less coercion	**More coercion**
Family and child focus	Family casework with negotiation 14 cases	Family casework with coercion 14 cases
Focus on child	Child-focused casework 5 cases	Child rescue 11 cases

[1] The remaining seven cases could not be classified in this way, or there was inadequate information

The casework service did not always remain static, so the degree of coercion imposed could (and did) move back and forth along the continuum of less to more coercion and vice versa. Family casework with negotiation could be continued throughout the intervention, with a balance of help offered to the child and other family members and a minimum of coercion. This pattern became harder to sustain, however, if parental co-operation was lacking or if a child was not developing well and the harm, or risk of maltreatment, was not diminishing. When lack of co-operation was coupled with increasing danger to the child this could direct the focus away from the parents to a member of the extended family or to the other parent, who might be able to provide care for the child. Where the needs of at least some members of the family were still to the forefront, but the degree of coercion had increased, the pattern shifted to the 'family casework with coercion' quadrant. Where the practice focus turned overtly to the child and away from the parents and family, often with the backing of a court order, the pattern of help would sometimes shift from 'family casework with negotiation' directly to 'child rescue'.

Examples of work with children and their families in each of the four quadrants are given below:

Family casework with negotiation

There was ample evidence of medium- and longer-term supportive work that encouraged and facilitated families in caring for their children in very difficult circumstances. For one family of three children, where serious neglect and developmental delay was a concern, help was offered outside the formal child protection system with the active participation of a multi-agency core group. The social worker described this rigorous but supportive work:

> The thrust of the work is twofold: firstly, to maintain adequate standards in the house to prevent what had happened, happening again, and secondly, to check on the general development of the children and get the parents involved in doing that too. I checked on the number of accidents they had, and how many times they had to be taken to or admitted to hospital, and compared it to RoSPA [Royal Society for the Prevention of Accidents] figures. These children were within an acceptable standard so this provided a benchmark. The bruises they got were not serious and were to do with chaotic parenting, not dangerous parenting. We are also doing other things to help their development, for example providing family aide, nursery places and summer schemes, and cash – all from Section 17. What prevented this case becoming child protection was to call meetings with all the agencies involved and to have the issues firmly placed out there so that the family were under no misapprehension that by what they were doing they could be heading towards a child protection conference.

The possibility of coercion was present in this case as in many others, and very few cases in this 'significant harm' sample were worked with in an unconditionally supportive manner. Work with baby Carys started as family casework with negotiation, and a touch of coercion. Over time, the extent of coercion increased and a court order was sought:

● ●

Carys' name was placed on the Child Protection Register at birth and she was born below the third centile in weight with heroin withdrawal symptoms. Her mother, Debbie, discharged herself from the drug detoxification unit within two weeks of Carys' birth, and intensive family casework and monitoring from the social worker and health visitor was offered and initially accepted. Debbie and her partner became reluctant to accept this monitoring, however, and failed to keep appointments at the clinic. When Debbie did not collect Carys after leaving her overnight with her mother, an Interim Care Order application was made and Carys remained with her grandmother. Concerted, but largely unsuccessful, efforts were made to work with the parents, and a high level of emotional and financial support was offered to the grandparents (family casework with a degree of coercion because of the order). Work continued in this mode for the rest of the year, with Carys remaining within the family on an order.

● ●

Family casework with coercion

● ●

A baby with a fractured limb was placed in a residential setting with her mother after being taken into police protection. Subsequently, care proceedings resulted in a Supervision Order. The young age of the child and the extent of the injury influenced the need for a degree of coercion in this case, as did the history of violent marital conflict. Concerted attempts were made to work with both the parents and the extended family, placing this case within the family casework with coercion quadrant (rather than child-focused or child rescue work). Working through interpreters, however, made it extremely difficult for professionals, and the social worker in particular, to establish a relationship of trust with either parent. At this stage, neither parent felt properly involved in the work or fully understood it. Social Services did acknowledge the isolation and the need for support so funded a visit from a member of the mother's extended family from abroad. The social worker explained the early difficulties:

> Harvinder said she did not want social work involvement but she's moved on considerably now. She came from not only a different culture but also moved from the countryside to the city when she came to the UK. It was a phenomenal change for her, plus not knowing what this system was. It was all quite alien to her and it was perfectly reasonable for her to be mistrusting because she didn't know what was going on. But now things have moved on. . . . We tried using a family group conference but it didn't work because Dad just bullied Mum into what he wanted – that's not negotiation as far as I'm concerned . . . Then we encouraged mother to get an injunction with powers of arrest and we provided a phone for her. Dad tried to get me on his side, but basically I can't be on anyone's side. All in all it was a massive piece of work.

● ●

Towards the end of the year, however, the worker's tenacity was rewarded and coercion was not necessary. The work had moved to being within the 'family casework with negotiation' group, with the end of the Supervision Order in sight.

Child-focused casework

In this pattern there was more of a focus on the child than the family as a whole. Often there was a tendency to concentrate on the abusive incident rather than the broader family context.

● ●

> For 13-year-old Neil the focus of the intervention was on his alleged sexual abuse of a younger child. Neil was offered group work to tackle his behaviour. No help was offered to his brother, Howard, who caused a great many problems at home and school because of his difficult behaviour. Howard attended a residential school for children with emotional and behavioural difficulties, coming home for weekends. The family was under additional stress because Neil's mother had a chronic illness. Neil felt responsible for looking after his mother, who was a single parent. Neil's mother said:
>
> > I don't think anyone's done anything to help. But my impressions of the social worker have picked up a bit. She's not as snotty as I thought she was. But I'm going to need to get on to Social Services about Howard's schooling because he's going to be kicked out of that school.

● ●

In another case, child-focused casework and concentration on a single incident of physical abuse had some positive aspects. Cultural relativism was spurned by challenging some Muslim parents' right to beat their teenage daughter for transgressing cultural rules. Reference has already been made to the young woman, who refused to go home after being beaten by her father. She was accommodated, at her request, but chose to go home within days. The social worker commented:

> Although I appreciated the family's culture and their religion, their children also had an English side to them which had developed through their mixing with people at school. She had an idea of her own rights, and said her dad had no right to beat her up, and she was glad he was told that.

To an extent, however, this approach had the negative effect of pitching the child and the helping agencies against the family. This young woman said that she now feels more distant from her family and less loved but, should the incident happen again, she would know who to contact and that she would be helped.

Child rescue

In this pattern there was a concentration at the time of harm or suspicion of harm on the needs of the child. The degree of coercion was high. The needs of the parents and other family members were secondary or unmet. In the following example, services were provided to the baby and her carers; her mother's needs remained unmet:

• •

Tara was removed at birth from the care of Dawn, her 16-year-old mother, because no place could be found to take the mother and baby together to assess Dawn's ability as a parent. A decision was made to place Tara outside the family for adoption, as the option which would have the best chance of a good enough outcome for this vulnerable baby. The work in this case was very clearly child-focused, with the backing of legal orders. Tara was in foster care for a year and then adopted. Support to Dawn was minimal and no counselling was provided to help her come to terms with losing the baby. Dawn's contact with Tara was terminated by a court order, against her wishes, when the baby was 5 months old. In this case, the wishes and feelings of one child, the 16-year-old mother, were overruled in the interest of the child who was the subject of the court proceedings.

• •

This case raises a question that arose in at least two other cases – the respective duties towards two children when the child's mother is a child herself, as defined by the Children Act 1989. The facts supported the conclusion that it was necessary to protect Tara by removing her from her mother's care, but there was little evidence of serious consideration by the agencies of their duty to provide services to Dawn as a 'child in need'. It could be argued that more attention should have been given to the fact that she was highly likely to suffer significant impairment to her future emotional development unless a serious attempt was made to provide her with support and services. Practice which focuses so single-mindedly on the child, at the very least, does not store up goodwill or engender trust with young parents, a large proportion of whom are likely to need social work and other services in the future, when other children are born. The long-term outcome for Tara and others like her is discussed in Chapter 9.

The direction of work with babies was not always towards more coercion, however. For another baby, Frankie, intervention that started in the 'child rescue' mode, and was seen by the parents as highly coercive and distancing, moved to the 'family casework with negotiation' pattern. The outcome for this baby was not permanent care away from his birth mother but a return home:

With Frankie, the work at the start of the research period was driven by suspicions of severe neglect, which was thought to have exacerbated serious ill health. Frankie was removed from his mother, who had been staying in bed and breakfast accommodation (child rescue). When it was realised that Frankie's poor health was not attributable to poor maternal care, closer links with the mother were forged and a return home effected (family casework with negotiation).

Nine-year-old Steven was accommodated at the time of an incident of sexual abuse by someone outside the family. The social worker demonstrates very clearly that he sees himself as Steven's social worker, not the family's, even though no other worker was allocated to support the parents:

> I don't want the roles to get muddled, which is why I wasn't keen to be their support because I'm Steven's social worker. I don't want them to think I'm taking their side, if you know what I mean. So I try to keep it that I'm Steven's worker but will be there for them if they need me – but not in a friendly capacity. They prefer to be friends with people rather than keep it on a professional basis. I think you always have to keep that distance. It would be a lot easier to go in and be chummy and friendly, and talk about what they wanted to talk about, but really you've got an agenda and things you want to sort out, and you have to do it.

In spite of Steven being an accommodated child, attempts to work in partnership and let the parents share the agenda, were clearly not part of this worker's practice. Not surprisingly, the parents expressed disappointment at not receiving the help they knew they needed.

Multi-agency co-ordination and practice

Another issue to be taken into account when analysing the service provided was interagency co-ordination (Hallett 1995). Table 6.2 shows a high degree of agreement between professionals about significant harm, indicating that the groupings were becoming familiar with the terminology but showing, also, a healthy percentage of minor disagreement. Different patterns of interagency co-ordination and collaboration were evident in practice at the time of determining significant harm and in the follow-up support and monitoring. Two overlapping teams of professionals were involved, which could be described as the 'support' and the 'forensic' teams.

Table 6.2 *Level of professional agreement about significant harm at Stage 1*[1]

Agreement level	%
Much disagreement	4
Midway split	15
Minor disagreement	38
Full agreement	43

[1] Includes 48 interview sample cases where there was adequate information

The support team was usually in evidence prior to the initiation of child protection enquiries. In most cases, it became the 'core group' after a child protection conference and assessment had taken place. If the child's name was not placed on the Register following the conference, this team sometimes continued as a multi-agency support team. In cases where the formal child protection system was not used at all, this grouping remained the 'support team' with some additions and some drop-outs throughout the year. It was evident in all cases, however, that the extent and intensity of multi-agency co-operation increased at the time that the possibility of significant harm was put onto the agenda.

Typically, the support team comprised different combinations of health visitors, GPs, family aides, playgroup leaders, family centre workers, voluntary agency workers and social workers from statutory and voluntary agencies for the younger children, with the addition of school nurses, education welfare officers, and class teachers or school counsellors for the older children. For a child with a chronic illness, disability or behaviour problem, a community or hospital paediatrician, community medical officer, child psychiatrist or probation officer might be involved. Probation officers, addiction specialists, or adult mental health workers might also be involved in the support team. In a few cases, the local police officer played an important part in the community support provision.

The second multi-agency team was the 'forensic team', which dominated the decision-making process at the time of the child protection conference. Health visitors and social workers, community medical officers, paediatricians and school nurses provided continuity in that they usually belonged to both teams. GPs, in theory, belonged to both but rarely attended the child protection conference and made a more important contribution to the ongoing support team. Headteachers were also members of the forensic team (it was rare for class teachers to attend conferences), as were officers from the specialist child protection police unit and doctors who had examined injuries or been asked to comment on physical development or the impact of neglect. In some cases, specialist child protection investigation or assessment teams, often provided by the NSPCC but sometimes by child psychiatry departments or a specialist section of the social services department, joined together for this 'forensic' stage of the case. They sometimes remained involved until a 'comprehensive assessment' (DoH 1988) had been completed. In the minority of cases where a court application was made, a guardian ad litem and a solicitor for the child, although not a part of the 'forensic team', would be involved at this stage.

The age of the child

The information collected about all 105 children, with detailed material from the intensive sample of 51 cases, provided insights into the nature of inter-agency work with children of different ages.

Babies

All the 18 babies had active support from health and welfare agencies in determining significant harm, or more often, likely significant harm. The child protection conference was, in this sense, a meeting of the 'forensic team', but many participants continued to have a role with these families. On the whole, intervention was well co-ordinated, with the active involvement of a range of professionals. There was no evidence of drift and all the babies were the subject of good multi-agency planning.

Some parents found support from health visitors easier to accept than from social workers:

> The health visitor has given me lots of advice about the baby and her tantrums, and she tries to support me as much as she can. Every week I go to the clinic with the baby as well. I like her. I didn't at first, till I started to see her a lot. I went to the clinic every week with the baby and when I stopped, she came to see me at my mum's.

> I don't think anything would have been helpful really. I just wanted to get Social Services off my back. We couldn't have refused to have a social worker because of it being child protection. It's probably when they would have started thinking about taking the children off us if we had.

The probation service was involved in a forensic capacity with only one family, where a father who was the subject of a Probation Order for theft was offered anger management but did not attend the programme. It was alarming to note that the probation officer did not work with other agencies, or alone, to try to address the violence between the parents, which was a source of emotional and likely physical harm to the baby.

Children aged 1–4 years

The services provided to this group of 30 pre-school children were often numerous and of long duration, but were rarely well co-ordinated. Funded day care was the typical service and it was offered to all but one of the children. Rehousing during the year was achieved for almost two-thirds of the families but some were still in urgent need of new accommodation. Families were regularly offered practical help, often connected with the move, for example the provision of furniture.

Specific parenting assistance was also offered by a range of professionals and was usually valued by parents:

> I've seen a child psychiatrist with the kids, and the social worker and the family support worker. We've had quite a few sessions, sometimes with their grandfather as well. I saw the social worker on Tuesday and we drew up a care plan, like the subjects that were to be discussed, so that we could build up my self-esteem to help with the kids' behaviour. It's to help me to help them get on.

Much of the parenting assistance was in collaboration with day nurseries, family centres, foster carers and, in one case, a women's refuge. The social worker was the key figure in establishing mechanisms whereby parenting advice and support could be offered, but it was more often delivered by the nursery workers who had good day-to-day knowledge of the child.

Removal of a child's name from the Register often signalled an end to social work support for children of this age. Health visitors, in particular, felt they were carrying worrying cases without support:

> No, I didn't agree with him coming off the Register. I knew that would mean I'd be left to support this family on my own, and their problems haven't disappeared. People think we're social workers with all those connotations and we're not. We're there for the health and well-being of the family.

Children aged 5–11 years

There were 31 children in this age range. Twelve of the children lived away from home at some point during the study; 6 were away on a long-term basis by the end of the year; and a further four were living with the extended family or their care was being shared between parents and grandparents. Similar patterns of discussions between 'forensic' and 'support' teams were evident with this group of children. The bulk of the activity, however, was in liaison within Social Services because of the high numbers of these children accommodated.

Twelve of the parents in this group had problems with alcohol, drugs or mental health. Well-co-ordinated help was provided to most of the families with these difficulties. Support came from specialist services including drug dependency units and family consultation services; schools were also significantly involved:

> The school's been excellent. The professionals all keep tabs on me and
> I can't even sneeze without them knowing. The GP has been good with
> the medication. I've collected it every day to prevent people worrying that
> I won't take it right. The chemist tells my social worker or my health visitor
> if I don't collect it. That was my idea.

Teenagers

There were 26 young people in this 12+ age range. More than a third were living away from home for long periods of time. One in five of the parents had significant physical or mental health problems, and two had alcohol or drug problems. For one 15-year-old girl there was a very active multi-agency support team, which operated outside the formal child protection system, providing co-ordinated special services and high-status residential care. This team hovered on the borders of becoming a forensic team as the question of significant harm was frequently discussed, as was the possibility of moving the case into the formal child protection arena and providing help with a greater degree of coercion.

The service to families of minority ethnic origin

Several of the case descriptions in this chapter have concerned families from minority ethnic groups. Some spoke specifically of the impact of racism or the fear engendered by the child protection process. In one situation, where a baby had been caught up in an episode of domestic violence in which her arm had been fractured (described earlier as an example of family casework with coercion), the mother described her confusion and fear about the child protection procedures:

I was so worried and unhappy. First it was my mother-in-law and all of that, and then the Social Services. I don't know the law and the language. I'm very worried about the court. I class it all as racism and that goes on. I only want to bring my children up. It's the only thing I can do. I can't fight with the government and the court. I am a mother and I am worried for my children.

This young mother found the interference of the authorities outside her experience and comprehension. It was extremely difficult for the social worker to explain why Social Services were involved, and it took time and patience to establish with both parents the basis for intervention. Had this been possible earlier, recourse to the courts might have been avoided, or better understood.

One African refugee couple spoke articulately of the urgent need for a service for recent immigrants and refugees to explain the law in respect of the punishment of children. The father said:

The relationships between the Europeans and the Africans – you have a lot of work to do. We Africans have our way of living which has been badly understood right from the start. It is necessary to explain clearly, to advise how to do things from one situation to the next. I am a man of good education, I have a university education, but when I come to England I have difficulty adapting myself to a different regime, because we don't have any instruction, nobody tells us how it has to be.

You receive us into your country but suddenly if there is a family problem, the police are at your doorstep, the social workers arrive. In our country we don't have social workers. The police don't come for family problems. So if there is a problem and the social workers put the wife somewhere else and put the husband somewhere else there will always be a grave problem for African families. We can't accept this because, firstly, it's a question of security, the wife is a woman. For Europeans it's normal if there's a problem in the family, the marriage breaks up. When the family gets together the husband says, 'Has another man been with you?' He is jealous. So the social workers cause serious problems.

The first thing you should do is to get well-established families from my country when Africans arrive here. You should get them to say to them, 'If you do this this will happen; if you do that, that will happen.' It should be written down with the help of other people from my country so that they can say, 'Yes, I understand that, I accept that.' It should say and be given to all Africans who come here, 'If you hit your wife, then the authorities will be able to take her and give her somewhere else to live, etc. etc. The children, you should speak to them, you should not hit them; if you do, they may be taken away by the police.'

Translation/interpretation

Great efforts were made, in the different areas, to meet the needs of minority ethnic families, but not all were free of problems. Language is the key to understanding any situation, especially situations as sensitive as those where abuse and neglect are alleged. The provision of interpreters was patchy, although in one area an interpreting and translation service was provided by the local authority. The difference such an accessible service made to parents and staff alike was marked.

The role of the interpreter is crucial. There are issues of confidentiality and cultural acceptability, not just within the family but within the broader community. The interpreter needs to be able to respect confidentiality, and for many ethnic groups it is important that the interpreter is known to be an outsider to their own network. The logistical problems of achieving this means that it is tempting to involve another member of the family to translate in an emergency. This is particularly inappropriate if children are brought in to act as interpreters. A 14-year-old boy, used as a translator, told the researcher how worried he was about it:

> I was only 14. I got confused. My mind was muddled up and I was frightened a bit. I cannot explain how I felt.

In another case, difficulties between an Asian woman and her husband were exacerbated when an Asian man was employed to interpret for the wife.

Another subtle problem is whether the person will *translate* or *interpret*. One researcher, who was fluent in French, attended a conference where the family required the service of a skilled interpreter, but received a muddled combination of translation and interpretation. The meaning and context of the child protection procedures were not conveyed to the family and occasionally the actual translation of the words was incorrect. At one point, the interpreter took on the role of advocate: advising the mother against making a particular point, and failing to interpret a sentence which would have been very helpful to the conference. This was not an isolated incident. In another conference, where an interpreter was used, an Asian father described how the rest of the all-white conference were unaware of the interpreter's admonishments to him:

I tried to explain, but no one would listen to me. I was not very well so became very anxious. The interpreter told me that it [was] my fault, as I should not have hit the child, and that I should just accept what was being said.

This father was also concerned that what he said was not accurately reported to the social worker:

My social worker is very good but I cannot talk to her myself. It always has to be through the family worker, and I am not sure what they say or whether the social worker knows what I am asking for.

When all the members of the conference are dependent on one interpreter, error and misunderstanding may occur.

Workers from the same ethnic community

The employment of workers from the ethnic community in one area, whilst very positive in one sense, also caused some problems within the community – for the workers as well as the families. Their task was to report incidents of abuse or neglect, and such was their vigilance that the families felt that they were being spied upon. Workers would assiduously preserve confidentiality, but their actions, and any negative reporting, would often be passed on within their community, causing the potential for division and resentment:

Sitara used to come every day to observe us, especially the children's behaviour. She took them to school and brought them home. She then wrote a report for Social Services informing them that I am OK as a mother but that the children don't listen to me. At present the children's names are off the Register but I am still visited. In fact, every time I go out even to the shops, which are a minute away, on my own without the children, they are there. I don't like this continual interference. Sometimes they come when I have visitors or friends or relatives. They start questioning me in front of visitors, which is an insult in our community and culture, as they think my children are really bad, which in turn is a reflection on me, their mother. . . . Once my cousin came round so I left the sleeping baby with her in order to go to the shops. The worker saw me out, did not ask about the baby but came to my house with a social worker as she thought I had left him on his own. It was embarrassing. My cousin asked questions and wondered what was wrong. My husband was angry about this incident, so when the worker went into our shop he told her off, which she didn't like.

The issues of community loyalty, confidentiality and clarity about the role of the family workers in relation to the community seemed ill-defined in this new project, which was still establishing itself.

What emerges from the data from the families of minority ethnic origin is not so much the need for a set of guidelines about race or ethnicity for workers to follow, but a leap of imagination and extra sensitivity to be made in order to empathise with families. Matching language may be more important than matching race; consideration of class also needs to come into the equation. There is an inverted tact, which becomes tactlessness, when black or Asian workers are asked to resolve problems for other workers that may be handled with a little forethought and information-gathering by the workers' themselves. There were shining examples of social workers in the study, however, who had made the effort, taken time to think through the situation, and put their values into practice, which made the client–worker relationship meaningful, often despite ethnic and cultural difference.

Children's views

We conclude the chapter with a summary of the children's views about services. The children as we have said, were happier with the services offered than were their parents. Well over half of the 29 children asked said their social worker was helpful, and a further quarter had mixed feelings. When asked who was the most helpful professional, social workers and teachers came top of the list (nine said social workers, eight said teachers). For two, it was a police officer, and one said their doctor (who had helped with incontinence problems). Four children mentioned another professional by name, but they did not know the details of this person's role. Although children's views can change from day to day, and younger children in particular will tend to remember what has happened most recently, they were clear about what they found helpful:

> I've got a teacher at school I can talk to when I want to talk to someone. She's more helpful than the social worker. She told me about the same problems happening in her family when she was my age. It's not just that she's Asian like me – it's just who she is. It wouldn't matter if she was English or not.

Children do not always want to be reminded of their difficulties:

> The most helpful person was Mr Smith, the school counsellor. I saw him for a couple of months. He wouldn't just talk about my dad, he'd talk about other things as well, like a football match.

Nine-year-old Katy did want specific help, however, when her parents were fighting. She got it from the police, whom she said 'stopped the rows'.

All the children who were asked knew their social worker's name. This in itself may not seem over-impressive, but the children were extremely confused about the other professionals they had seen. Only three children said their social worker did not help them. Three children also said they did not get on with their social worker. The bulk of the children, however, said they got on well or very well with their social worker and were able to describe the sort of things they did together:

> We play paper games and that sort of stuff – and I talk to her. It's helpful to see her because she sorts things out for you.

> My sister and my mum and I go to a place once a week. They tell us about what will happen and they help you to get along with your sisters or your friend, and we draw a tree chart of our family and we talk about things that make you get cuddled and smile. It was OK, but I wasn't by myself and I prefer being by myself. You get to talk about more things about you, without other children interrupting you. The best person is my social worker because she doesn't talk about the abuse so much, and she asks questions, but not just about the abuse, and she takes us out. She understands best how I feel.

Many children commented that they liked to see their social worker regularly and enjoyed doing familiar, ordinary things like going to a café or 'just talking'. Children were disappointed if the level of visiting dropped, saying, 'If you don't see much of your social worker, how can they know you?'

Twenty-six children were asked whether they were involved in decisions made about them, and over half said their social worker helped them to feel part of decisions made. Five were helped to be included by someone other than their social worker, but four children did not feel involved. Three children who were asked could not grasp the question. In terms of attending meetings, two children went to the child protection conference, and they were glad to have done so. Six children went regularly to reviews and planning meetings, but most of the children we spoke to had no wish to be involved in more meetings and did not on the whole find them productive or enjoyable experiences.

Children were asked whether they knew how to complain about their dealings with professionals. Although attempts were made to simplify the language, the concept of a right to complain seemed alien to most of these children. Four young people, however, said they did know how to complain but hadn't wanted to do so. No children were in contact with organisations for young people in care, although one child said her social worker had given her information about this. This is not to say that social workers had not provided this sort of information, but children could not recall it. It was noted in Chapter 5 that a small number of the children felt they had no one to turn to or talk to. While the small cards available from 'ChildLine', with a special telephone number for children in care, are unlikely to be sufficient on their own to resolve contact problems, children might feel able to use this sort of distant contact as most had access to a telephone.

Summary

This chapter describes the intensity and duration of services offered to the sample families. At the time of coming into the sample, almost half of the cases were already 'open' long-term cases, which were either kept open or received an intermittent 'revolving door' service, often via a duty system. During the course of the study almost a fifth of the sample had a low-intensity service, either because little in the way of help or services were offered (often in spite of registration), or because little was accepted. A large majority of families, however, did receive a consistent service of longer duration.

Work that was focused on the child – with the needs of parents and other family members treated as a low priority – tended to be more coercive. This style of work made the child's return home difficult, and caused problems if the child returned home after a spell of accommodation.

For one in four families, co-ordinated help was not available until the incident that prompted the conference galvanised the agencies into action. These cases fitted into a pattern of waiting until 'need' became 'harm' before a service was provided.

Multi-agency help was offered in 52 of the 105 cases. Multi-agency working intensified in all cases at the time when the possibility of significant harm came onto the agenda. Two overlapping teams of professionals were involved: the 'support team', which could provide long-term support from within or outside the child protection system, and the 'forensic team'. The 'forensic team' was in operation for a briefer period of time and dominated decision-making at the child protection conference.

There was evidence of extensive efforts to meet the needs of minority ethnic families and to provide a culturally sensitive service, but there were many problems in delivering this service. Little information about laws, in relation to parenting and violence, was available to parents and this would have helped families new to the UK. There was also confusion when using interpreters, who sometimes acted as advocates for the families and sometimes failed to translate accurately. Employees recruited from the communities in which the families lived were felt by some families to be acting as 'spies'. The workers themselves felt uncomfortable in their role, which had the potential for division and resentment in their own networks.

Half of the families felt they had been helped to some extent over the year of the data collection, although many parents were ambivalent about the service provided by the social worker. A significant minority were dissatisfied by their contacts with the child protection and family support services.

More children than adults made it clear to the researchers that they felt supported by social workers over the year. The positive responses from the older children suggest that social workers have invested time and energy in their contacts with children, which have in turn been valued. Social workers and teachers were listed by children as the most helpful professionals. On the whole, the children did not like to be reminded of any abuse and wanted to be able to play, do ordinary things, and discuss other issues of importance with their social worker. About half of the older children said their social worker helped them to take part when decisions were made about them.

7 *The use of out-of-home placement*

For several years before the implementation of the Children Act 1989 strong criticism had been expressed of the legislative provision whereby the local authority could assume parental rights by passing a resolution of the Social Services committee. Although parents could appeal to the courts, this was rarely done, and was even more rarely successful (Millham et al. 1989). The grounds for the assumption of parental rights were different from the grounds under which a Care Order could be made. However, once a child had been received into voluntary care it was held to be no longer possible for an application for a Care Order to be made. The only recourse for the local authority was to assume parental rights, if it could be demonstrated to be in the interests of the child that long-term plans should be made to which the parents were not willing to consent, and if legal grounds were satisfied.

Out-of-home placement and the 1989 Act

The Children Act 1989 sought to address the criticism of this situation by ensuring that the local authority could gain parental responsibility only by virtue of a court order. Prior to the Act's implementation in 1991 there was a tendency not to provide voluntary care if there were reasons to believe that the local authority might subsequently need to increase its control over the situation. Most often this occurred in cases of abuse or serious maltreatment, or where a child had already been received into care on one or more occasions and discharged inappropriately. Packman et al. (1986) found that the 'victims' who went into care almost always did so following a Place of Safety Order, and that Care Orders usually followed. The opening up, by the 1989 Act, of the possibility of seeking a Care Order on a child already accommodated under Section 20 was held by many child care practitioners to be a step forward. It was anticipated that it would allow greater scope to use the less coercive procedure of providing accommodation for the child in the first instance. With the child in a safe situation, time could be taken to clarify whether continuing to work under voluntary arrangements would be feasible and in the interests of the child. If this proved not to be the case it would then be possible to seek a Care Order in court.

The other group for which accommodation under voluntary arrangements was likely to be extensively used, following the implementation of the 1989 Act, was children with disabilities who needed regular respite care with the same carer. Various informal arrangements had grown up outside the provisions of previous child care legislation to avoid the stigma that had become associated with reception into care. In order to minimise the risk of stigma, certain restrictions on the parental rights of children who were received into care under voluntary arrangements were removed when the new legislation was implemented, most importantly the requirement for parents to give notice of their intention to resume care of their child. This aspect of the new legislation was hotly debated, with a strong consensus that the removal of the duty to give 28 days' notice would make it difficult for the authority to make long-term plans for children who were accommodated. These perceived difficulties, it was believed, might discourage social workers from using accommodation and encourage the routine seeking of Care Orders in cases where there was any possibility that the child's long-term future may not lie with the family of origin.

The appropriate use of accommodation has been widely debated in the professional and legal literature since the Act was implemented. In particular, the question of whether accommodation should be used only when it is totally voluntary on the part of parents and child, or whether it is legitimate to exercise a degree of coercion by limiting the choice available to parents has been discussed. Packman and Hall (1998) revisited the two agencies that took part in the study *Who Needs Care?* (Packman et al. 1986). They reviewed 177 admissions to Section 20 accommodation and found that this type of accommodation was used much more frequently with protection cases (categorised as 'victims' in both studies) than was the case in the original study.

> Twelve per cent [of the accommodated children] were known to have been on the Child Protection Register in the past and nearly a quarter (23%) were either on the CPR at the point of their admission, or were registered soon after they entered accommodation – a total of over a third of the children in the sample. Again, this is a sharp contrast to the situation ten years ago, when only one per cent of children entering *voluntary* care were registered.
> (Packman and Hall 1995, p. 71)

Other researchers (Lindley 1994; Hunt et al. 1999) have considered cases where applications for public law orders were made following a period of accommodation, alongside cases where a direct application for a Care Order was made without a period of accommodation. These writers cite social workers and solicitors who were influenced by the anger and the sense of powerlessness or betrayal of parents who thought they had willingly consented to their child being accommodated only to find that a Care Order was subsequently sought. These professionals questioned whether accommodation should be restricted to cases where there is no element of coercion.

A second area of interest and debate about the use of accommodation concerns the provision of short periods of respite care, usually in the same family or within a residential establishment, in order to support families and provide additional stimulus to some children. Stalker (1990) and Robinson (1987) discussed the use of respite care for children with disabilities prior to the implementation of the Act. Aldgate and Bradley (1999) reviewed the use of respite care for children who may not themselves have a disability but whose families are under pressure. These authors conclude that Section 20 respite care is an important part of family support, as is the use of accommodation outside the home on a specific occasion for families where this might reduce the stress and facilitate the long term care of the child by his or her parents. The *Guidance* on the Children Act is specific about the importance of emphasising parental responsibility and involving parents, siblings and relatives in the plans for the child who is looked after in this way.

Our study included some children who were provided with respite care and others for whom periods in accommodation were provided in order to help alleviate stress and improve the chances of the parents providing a high enough quality of parenting for their child in the long-term. Placement away from home was also provided as part of the assessment process, and as a means of achieving short-term protection until a doubtful situation was clarified. For a small number of children, Section 20 accommodation was the legal basis for planning permanent care for them away from the family home.

The use of out-of-home placement in the cohort of 105 cases

There was evidence in the study of the flexible use of legislative provisions to secure care for those children who could not remain safely within the family home. During the 12-month period after serious concerns were identified, 71 of the 105 children lived away from the family home at some stage, though this was sometimes only for a day or two. In six cases the child was accommodated, together with a parent, either at a residential unit for families or with relatives. Just under one in three of the children lived away from their parents for a week or longer, although a substantial minority of these lived with relatives or friends. The interventions that were made were diverse and illustrate the wide range of possibilities available to protect children from harm. Using accommodation creatively enlarged the scope for child protection professionals to take account of the uniqueness of each child, family and situation. There were:

♦ immediate short-term placements with foster carers or members of the extended family, sometimes following on from police protection or Emergency Protection Orders at the time of the incident or crisis;

♦ medium-term placements with foster carers or members of the extended family while efforts were made to trace the child's parent(s) or to assess the nature and quality of parenting;

♦ shared care arrangements between parents and grandparents or foster carers; and

♦ long-term placements with a view to adoption or (for teenagers) independent living.

Most of these arrangements were made by agreement but a substantial minority took the compulsory route through court: eight began with accommodation under Section 20 but ended with Care Orders. In view of the debate about whether the 28 days' notice provision of previous legislation should be retained in order to prevent children being removed inappropriately by parents, it is interesting to note that in none of these cases was emergency action needed to stop this from happening. Four cases started with the child being taken into police protection and moved to a voluntary arrangement for the child to be looked after. One started as an Emergency Protection Order, moved into accommodation and ended with a Care Order. These reflect the fluidity of family life when parents are under pressure or in crisis, and the attempts by workers to incorporate into practice one of the principles of the Act that the child should, wherever possible, live with his or her own family. They also demonstrate the use of coercive measures for short periods to protect the child or secure continuity of long-term plans until it becomes clear whether voluntary arrangements can be agreed and sustained or it becomes necessary to limit the parents' parental responsibility on a long-term basis.

The views of parents about Section 20 arrangements differed widely, depending on how they felt they had been consulted and treated by Social Services during the child protection procedures:

I was completely devastated when my friend 'phoned up school. I just couldn't cope with it. I mean she's [the child] all I've got [cries] and they're intending keeping her away from me. I just can't take no more.

She's [an 8-year-old] still very difficult. It got to the point where she was trying to take her own life – pieces of glass at her throat, sitting out in the middle of the road, just generally hurting herself, and it just got to the point where I thought, 'Well this child needs help and I can't give her the help she needs', so I put her in care. I asked for it. I couldn't cope any more. It all got too much. I thought I was coping but I wasn't. I'm going for counselling tomorrow. I've got Becky out of the way so I can do it.

The reasons for, and purposes of, placements away from the family home varied greatly, but there were enough similarities in some of the cases to categorise them (see Table 7.1).

Table 7.1 *Uses of out-of-home placements during the 12 months*

Use of placement	No. of times Section 20 used
Already accommodated (all older children)	3
Regular, planned respite care (including respite with relatives)	9
Periods of accommodation as part of support service	4
Planned accommodation of parent and child together	4
Assessment or long-term placement with relatives	11
Accommodated for longer period (likely to return home)	4
Accommodated for longer period (not likely to return home)	4
Accommodation requested by child	3
Accommodation agreed as alternative to Care Order application	12
Accommodation with threat of court action	2
Care Order sought for protection or to secure long-term plans	15
Total	71

In summary, out-of-home placement was used in five broad ways:

♦   as short-term protection;

♦   to provide respite as part of family support services;

♦   as a longer-term measure to help parents and children experiencing difficulties but where there were positive family links;

♦   to help older children move towards independent living; and

♦   to provide permanent substitute family care.

Sometimes a placement was used in more than one of these ways in the space of 12 months. For example, two children were already accommodated when serious concerns about their long-term well-being were raised. A boy, aged 14, was having a regular period of respite care when concerns about his serious problems at home were heightened. This led to a child protection conference. The likelihood of harm resulting from a sexual assault by a fellow resident in a children's home led to a conference on a 10-year-old girl, who had been accommodated for over a year. Another child already looked after was Louise:

● ●

Louise (aged 2) had been in accommodation for four weeks, at her mother's request, when the initial child protection conference was held on all three children in the family because of a build-up of concern about the quality of care the children received at home. All three children were registered in the category of neglect. The local authority solicitor advised that this was appropriate for Louise, as well as her brothers, because her mother could remove her from accommodation at any time. He argued that Louise needed the protection offered by the Register as much as her brothers, even though she was not living at home and there were no immediate plans for her return.

● ●

There was no clear pattern about the use of a legal order or accommodation in these different sets of circumstances. There did, however, appear to be a difference in the way in which the agencies, or area teams within agencies, used accommodation or court proceedings in similar cases. Figure 7.1 shows that of the 68 children who left parental care for more than a day or two, 38% were provided with accommodation under Section 20, whilst 25% were provided with financial support and advice or assistance to facilitate informal arrangements. (Additional details of the legal orders used are provided in Chapter 8.) In addition to the 22 children subject to a court order at the end of the 12-month period, there was discussion about a possible application for a Care Order in respect of three more of the accommodated children. For one of the children, already accommodated when concern was raised because of a sexual assault in residential care, the question of whether a Care Order should be applied for was a recurring theme throughout the 12-month research period.

The following cases give examples of how the voluntary provisions of the Children Act 1989 were used:

Figure 7.1 *Legal arrangements for the children who left the care of their parent(s)*[1]

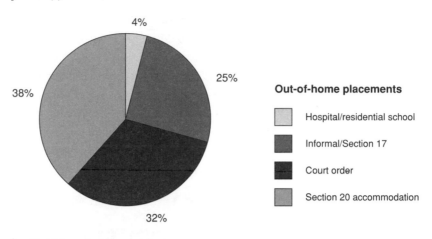

Out-of-home placements

- Hospital/residential school
- Informal/Section 17
- Court order
- Section 20 accommodation

[1] n=68 children who left parental care

Short-term protection

There are different reasons why children need to be protected by using accommodation, but most of the arrangements studied were made with the agreement of members of the respective family. These cases included: a baby who was being left alone and neglected by an unpredictable young mother; a young man who had to be separated from his siblings because he was involved in their sexual abuse, having been abused himself by their father; a young person at risk of offending and beyond the control of his mentally ill mother; a toddler who was being neglected as a result of her mother's addiction to alcohol and drugs; and a teenager who was bailed to a residential unit following his arrest for the alleged abduction of a toddler.

● ●

Iqbal had his arm fractured when he was 4 months old during a fight between his parents. His older sister had also sustained a fractured arm as a baby and her name had been placed on the Child Protection Register, although there were uncertainties about whether it was accidental, or intended. Domestic violence was a feature of family life and Iqbal's mother had stayed in a number of women's refuges. The child was taken into police protection following a change in diagnosis from the hospital casualty department after they had allowed him to go home. To prevent a traumatic separation of mother and baby while effecting the separation of the parents, Iqbal, his mother and sister were accommodated in a residential unit, with supervised access for his father.

Cassie, a 6-year-old who had never attended school, was referred by the staff of an inner-city bed and breakfast hotel because her mother was often under the influence of alcohol and drugs. The residents reported that Cassie was not being fed properly and that she had been kicked in the chest and chin. Cassie's mother agreed to Cassie being accommodated under Section 20 of the Children Act while further assessments were made. Cassie was placed with foster carers. She was described as extremely thin and only able to eat tea and toast. Subsequently, her mother disappeared. A year later Cassie was waiting to be placed permanently with a substitute family. Her attachment to, and concern about, her mother was undiminished.

● ●

Regular respite care

Aldgate and Bradley (1999) conclude from a study of respite care provided to families under stress that such care is not frequently used when there is a question of maltreatment. It was therefore interesting for us to note that it was used as a family support and child protection measure in an important minority of the 105 cases, although most often it was a relative who provided the respite care. It was used with children who had disabilities as well as in cases where parents were in need of respite because of their own difficulties:

● ●

Hannah suffered from Asperger's Syndrome which meant she was exhaustingly difficult to supervise. Her parents were under constant stress and hoping for a special boarding school place, which neither Social Services nor Education were willing to fund. The respite care once a month went only a small way towards what was really needed.

● ● ●

Stevie was a baby on whom there had been a pre-birth conference. His young mother's first child had been made the subject of a Care Order because of neglect and under-stimulation. Plans were made to assist his mother to keep Stevie and to look after him herself after his birth. Stevie's mother had been in care as a child and had a history of self-harming. She married a young soldier, not Stevie's father, and travelled to an army camp in another area where she soon left him. Her husband had undertaken a great deal of Stevie's care and Social Services helped out with periods of accommodation under Section 20 of the Children Act. However, when Stevie's mother was evicted from the tenancy of the army house it was decided, in the light of her lack of care for, and interest in, Stevie, that care proceedings should be initiated. Eventually, Stevie went to live with his maternal grandparents and half-brother, this arrangement being secured by a Family Assistance Order and a Residence Order.

● ● ●

Ricci had been deeply upset by his parents' violent marriage and subsequent divorce. As a result of the ongoing battle between his parents he assaulted his father, expressing some of his uncontrollable rage. Although only 14 years old, Ricci was physically fully grown. In defending himself the father injured Ricci. This incident was the reason for the initial child protection conference.

Ricci's mother explained that he often needed calming down, which she felt unable to do. Instead, he went frequently and sometimes for weeks at a time to her parents' home. They would often stay up all night talking to him when he was upset. The conference did not register Ricci and the case was closed fairly swiftly after referral to the child and family psychiatric department for therapy. Sessions there did not materialise and in the end the family managed to sort out its own problems.

● ●

A longer-term measure to avoid the permanent breakdown of family relationships

Out-of-home placement was also used as a longer-term measure to help parents and children, who were experiencing difficulties but where there were positive family links, to avoid the permanent breakdown of their relationship. There were two families where lone mothers were placed with their school-age sons in residential units for assessment, given help with parenting skills and special help for the boys. This was a way of avoiding the removal of the children and placing them in foster care. Both mothers had asked for their child to be accommodated. Neither rated the residential placement as successful or helpful. One said she needed a break from a demanding child while she moved house, and the other wanted placement for her son and herself separately so that she could make a concerted attempt to break a drugs habit.

A step towards independent living arrangements

● ●

Jacob, a 15-year-old, known to have abused his younger siblings and to have been abused himself by his stepfather, was accommodated at a residential boys' unit. He needed to be separated from his younger brothers and sisters. Jacob settled well and liked the unit. He was excluded from his usual school but transferred to the unit's school and did well. Therapy was arranged for him at an eminent local centre. He had contact with his mother and older sister when he wanted it and was preparing for independent living.

● ●

Part of a plan to secure placement with a permanent substitute family

When accommodation was used as part of a plan to place a child with substitute parents the children tended to be older, whereas Care Orders were most likely to be sought on younger children.

● ●

Joel (aged 11) had been 'running wild' with his older brothers on the fringes of the law since his mother's mental state had deteriorated. She was unable to exercise any control over him. The social services department had used a wide range of resources in an attempt to keep the family together, but the situation worsened markedly and Joel and his next-eldest brother were accommodated with foster carers. After three days the two boys took the law into their own hands and returned to the extended family. They asked to be allowed to live with them. At this point, an initial child protection conference was called to consider the risks to the boys and whether the arrangements would protect them. Joel went to live with his aunt and her children.

● ● ●

Ten-year-old Angie was accommodated at the time of the child protection conference. She had been abused by a play leader and had become increasingly difficult to care for. Her father and stepmother had requested that she be accommodated after she had started to play in an overtly sexual way with her younger half-sister. The local authority finally agreed on condition that she should be placed with a permanent substitute family. The placement broke down and she was in a children's home when a sexual relationship with an older boy led to the conference.

Angie was clearly suffering, and likely to continue to suffer, significant harm as she was vulnerable to abuse in residential care, but her family felt unable to care for her at home. Her father agreed for another permanent foster placement to be sought, provided that he and his wife could continue to see her on a fortnightly basis. Angie was confused about where she wanted to be but did not want to lose her close relationship with her family. When the local authority suggested reducing the amount of contact in order to make it easier to find a placement, the father objected and said he would ask for Angie to return home. The local authority told the father that they would initiate care proceedings if he did so. A period of negotiation followed, contact remained as it was, and Angie was placed on a permanent basis with experienced long-term foster parents by the end of the study.

● ●

Table 7.2 provides details of long-term plans and the legal status of the 68 children who were cared for away from home during the 12 months of our study. By the end of the study period, 32 of the 68 children were at home and a further four were due to return very shortly. Fifteen children had been placed or were about to be placed with permanent substitute families. The table shows that Section 20 accommodation was used predominantly with those who returned home. However, it was also used as often as Care Orders with children who were likely to be placed with permanent substitute families.

Table 7.2 *Long-term plans and legal status of the children 'looked after'*

Legal status	At home or return soon	With relatives, long-term	Moving towards independence	Permanent substitute placement	Uncertain	Total
Section 17/informal	11	2	—	1	3	17
Section 20 accommodation	14	2	3	7	—	26
Hospital/boarding school	2	—	1	—	—	3
Court order	8	2	2	7	3	22
Total	35	6	6	15	6	68

Since the implementation of the 1989 Act there has been much debate about whether the requirement to consult and give due consideration to the wishes and feelings of family members is increasing the numbers who are drifting in unplanned care. In this study, only six of the 68 were in unplanned care at Stage 2.

The children for whom permanent substitute families were sought included all age groups but they were predominantly younger children. Six were unborn or under 1 year old at the start of the study, six were aged between 5–11 years, and three were 12 years years or over. It is a cause for concern that plans were uncertain at Stage 2 for two children who were under the age of 1 at the start of the study and who were away from home and on Care or Interim Care Orders. Plans were also unclear for two children in the 5–11 age group and for one teenager, but were clear for all those aged 1–4 years at the start of the study.

Type of placement

Figure 7.2 indicates the main placement of the 68 children who were cared for away from home for any length of time.

Figure 7.2 *Main placement of the children who experienced out-of-home care*[1]

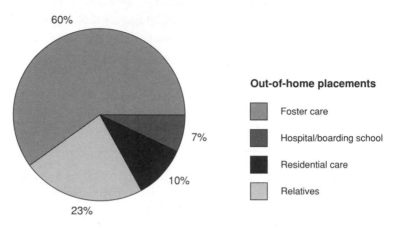

¹ n=68 children who left parental care

The way in which relatives were brought in to provide care has already been demonstrated in the case examples. It was noticeable, and frequently commented upon by relatives (who were mainly grandparents), that little practical or cash assistance was made available to them. Table 7.3 shows that no children were accommodated under Section 20 with family or friends, and therefore, it was only the two sets of carers whose young relatives were on Care Orders who received the full foster care allowance. Even the grandmother whose grandchild was the subject of a Supervision Order and a Family Assistance Order received no help with the costs of care. Relatives resented this, but told us they were afraid to ask in case they appeared ungrateful or unsuitable and thus risk having the child removed from them. One young aunt with five children of her own took in her 11-year-old nephew when his foster placement broke down. She agreed to continue with the arrangement only to find that the small Section 17 allowance (well below the foster payment rate) was time-limited to one year, after which she was expected to apply for a Residence Order and claim income support (no mention was made to her of a Residence Order allowance):

> I think they pay great attention to what you have to say and truly, at the conference, things were much easier to understand. The only thing I find, looking after kids, is because you are family they tend to not want to give you much. I know

the rate because my gran used to foster. They want to give me £20 a week and go to Social Security. At the moment they give me £48 a week. I went to a woman at the advice place and she told me that the Social want me to go for a Residence Order so that way they get me off the books and don't have to pay me. She goes, 'It shouldn't be like that.' They should help me.

Table 7.3 *Types of placement, by legal status (main placement)*

Placement	Informal	Care Order	Supervision Order	Accommodated	Residence Order	Total
With family/friends	13	2	1	—	1	17
Foster carers	—	18	1	21	—	40
Residential unit	—	2	1	4	—	7
Hospital/boarding school	3	—	—	1	—	4
Total	16	22	3	26	1	68

Hospital was used briefly as an emergency protection placement but boarding education was used for longer periods. It was a preferred solution for parents whose children were placed there, but resisted as a placement by professionals:

● ●

Ginnie, aged 10, suffered a mild cerebral palsy at birth, which left her slightly disabled in her speech and mobility. During her early school years she was satisfactorily placed in a mainstream school, but when her parents moved area and she had to move from first to middle school the local education authority concluded that she should attend a special school. Day after day she came home distraught, frustrated and unhappy. Her mother responded to her distress by trying to secure an assessment of her unhappiness from a number of professionals. During this process she discovered that Ginnie's IQ level was over 140. Finding an acceptable school became a battle and eventually Ginnie was taken out of school but taught at home by her mother, for over a year.

The initial child protection conference was called because it was thought that Ginnie was being emotionally abused by her parents' persistently seeking a diagnosis for her in order to place her in a school of their choosing. By the time the conference took place, Ginnie's parents had found an independent boarding school willing to accept her, where she had settled happily. Ginnie was not registered but the conference supported the placement. However, it took an application to the Secretary of State for Education to direct the local education authority to provide a Statement of Educational Needs for Ginnie, which resulted in an agreement to pay the school fees. Ginnie's mother said, 'Manky as we are, we're still paddling our own canoe!'

● ●

Partnership or coercion?

The statements from parents and case studies cited in this chapter indicate the very different situations which lead to children being accommodated. With the Children Act's emphasis on partnership, a closer examination of the element of agreement to accommodation arrangements was made by the researchers. In respect of the intensive sample of 51 we were able to reach a conclusion as to whether parents, children and social workers agreed that a particular placement was an appropriate response in the circumstances. Including the children who were subject to Interim or Full Care Orders, there were 40 families in the intensive sample who experienced a total of 44 placements away from home within the study period. Table 7.4 shows the level of agreement to such placements.

Table 7.4 *Agreement of parties to decision to use out-of-home placement (including Care Order cases)*[1]

Agreement to placement	Parents	Children	Social workers
Requested it/fully agreed	26	11	38
Reluctant to agree/ambivalent	1	5	5
Did not agree	17	7	1[2]
Child not consulted		7	
Child too young to be consulted		14	

[1] Forty families and 44 placements in the intensive sample; regular respite is counted as a single placement; view of social worker not known in one case

[2] No choice; child bailed to residential unit

There were 17 placements where all three parties agreed (including cases where the child was too young to have an opinion or had mixed feelings). In common with Aldgate and Bradley (1998) and Packman and Hall (1998), it was found that the children were more likely than the adults to be wary about leaving their parents. However, in this present study of significant harm cases, social workers were less reluctant than those in the Packman and Hall 'accommodation' study (1998) to place children away from home.

Turning specifically to the question as to whether accommodation is, or should be, used only in cases where there is no element of coercion, it can be seen from Table 7.5 that 'forced accommodation' was used in two of the

105 cases in the cohort, both of which involved placements with foster carers. In one such case the parent was not given full information about the alternatives and it seemed unlikely to the researchers that an Emergency Protection Order would have been made had she refused to agree. The mother was given no information as to the whereabouts of her children and no contact was arranged for a period of days. Children and parents were greatly distressed by the separation, which proved to have been unnecessary.

Table 7.5 *Use of coercion for out-of-home placement, without a court order*[1]

Circumstances of placement	No.	%
At request/with agreement of parent	26	57
Coercion appropriate – explanation of alternative and limited choices given[2]	13	28
Coercion appropriate (see above) as short-term measure, but lasted longer than needed[2]	5	11
'Forced' accommodation – no clear explanation of alternatives given	2	4
Total	46	100

[1] Includes placements with relatives and two in boarding school

[2] In eight cases, when coercion was used appropriately, the placement was with relatives

In a number of cases where there was an element of coercion, the alternative of an application for an Emergency Protection Order or Care Order was explained and limited choices were given. Although some of these parents were either reluctant to part with their children or would have liked them to return from accommodation, most agreed at the time or subsequently that it was the 'lesser of two evils'. This father was very clear that he preferred accommodation to a Care Order:

> We agree that she needs foster parents and we agree about the sort of foster parents, but what we are at loggerheads about is the contact. He's given me a choice. I've got a letter from him. I went up there to see him to discuss it. You see, that's what I'm like, I don't like being threatened, that's one thing I don't like, and it's best to still have parental responsibility. I feel involved. If it went to court and they did do that, I wouldn't have anything to do with them basically. He was on about this court order thing and basically said, if I interfere or make waves he is going to take it to court. It's he wants his own way, Social Services want it their own way. But I'd rather have it this way, oh yes, because I've got parental responsibility. I can't do everything I want, but I can go up there and argue with them and they have got to listen.

Because if it went to court I wouldn't have anything to say about it. I could go up there and say, 'I don't like that idea', and they could say 'Tough'. They didn't tell me, I worked it out for myself. That is what they are basically saying, if I don't co-operate, they will take it to court.

Summary

A placement away from home for any child must be one of the most traumatic experiences, even if it brings relief and protection from maltreatment. For parents, too, it is likely to arouse deep feelings, however well it is arranged. Therefore, coercion – with its overtones of pressure and loss of control, often resulting in emergency and unplanned placements – is best avoided if at all possible.

From our study of these cases it appears that Section 20 accommodation and voluntary arrangements with relatives are being used, as the Children Act 1989 intended, to avoid the need for emergency procedures and court orders. Our conclusion in this respect is similar to that of Packman and Hall (1998). Like them, we found that emergency and unplanned placements were more frequent than they need have been, especially with school-age children when the necessity for out-of-home placement could have been predicted and planned for.

As elsewhere in our study, the term 'partnership' was rarely an appropriate description of the decision-making and social work process at the time that the child left home. In only 17 of the 44 placements of the children in the intensive sample (including those where court orders were used) did the parent(s), child (if old enough) and social worker agree that the move from home was necessary or desirable. Even when decisions were reached without the sanction of the court, these arrangements were often achieved with a degree of coercion. Just over half of the parents were in agreement with decisions to place a child with relatives, in hospital, boarding school or Section 20 accommodation. The children were even less likely to be fully involved in these decisions. Within the intensive sample of 51 children, 30 were old enough to be asked about their placement. Only a third of them agreed with the decision.

Despite these limitations – on the possibility of working in partnership and unease with the extent of coercion in arrangements which are not reviewed by the courts – we conclude, as do Packman and Hall (1998), that the use of Section 20 accommodation in protection cases can provide valuable breathing space and, in some cases, is an appropriate staging post towards placement with a permanent substitute family or with relatives.

8 Protection and coercion: the use of legal orders

The provisions of the Children Act 1989 and its accompanying *Guidance* are based on one of the fundamental principles of the *UN Convention on the Rights of the Child*: (UN 1989) that is, children are best looked after by their own parents whenever this can be achieved without serious detriment to their welfare. Consequently, parents should be allowed and, if necessary, helped to fulfil their natural and legal responsibilities. Voluntary and co-operative working relationships between health, welfare and education services, parents and older children are to be aimed for. A new balance is to be struck between family autonomy and the protection of children; and coercive intervention in the family is to be kept to a minimum.

Local authority social services departments have been given the lead role in promoting the upbringing of children within their families by providing or co-ordinating support and therapeutic services for parents who are unable to meet the needs of their children without additional help. This help may be in the form of extra resources or services, or it may be to help parents make full use of the services of health, education, income maintenance, housing and general community support. Section 27 of the Children Act empowers workers from Social Services to call upon these other services to assist them in their duty to promote the welfare of children in need, including, as is made clear in Schedule 2, those who may be in need of protection. There are also provisions for interagency assessment of the needs of children. Schedule 2 lists services to be provided and these include accommodation away from home, if this would help the child directly, or strengthening the ability of the parents to provide good enough parenting in the longer term. The *Introduction to the Act* (DoH 1989a, p. 2) states that accommodation is appropriate 'for a shorter or a longer period' if the parents need respite and also if they 'are unable to care for him properly'.

Thus, even when there is some risk to the child, the policy is to avoid coercive measures if this can be done without increasing the harm, or the risk of harm, to the child. If coercion is needed because plans to prevent a child from suffering significant harm cannot be agreed by negotiation and discussion, the involvement of parent(s) and the child in decisions about his or her well-being is still to be encouraged (Kaganas 1995). *Guidance* on the Act provides the background against which social workers were acting in relation to the children in our research sample who became subject to an application for a court order.

In this chapter the numbers and types of orders are described and the use of other legal proceedings outlined. We also discuss who influenced the decisions when applications for orders were made and whether the orders were, with the benefit of hindsight, necessary. Linked to applications and the need for court orders is the key question of whether parents and older children were considered to be willing to work co-operatively with professionals in ensuring the effectiveness of protection plans.

Emergency procedures

At the first stage of child protection procedures it might be necessary for emergency measures to be taken, either as a result of a Section 47 enquiry after a child abuse referral or in the course of the routine work of police officers, social workers and health visitors. Such measures are not taken with the frequency of calls to the ambulance service, although child protection work is often portrayed like this. It should be noted that in the eight busy teams in our study, mostly working in areas of high deprivation, such formal protection measures were used only 20 times during an eight-month period. National figures confirm the large drop in the number of emergency orders issued since the introduction of the Act when compared with Place of Safety Orders made in the 1980s. This change was one which was specifically sought following a series of research studies and inquiries that showed the unnecessary use of these orders and thus the unnecessary harm caused by precipitate removal of children from their homes. In this study of 105 cases, ten instances of a child being taken into police protection were recorded and ten Emergency Protection Orders were granted during the study period.

It was more common, however, to make temporary arrangements to ensure that the child was safe until further enquiries could be made and, if necessary, a court date fixed to hear an application for an Interim Care Order. Informal arrangements were made more than twice as often as formal emergency procedures were used.

Although some studies and inspection reports published shortly after the implementation of the Act found police protection being used in circumstances where an Emergency Protection Order might have been more appropriate, this did not appear to be so in this present study. The ten children taken into police protection ranged from less than 12 months old to 16 (with only half being under 5). Our overall impression was that in most cases these powers were used in difficult situations to allow time for parents, police and social workers to work out informal protective arrangements, with varying degrees of involvement and/or coercion of parents. In all except two of these ten cases the child was at home at the end of the study, and in one case the young person was living independently. In five cases, accommodation with relatives or foster parents had been used in the interim period, and in one case there had been a court application that led to an Interim Care Order and then a Supervision Order.

In only two cases (involving a 16-year-old and an 8-year-old) did taking a child into police protection lead to a full Care Order. At the end of the 12 months the 16-year-old was living independently with social work support and the 8-year-old was in foster care and unlikely to return to her family.

In contrast, nine of the ten children on whom Emergency Protection Orders were made went on to become subject to further court orders. These children tended to be younger and included five who were not born at the time of the initial conference. At the end of the study four of these babies were with foster parents (three with plans well advanced to place them with permanent substitute families, and one whose future was uncertain); and the fifth was living with relatives. Care Orders were obtained on all five of these infants. Of the four other children (aged 3–11), three were subject to Care Orders (two placed at home, one with foster carers). The fourth child (who had been subject to Interim Care Orders) was living at home but his future was uncertain. The only child who did not become subject to further court orders was well settled at home.

It is impossible to tell whether children would have fared worse, as well, or better if emergency measures had not been taken, as was the case in similar circumstances. There were clear reasons for the use of Emergency Protection Orders in all of these cases, but it is interesting to note that different agencies made differential use of emergency measures and negotiated protection arrangements, as is shown in Table 8.1.

Caution is urged in view of the small numbers, but, since this was a total cohort of the significant harm cases in these areas, the trend may be worth considering. Fieldshire and Hillborough used protection measures involving a move for the child in a smaller proportion of cases. Woodborough,

Table 8.1 *Use of formal/informal protection, by authority*

Authority	No. of procedures					No. of children
	Police protection	Emergency Protection Order	Section 20 accomm-odation[1]	Protective placement with relatives	No emergency protection	
Coastshire	4	4	3	3	12	26
Fieldshire	—	2	3	2	10	17
Hillborough	4	4	8	6	26	48
Woodborough	2	—	3	2	7	14
Total	10	10	17	13	55	105

[1] For all three Coastshire cases, parents acquiesced reluctantly; in all three Fieldshire cases, parents agreed; in five of the Hillborough cases, parents agreed and in three they were reluctant; in two of the Woodborough cases, parents agreed and in one case they were reluctant

Fieldshire and Hillborough were more likely to use *negotiated* arrangements, especially Section 20 accommodation, than was Coastshire. Equal use was made of placement with relatives by the authorities.

Orders already in existence

Table 8.2 shows that before the incident or heightening of concerns which led to the initial child protection conference or planning meeting (Stage 1), 86 of the children were at home with one or both parents and there was no court order in force (other than a Section 8 Residence Order). Although, we have already noted that most of our families were well known to the helping or protection agencies.

The adopted child was a 15-year-old who alleged her adoptive father had sexually assaulted her. She was subsequently placed with another family prior to a move to independent living when she was 16. One 12-year-old girl was already subject to a Care Order at the start of the study: she had virtually been abandoned by her mother when she was 6 years old, following years of serious domestic violence at home. The mother took the two youngest children with her to a refuge in another town, leaving the two oldest siblings together with friends of the family. The mother felt unable to provide for the two older children and eventually Social Services became involved at the request of the friends and approved them as foster carers for these children.

Table 8.2 *Legal status of the children at Stages 1 and 2*

Legal status	Stage 1	Stage 2
At home with parents or relatives/no order	86	66
At home with adoptive parents	1	3
Accommodated	3	8
At home – Supervision Order	2	2
With relatives – Supervision Order	—	1
At home, Section 37 directions	2	—
At home, Residence Order to mother	1	1
At home, Residence Order to father	—	1
Residence Order to relative	—	1
Interim Care Order	—	3
Ward of Court (1 with relative, 1 outside family)	2	—
Care Order/living away from home	1	13
Care Order/placed with relatives	—	2
Care Order/living independently	—	1
Care Order/placed with parent(s)	—	2
Child not yet born	7	—
Total cases	105	104[1]

[1] Not known in one case

Table 8.3 *Conference recommendations for legal action, by emergency action (no. of cases)*

Recommendation for legal action	Emergency action			
	Not used	Police protection	Emergency Protection Order	Total
Care proceedings	9	2	6	17
Residence Order application	4	—	—	4
Contact Order	—	—	1	1
Intervene in private law proceedings already in progress	8	1	—	9
Total cases	21	3	7	31

Conference recommendations for legal action

It is often assumed, but not a requirement in law, that cases should be considered by a child protection conference before a Care Order or Supervision Order is applied for. Recommendations to seek a legal remedy were made at the initial child protection conference in 31 cases. Table 8.3 shows that Emergency Protection Orders or police protection had already been invoked in respect of eight of the 17 cases when an application in care proceedings was recommended by the conference. In nine cases private law proceedings were pending in which the local authority might seek to intervene.

Orders made during the year following the initial child protection conference

Public law orders

Table 8.4 shows the range of legal measures and placement arrangements used at any time during the 12-month period of our study.

Table 8.4 *Legal and placement measures used during the 12 months*

Measure(s) employed	No.
No order used	54
Accommodation only	14
Emergency Protection Order → home – no order	3
Emergency Protection Order → Interim Care Order → home – no order	1
Emergency Protection Order → Care Order usually following Interim Care Order	8
Interim Care Order → home – no order	4
Interim Care Order → Care Order	4
Interim Care Order only (continuing)	1
Accommodation → Interim Care Order → Care Order	7
Section 37 report	5
Ward of Court	1
Other combination	3
Total cases	105

Of the 105 children, 54 were at home throughout without any order being in place, and eight went home after Emergency Protection Orders or Interim Care Orders had ended. An Interim Care Order was made in one case which was still in place at the end of the study. In total, 21 children were made the subjects of Interim Care Orders, 15 of which led to full Care Orders. The national trend for more applications for public law orders 'on notice', with the child remaining with parents or safeguarded by informal arrangements often involving relatives, was evident in our study with 16 Interim Care Orders made on notice. Seven of these were in respect of children who were initially accommodated under the provisions of Section 20. Five children were the subjects of Section 37 directions which required the local authority to consider whether they should apply for a Care or Supervision Order. Two other children became subject to a combination of private law orders.

Given the criteria for including the 105 children in our study (suffering or likely to suffer significant harm as a result of what had happened to them prior to the initial child protection conference), the fact that around a third of them were subject to a range of legal provisions within a relatively short time-scale suggests that social workers were mindful of the wide choice of court orders and informal arrangements available to protect children and that they were using them. Notably absent were Child Assessment Orders, which were so hotly debated when the Bill was before Parliament (Dickens 1993). Only one Family Assistance Order was made, though they may have been helpful in other cases but seemed not to have been considered.

Criminal prosecutions of a parent or other person alleged to be responsible for the maltreatment were being considered in respect of a quarter of the whole sample at the time of the initial child protection conference. This suggests that a substantial minority of the cases had developed sufficiently by the time the first conference had taken place for definite decisions to be reached within the conference. It also suggests that earlier decisions must also have been made about the possible use of an order and legal advice sought. The information appears to refute the idea that social workers have been reluctant to use the Act to protect children early on in child protection procedures. However, there was considerable variation between area teams with a range between 3% and 18% of cases in which Interim or full Care Orders were made. Combining area teams in each authority the proportions were 16% for Coastshire, 15% for Fieldshire, 8% for Hillborough and 12% for Woodborough.

A researcher rating of the influences upon the decision as to whether or not court action should be taken indicates that team leaders, team managers or senior social workers were most influential (13 cases), but nearly as important were *groups* of professionals in either strategy meetings or child protection conferences (ten cases). In one of the authorities that made heavier use of courts, the authority's legal adviser routinely attended initial child protection conferences and strategy meetings, and there is qualitative interview data to suggest that local authority solicitors were more influential in this authority. However, in no case were they said to have had the *major* influence on the decision.

A member of the police service was most influential in five cases and a parent (or in one case the parent's legal representative) in six cases. These were most often where a Section 8 private law application was being considered or already pending. The investigating social worker was only thought to be most important in one case and that also applied to the conference chairperson.

The application for a Care Order was considered by the social workers interviewed not to have been necessary in almost half of the cases in which it was recommended. It would appear that it is, therefore, not unusual for the key social worker to be overruled when decisions are made about applications for court orders. Fifteen of the other professionals interviewed, who were involved in cases in which an application for a Care Order was recommended, thought an order was necessary, but 14 were unsure or thought it was not necessary. Thus, we find a slightly different picture from that identified by Hallett (1995). There was much agreement, but some important dissent, which might be expected to have an impact on the way in which professionals subsequently worked together and with family members. The role played by a social worker in court proceedings when he or she does not believe that the application for an order is necessary, might be an appropriate focus of study. It is our impression that although they disagreed about the necessity for court proceedings, these workers went along with the conference decision and got on with picking up the pieces in their work with the families.

Private law orders

Apart from the Section 37 directions provisions, the other orders used in these cases fell under Section 8 private law provision. There were no examples in the study of a Specific Issues Order and very few Contact, Residence or Prohibited Steps Orders.

Section 8 Contact Orders

As might be expected, it was more frequent for absent parents to have informal contact with their children than to have applied for Section 8 Contact Orders. A Section 8 Contact Order was in force before the incident in respect of four mothers and nine fathers, but was ended in respect of two fathers after the incident. Nearly a quarter of the children did not have contact with their father. It was not possible to tell whether encouragement to use Contact Orders would have improved that situation, or what proportion of these fathers had been refused contact for an appropriate reason.

There were 16 families where it was known that there had recently been a dispute, or there was an ongoing one, about residency and contact. The arrangements varied widely according to the circumstances. For some children the lack of contact arrangements was a relief, but sometimes it was a source of distress. A 10-year-old refugee had left a civil-war-torn country with her father, stepmother, sisters and stepsisters. The separation between her parents pre-dated this flight but she was deeply distressed, not only by not seeing her mother but also wondering about whether she was still alive. She suffered when she saw the suffering in her country displayed on television. Her maternal grandparents, who had had a big part in her upbringing, and her two siblings were also left behind.

Less dramatically, a teenager whose mother was white and father of African-Caribbean origin had stayed in rather spasmodic contact with her father. There was no address for him recorded on the social services file, even though she had regular periods in accommodation because of her many difficulties. However, she was able to track him down when she needed to see him and made it clear that she did not wish him to be told about her step-father's attempt to sexually assault her.

In other cases the separation was the result of the allegation of maltreatment which occurred at the time of our study:

● ●

Belinda, aged 14, lived with her mother throughout the period of the research. She used to see her father every weekend after he and her mother separated and divorced. An allegation of sexual abuse was made against him by the daughter of the woman he was living with, but no prosecution took place. All contact was stopped immediately for several weeks and then, despite the fact that the police were not pursuing the matter, Social Services allowed only supervised contact. Belinda's father said to the researcher:

> They decided that contact had to be with a Social Services woman, which I totally disagreed with. When we were out and about she was there taking notes. I took the children into the Kentucky Fried Chicken and she was sitting there making notes. Yeah, she sat at the table with us and it was really uncomfortable. I made such a fuss about it. I was really fuming and it was only then on the understanding if my cousin would have sessions at their

family centre that they would allow her to be the supervisor of the contact. I think if I'd had to just go on, and take it, I'd have gone spare. It was really uncomfortable. My cousin's had to make reports out about the sessions. She thinks it's appalling like. She's only helping me out for the children's sake, really, and my sake. I'm just in a vicious circle. I wanted to take Belinda out for a day just before Christmas and I couldn't just go and ask her. I had to go all the way through Social Services to get permission off of them. I couldn't do it off my own back.

● ●

It should be remembered that, whether fragmented by marital or partner separations or the traumas which lead to state intervention, children lose siblings and relatives as well as parents when families fragment; also, that unsatisfactory contact arrangements with parents usually mean unsatisfactory contact with grandparents and siblings. Twenty-five of the children in our sample did not have a sibling, but another 25 were already living apart from at least one sibling before the incident in question. After the event which led to the conference or planning meeting less than half of the 80 who had a sibling lived with all their siblings, 24 who were away from at least one sibling had some contact, two had indirect contact, and seven had no contact with their siblings. Information on ten children was not available.

Section 8 Residence Orders

At the time of the incident, three mothers and three fathers had Residence Orders in their favour. By the end of the study, three mothers, four fathers and three other relatives held Residence Orders. The orders were used in very different circumstances:

● ●

One father had fought for a long time to be granted a Residence Order in respect of his two children because he was so concerned about the level of violence between his ex-wife and her new partner. The Order was made as a response to the child protection concerns at the start of our study.

● ● ●

A grandmother was asked by a transfer conference to apply for a Residence Order for her three grandchildren because they had been seriously abused by her daughter's partner in the past and the daughter had removed them from her mother's care on a previous occasion.

● ● ●

Grandparents were granted an Interim Residence Order prior to the initial child protection conference on their 4-year-old grandson while a Section 37 Directions report was being prepared. There was a bitter and vindictive parental struggle for custody of the little boy.

● ●

Regrettably for the relatives and children, none of these three placements with relatives was supported by a local authority Residence Order allowance. Some of these children were difficult to parent, and there was cause for concern that the stability and thus the child's 'sense of permanence', which has been found to be so important for children's long-term development, may in the future be jeopardised by stress resulting from low income.

Prohibited Steps Orders

The Children Act provides that 'No step which could be taken by a parent in meeting his parental responsibility for a child and which is of a kind specified in the order, shall be taken by any person without the consent of the court.'

There were three Prohibited Steps Orders granted during the research period. One story from a family in the study samples illustrates the limitations of the order in relation to protecting a child from a parent unwilling to abide by it:

● ●

Gina, aged 7, was included in the sample because, had the order not been made, she would have been likely to suffer significant harm from her father on future contact visits. Gina's mother, Linda, suffered mental cruelty and domestic violence at the hands of her husband, Gina's father. Linda left the family home and the town where she used to live with him and found safety in the women's refuge in one of the research areas. Separation occurred and the divorce was finalised before the Children Act 1989 was implemented. At the divorce hearing, the judge made a proviso that Linda's address was not to be divulged to her ex-husband.

Gina and her three older brothers were to have access visits with their father every month. After some months, the three brothers made it clear that they did not want to continue the access weekends because their father was hitting them as punishment. Their wishes were acceded to by the court. However, Gina, being still a toddler, continued to visit and only later began to show reluctance about going. Concerns were expressed about inappropriate parental behaviour during contact visits. When Linda tried to reduce the visits by not sending Gina, her ex-husband took the case back to court. The judge served a penal notice on Linda for not keeping to the arrangements, and withdrew the proviso about

actually result in Care or Supervision Orders being made. Table 8.5 shows that in our study there was a fairly close fit between what was recommended and what happened, with care proceedings being recommended in 17 cases and a formal order being obtained in 15 of them.

Table 8.6 shows that 12 of the 30 children that the conference recommended legal steps be taken remained at home during the assessment period, whilst

Table 8.5 *Conference recommendations for legal action, by legal orders (used during the 12 months)*

Recommendation for legal action	Legal orders				
	No order (includes lapsed Emergency Protection Order)	Residence Order	Interim Care Order/ Care Order	Supervision Order	Total
Care proceedings	2	—	15	—	17
Residence Order application	1	1	2	—	4
Contact Order	—	—	1	—	1
Intervene in other proceedings already pending – e.g. Section 8 application	2	—	3	3	8
Total cases	5	1	21	3	30[1]

[1] n=31 cases where recommendations were made for protective action via the courts; information on one child missing

Table 8.6 *Conference recommendations for legal action, by placement during assessment*

Recommendation for legal action	Placement			
	At home	With relatives	'Looked after'/ (CO/ICO/ or accommodation)	Total
Care proceedings	3	1	13	17
Residence Order application	1	1	2	4
Contact Order	1	—	—	1
Legal proceedings outstanding – e.g. Section 8 residence application	5	—	3	8
Total cases	10	2	18	30[1]

[1] n=31 cases where recommendations were made for protective action via the courts; information on one child missing

three were placed informally with relatives and 15 were looked after by the local authority.

Table 8.7 shows that of the 51 cases where protective action was taken at some stage during the year (including 14 who were accommodated as a form of protection), 20 lived mainly with a parent (though some of these had short breaks away with relations or in respite care), five were mainly with relatives, and 26 were mainly in foster care or (in two cases) residential care.

Table 8.7 *Main placement, by court or placement action taken*

Action taken	Mainly with parents	Mainly with relatives	Mainly 'looked after'	Total
Emergency Protection Order only or Section 37 direction	8	—	—	8
Care Order or Interim Care Order	7	2	17	26
Accommodated	3	2	9	14
Supervision Order	2	1	—	3
Total	20	5	26	51

Table 8.8 gives the breakdown of orders by research area, illustrating how Coastshire made greater use of longer-term orders as well as formal emergency procedures. Although as time passed workers in the other three areas moved on to make court applications in a small number of cases (particularly for babies born after the initial case conferences), the difference was still significant. Coastshire used no Interim or full Care Orders in 31% of the cases, compared with 76% in the similar county of Fieldshire, 50% in Hillborough and 64% in Woodborough. At the end of the study, 38% of the Coastshire children were on Care Orders, compared with 18% each for Fieldshire and Hillborough, and only one out of 14 children in Woodborough.

Table 8.8 *Percentage of cases in which orders were used, by authority*[1]

Authority	ICO/CO/ wardship	Residence Order	Supervision Order
Coastshire	42	4	8
Fieldshire	17	—	—
Hillborough	27	2	6
Woodborough	14	7	14

[1] Does not total 100% as more than one order may have been used in some cases

The parents in Coastshire made it clear to the researchers that they felt the use of orders so early on, when they were struggling with illness, addiction or other severe problems, was precipitate and made it much harder to work with social workers and the other professionals they encountered at the child protection conference and afterwards. On the other hand, when social workers reluctantly decided they had to apply for a Care Order after working for months with a family to maintain a child at home, the social workers reported to researchers that they sometimes felt that they had failed their clients and had somehow betrayed them by gaining information which, in the end, removed their child from them:

> I was horrified because I realised I was putting this mother in a situation where we were abusing her because she can't help how she is (she has a learning disability). But I gathered all this negative information about her by helping her.

Whether this case could be described as 'manipulative', when considering the issues of partnership, would depend on whether the mother continued to be helped and supported as a parent of a looked after child (as required by the advice in the *Principles and Practice in Regulations and Guidance* (DoH 1989b)) and whether the social worker had been open and honest with the mother about the reasons for any particular action or decision.

There seems to be no way of making such work easier. The use of orders early or late is a painful business. In terms of the necessity of using coercive measures, it would seem that, in this study, the later they were used, the more likely it was that parents would recognise them as necessary.

Were the Care Orders necessary?

Whether or not an order is made (once the threshold conditions are crossed) depends on a court being satisfied that doing so 'would be better for the child than making no order at all' (Children Act 1989, Section 1 (5)). In the majority of cases, local authorities concluded that a public law order would not have been helpful and made no application. In other cases, applications and Interim Care Orders were made but the court decided on the recommendation of the social workers and guardian ad litem, that either an order was not necessary (six cases), or that a Supervision Order was more appropriate than a Care Order (three cases) at the final hearing. There was only one case in which the local authority's application for a Care Order was rejected by the court.

With the benefit of hindsight, and (for the intensive sample) following lengthy conversations at the two stages with parents and older children, it was possible to reach a tentative conclusion as to whether the orders really had been better for the child than making no order at all. We concluded that in 46% of the 28 cases in which an Interim or full Care Order was made it would probably have been possible to achieve the same result, with less stress to all concerned, without making an order. An agreement for a child to remain in hospital or with relatives, or the provision of Section 20 accommodation until a further assessment could be made, would probably have resulted in less hostility and better planning.

Arrangements for family contact for looked after children

The information available on contact between children separated from one or both parents at any time during the research period indicates that of the 49 mothers having contact, 20 had supervised contact and 29 unsupervised; and of the 46 fathers having contact, 15 had supervised contact and 31 unsupervised. Of the 39 children who had periods in care or who were looked after under emergency protection or Section 20 accommodation provisions, there were ten who had no contact with either parent, 13 who had supervised contact, and 16 who had unsupervised contact. The arrangements varied widely according to the circumstances, and differed over time.

So far as we could tell, there was only one Section 34 Contact Order made alongside a Care Order, with the arrangements in the other cases left for negotiation between the parent and the local authority. The parents interviewed felt as if they lacked power in these discussions, and when they did assert themselves it was against a background of fear, that links with their children might be further curtailed. This applied in cases where a child was in accommodation for reasons other than respite care. Although they knew that, legally, they could take their child home (usually the older and more troubled/troublesome children), they felt unable to do so; or it had been made clear to them that if they 'did not co-operate' a court order would be sought. It was often not clear to parents exactly what requests about contact might be deemed 'uncooperative'.

● ●

Susan, aged 10, and her two younger brothers were removed from home because an allegation had been made that she had been used for pornographic photography by a man known to her mother. Accommodation, with the threat of an Emergency Protection Order if parental agreement was not forthcoming was used. The police thought that her mother was involved so no contact was to be arranged over a full weekend, even with the two little ones (one of whom was only 2), until a video interview had been conducted with Susan. It was only when Susan's mother enlisted the help of a solicitor that contact was arranged.

● ● ●

Charlie, aged 5 months, was admitted to hospital with tubercular meningitis. His mother appeared threatening to hospital staff because she dressed as a punk, totally in black and with tattoos on her face. She found the hospital frightening and felt criticised by the staff because she did not fit into what she felt were their ideas of a parent. Charlie was in hospital for six months during which time his mother's visiting pattern had been unpredictable and eventually stopped. An Interim Care Order was made and he was placed in a foster home.

The social worker believed that Charlie should have a chance of being with his mother so she tracked her down through an advertisement in the *Big Issue*. She worked towards reuniting Charlie with his mother and persuaded the Housing Department to provide a flat and help with furniture. Charlie then began day visits with his mother, supported by a family worker, and in due course these visits were extended to overnight stays. Charlie was happily settled at home with his mother when the researcher visited a year later. No Section 34 Contact Order was made while the Interim Care Order was in force, but a 12-month Supervision Order was made to facilitate monitoring of his care when he returned home.

● ●

So far as siblings were concerned, 26 of the 33 children who were looked after by the local authority at any time during the research period, and had brothers and sisters from whom they were separated, had contact of some kind with them, seven had no contact with their siblings.

A researcher rating on whose opinion was most influential in decisions about contact shows that the children themselves were far more influential than any other person – twice as likely to be influential as the social workers. All but five of the 42 social workers responsible for arranging contact agreed with the decision about contact.

The 24 children in potentially dangerous situations

The pattern of help and services for the one older child in this group, the 15-year-old described in Chapter 4, continued during the year along the lines already outlined. No application was made to court, and services continued to be provided outside the formal child protection system. Her well-being did not deteriorate but a high level of concern remained for the family members, and the professionals all continued to be highly concerned.

Turning to the 23 younger children, a picture emerges of the extensive involvement of Social Services and the courts during this 12-month period. By the end of the year, 11 were living with one or both parents, and for eight of them there had been no Care Order application. Two children had been adopted and a further four were placed with prospective adopters; in all cases except one this followed the granting of Care Orders. Two children were living with grandparents (in one case under a Residence and a Supervision Order) and one was with a maternal aunt. Only one child, now aged almost 6, was in a short-term foster placement. The researchers concluded that she was likely to suffer significant harm because of the lack of a clear plan for her future and no contact with her mother, whose loss was still causing her distress. Originally accommodated, she subsequently became the subject of a Care Order and was the only young child in the sample who could be described as drifting in foster care. Two children had moved out of the areas and no detailed information about them was available to the researchers at Stage 2: one child was with parents, and a Care Order had been made in respect of the other.

Care Orders had been obtained for eight of these children (35% – a much higher proportion than for the cohort as a whole). Five of the ten Emergency Protection Orders were in respect of these children. Thus, the researchers' predictions of likely risk from the data available at the start of the study coincided with the conclusions of the social workers and the courts. Care proceedings led to two Supervision Orders, one for a child living with parents and the other with grandparents. There was a Care Order in respect of one child who was subsequently placed on a long-term basis with an aunt.

In seven cases where there was no order in place at the time of harm, or at the time of the initial child protection conference, emergencies followed or new situations arose which necessitated an application to the courts.

In the eight cases where no orders were used, the reasons for not making an application to the court varied. In three cases social workers made a major intervention in terms of family support, practical help and co-ordinating multi-agency involvement. The parents moved from being entirely or partly uncooperative to being partly or very co-operative so that the situation improved and the child was protected. In two cases the children's behaviour and emotional equilibrium were obviously disturbed, although their physical care was adequate. It would have been extremely difficult to provide sufficient evidence to convince the court of significant emotional harm due to the care 'not being what it would be reasonable to expect', although the evidence of impairment of emotional development was apparent to all the professionals involved. Social Services were already investing heavily in resources for the families, such as nursery places and parenting-skills advice, and the long-term and long-haul nature of the cases was recognised by the workers. In one case of rough handling by a young father, the incident was judged to be a one-off and, in the protection plan at the initial child protection conference, the extended family were charged with ensuring that the father should not be left alone to handle the baby. The baby was de-registered at the review conference. In another case, a baby was placed for adoption at the request of the parents. In the remaining of these eight cases the father was arrested and imprisoned for causing the death of his toddler son from another relationship. There were no concerns expressed by the agencies, and as help was not wanted, neither support nor monitoring followed.

Comments of parents and social workers on court applications

The following comments from parents give a flavour of their views and are very similar to those cited by Lindley (1994) and Hunt et al. (1999):

> We went to court and they kept us for hours and I wasn't opposing anything. Next time I shall oppose it. It wasn't what I wanted to happen, but for three years I've been asking for help for her [a 2-year-old] to have some foster carers, but they didn't listen. You get so much in your head when you're going to all these hospital appointments that you don't know what to do in the end. No, I didn't have any particular help or support to go to court. I felt no one was listening to what I had to say, not even my solicitor. I felt that all the decisions were more or less made beforehand. I was told this had been decided and I said, 'Yes, but he's my child.'

This mother, on the other hand, could see, with hindsight that the application for a Care Order had probably been necessary:

> I could understand afterwards why they put her on an Interim Care Order because at the time I wasn't stable. At the time, I think I didn't think that, but looking back now I think I was. I can understand they were scared that I would just get up and go again, because I was in that frame of mind then. It wasn't that I didn't care for her – I did. But you know when some people have got a problem, instead of facing it, they run away.

The following comments give a range of social workers' views:

> Yes, having the Section 37 Directions and going to court did help. The father instigated the whole thing, so he was committing himself to it, and it was kicking off on a better footing, about us being involved.

> It was an unusual and difficult case and it worked out far better to use 'significant harm' as the measure. The 'significant harm' meant, because we did not take a 'normal' order, we were able to use a private order to protect her [a 6-year-old]. The judge made a very clear judgement about the harm. We intervened to encourage the mother to protect the child with an order.

> We applied to the court for a revocation of the Care Order. I was watching Mum at court when the chair of the magistrates said to her that the Care Order was discharged, and during that little exchange it was really as if a huge weight had been lifted off her and she then really believed it. She left the court with a smile on her face.

Summary

This chapter surveys the use of legal orders. Numbers of emergency orders had already dropped dramatically nationally and this cohort illustrates that trend. Only ten of the 105 children had become the subject of an Emergency Protection Order. Only one of the ten children taken into police protection became the subject of a Care Order. The reverse was true for Emergency Protection Orders, with only one EPO not leading to a Care or Supervision Order.

There was a significant use of informal protection measures by means of Section 20 accommodation and placement with relatives. At the start of the study, 87 of the 105 children were at home with no order or a Residence Order only; at the end of the study, 70 were at home. There were public law orders in force in respect of four of these children (two Care Orders and two Supervision Orders).

For 28 children, major changes to their legal status occurred during the course of the year following the initial child protection conference. A range of legal orders was used overall, affecting just over half of the 105 children and suggesting that social workers were mindful of the way they could use the Children Act to protect children. One of the research areas used more orders at the start and overall than the others, but as the year progressed the other areas also moved on to use orders, particularly for babies.

All the parents whose children were made the subject of a Care Order were distressed and angered by the court process. However, those parents whose children were removed very quickly, via an Emergency Protection Order and Interim Care Order, were particularly distressed.

Most contact arrangements were informal but where orders were used they were mainly Section 8 private law orders.

9 *The impact of intervention on parents and children*

This chapter reviews the well-being of the children and parents at Stage 2 of the study. In order to link with studies completed before the implementation of the Children Act 1989, we use similar frameworks to those used for considering outcomes in the earlier studies (Dartington Social Research Unit 1995). In particular, when looking at service outcomes we follow frameworks developed by Thoburn et al. (1995) to consider whether the partnership principle in the Children Act 1989 *Guidance* became a reality in these cases. In looking at client outcomes we follow the broad headings used by Farmer and Owen (1995). Finally, we attempt to answer the question of whether any of the patterns of intervention or services are associated with positive change. (For most of this analysis the number of cases is 99, as data on six cases at Stage 2 were insufficient for reaching a conclusion about parent and/or child outcomes.)

The well-being of the children at Stage 2

Throughout this book we stress that, in assessing whether a child is being significantly harmed, any potentially abusive or neglectful parental behaviour has to be put in context: the circumstances of the family members' past and present lives together, any positive or negative facets of the child's temperament, and any disabilities or other special needs. Although identification of serious threats to the well-being of these 105 children led in most cases to more concerted and better-resourced attempts to help, the interventions often brought additional stresses. This was particularly evident in children who started to be looked after by the local authority and went to live for longer or shorter periods with people they did not know. Although all the children who left the care of their parents were insecurely attached to them, separation from them was an additional source of harm. This was especially so since the separation usually took place in an emergency, with no time for adequate preparation and choice of placement.

The term 'system abuse' refers either to the physical, sexual or emotional abuse of a child while being looked after away from home, or to the inadequacy, negligence or incompetence of Health, Education and Social Services, responsible for planning and meeting the needs of children looked after, away from their birth families. Leaving children in unplanned care and exposing them to harm – from a lack of security and to multiple changes of carer, often referred to as 'drift' – is the most common cause of further harm to children whose need for protection requires that they be moved from the family home. Inadequate attention paid to helping them to retain their links with their parents, siblings and other relatives and friends is another cause. All these factors were considered when we made an assessment of the interim well-being of the 'looked after' children at Stage 1, and actual and future significant harm 12 months after the start of the study, at Stage 2.

Table 9.1, when compared to Table 4.6, shows that the number of children at high risk of maltreatment decreased to a lesser extent than the number in high need. Figure 9.1 shows that, whilst the percentage of the 105 children considered to be at high risk of maltreatment had fallen from 48% at Stage 1 to 11% at Stage 2, the number in high need had fallen less markedly from 74 to 44. Only two of the 27 low-need cases were in the high-need group at Stage 2, whilst 36 of the 78 high-need cases were in the low-need group. Thus, once significant harm, or its likelihood, was identified, the intervention that occurred in most of these cases was associated with a reduction in the environmental and emotional stresses of most of the families.

Figure 9.1 *Risk of maltreatment at Stages 1 and 2*[1]

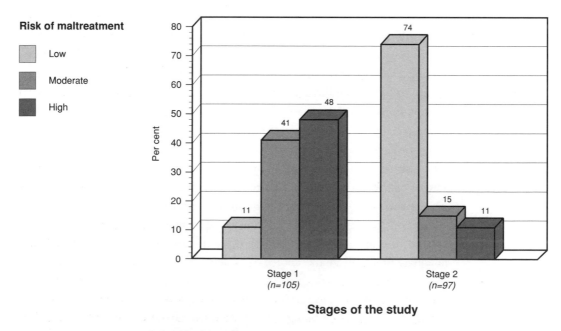

[1] x^2:85.96 df:2 p<.0001

Table 9.1 *Risk of maltreatment, and level of need, at Stage 2 (no. of cases)*

Level of need	Risk of maltreatment				
	None	**Low**	**Medium**	**High**	**Total need**
None	3				3
Low	4	7	1	1	13
Medium	2	27	6	2	37
High	5	24	7	8	44
Total risk of maltreatment	14	58	14	11	97[1]

[1] Missing data=8

Were the children protected from further maltreatment?

At the time of the initial conference or planning meeting it was not always clear whether the child had been maltreated or been exposed to danger through not being given the parental care 'which it would be reasonable to expect'. Children were included in the sample either if there was reasonable suspicion that this was the case or because they had been removed from home as an interim protection measure. At the end of the first round of interviews the researchers concluded in two cases that although the children were in need of services to avoid further impairment to their health or development, their needs did not result from parental maltreatment or lack of care. It was decided that since the parents had been interviewed and agreed to a second interview, they would remain within the sample. In each case, early concerns were such that an Emergency Protection Order was made.

Table 9.2 and Figure 9.2 show that, during the 12-month study period, 59 of the 99 children (about whom we had adequate information) had not been re-abused, and there had been minor injuries or less serious neglect in 25 cases. Fifteen had been more seriously maltreated during the year, necessitating further protective action. At the end of the study it was concluded there was no reason to believe that 14 children were being or likely to be maltreated, and the risk was slight for a further 38 children (just under half of the cohort). For the others, concerns about possible maltreatment or poor parenting of the children (some of them looked after by the local authorities) remained.

Table 9.2 Maltreatment during the 12 months of the study

Maltreatment	No.	%
No evidence of maltreatment	59	60
Serious sexual abuse	3	3
Serious physical abuse	2	2
Serious emotional cruelty	7	7
Serious/persistent neglect	3	3
Minor abuse/neglect	25	25
Total	99	100

Figure 9.2 Maltreatment of the children during the 12 months of the study[1]

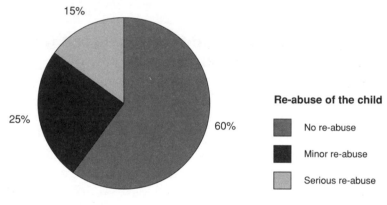

[1] n=92; missing data=13

Two of the low-risk-of-maltreatment cases at Stage 1 had become high risk by Stage 2, but 33 of the 47 high-risk cases had become low risk. Table 9.3 lists the child and family variables which were significantly associated with no further known episodes of maltreatment during the year.

The most striking characteristic of the children who were seriously re-abused was their age, with more of them being in the older age groups. Nine of the 24 especially vulnerable children (described in more detail in Chapter 4) were maltreated during this period, two seriously; seven experienced less serious maltreatment. As shown in Figure 9.3, only two of the under-fives were in the serious re-abuse or neglect group, the others being equally divided between the 5–11 and the 12+ age group. These two 1-year-olds were thought to have suffered serious emotional neglect during the year, one having been originally registered under the category of likely emotional abuse, and the other, actual physical abuse.

Table 9.3 *Variables associated with the non-maltreatment of the child during the 12 months of the study*[1]

Variable	Probability (x^2 test of significance)
The child was younger at the start of the study	$p<.01$
Alleged abuser at Stage 1 was the father alone[2]	$p<.05$
The significant harm at Stage 1 was likely rather than actual	$p<.05$
The actual or likely harm at Stage 1 was physical[3]	$p<.05$
The family was *not* in the 'multiple and enduring problems' group	$p<.05$
Child placed with relatives during assessment periods	$p<.05$
Child has no or few unmet needs at Stage 2	$p<.05$

[1] Because of overlapping variables and the small cell size in some tables, caution is urged when interpreting these data.

[2] Probably because in these cases the child was more likely to be removed, or the father was more likely to have left home. Maltreatment was *more* likely if the alleged abuser was the mother *and* father jointly (including stepparents) or a stranger or relative.

[3] Few in the sexual abuse group were in the *minor* re-abuse category. Maltreatment in the 12-month period was *more* likely if the harm at Stage 1 was emotional, behavioural or sexual.

Figure 9.3 *The ages of the children at Stage 1, and maltreatment during the 12 months of the study*[1]

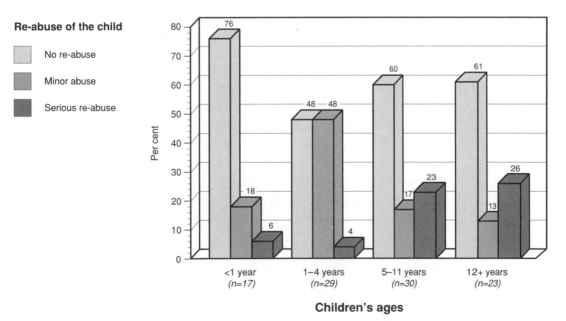

[1] Missing data=6; x^2:17.01 df:6 $p<0.1$

Not surprisingly, in view of their vulnerability to neglect, rough handling and punishments such as smacking, almost half the incidents of minor re-abuse or neglect occurred in the 1–5 age group.

Eleven white children were in the serious maltreatment group, compared with one of mixed ethnicity, and three with two parents of minority ethnic origin. These differences are not statistically significant and are explained by the other differences between the groups discussed in earlier chapters.

Serious maltreatment was most likely to have occurred during this period in cases where the original registration was in the categories of either sexual abuse or emotional abuse (29% of those registered in each category were re-abused) than in cases registered under physical abuse (12% re-abused) or neglect (10% re-abused). It is important to note that none of the 15 cases of serious maltreatment that occurred during the 12-month period were initially categorised as serious physical or sexual maltreatment or risk of death. This is partly because a substantial proportion of these children were living away from the person believed responsible for the maltreatment. However, the finding that five of the children originally in the serious neglect group were seriously maltreated during the year lends weight to the increasing attention being given to neglect as a cause of long-term harm (Stevenson 1998; Thoburn et al. 1999). All except two of the serious re-abuse cases involved children who were *actually* suffering harm at the earlier stage, suggesting that, by identifying *likely harm*, it might in most cases be possible to do something to prevent it happening. Only two of the 25 likely harm children were seriously maltreated during the year, and in three out of the 25 cases there were incidences of less serious abuse or neglect. Linked with this, most of the children who were seriously maltreated during the follow-up period were considered at the start to have behavioural or emotional problems or disabilities, which meant they needed especially competent parenting. This conclusion is in line with those from earlier studies such as that of Lynch and Roberts (1982), which followed up a group of children abused when under 5, whose parents received intensive multidisciplinary services. In that study, whilst the progress made by the parents was demonstrated by the generally average well-being of children born *after* the intervention, the well-being of the earlier abused children was, on average, poorer. A more recent eight-year follow-up of children physically abused or neglected when aged under 5 also concluded that, irrespective of whether they were placed elsewhere or remained at home, abused children, on average, were doing less well on a range of indicators than children who had not been abused (Gibbons et al. 1995b).

Nine of the 64 children who had been seriously maltreated during the year were living with a parent or relative at the end of the period, with no order in force. However, five of the 29 who were looked after by the local authority for most of the 12 months were seriously maltreated during this period, and five suffered minor abuse or neglect. In none of the cases in which a placement with a relative was used as part of the original protective intervention was a child seriously maltreated during the intervening period.

Incidents of maltreatment were more likely to recur amongst those children whose parents had multiple and long-standing problems than was the case for the 'acute distress' or 'single issue' families. All except one child were in families considered to be in high need at the start of the study, the other being in moderate need.

Three of the children (14%) who were the subject of a Care Order had been seriously maltreated, as had three of the seven who were accommodated at Stage 2. Sometimes, the maltreatment occurred while they were living away from home, but in most cases the re-abuse led to care or accommodation during the year.

Figure 9.4 shows that, in the serious re-abuse by Stage 2 group, there were more children who had not been registered by Stage 1 (20% – six cases) than had been registered (14% – nine cases). This difference is not statistically significant and is likely to be explained by the higher numbers of older children both in the non-registered and the serious re-abuse categories.

Figure 9.4 *Registration at Stage 1, and maltreatment during the 12 months of the study* [1]

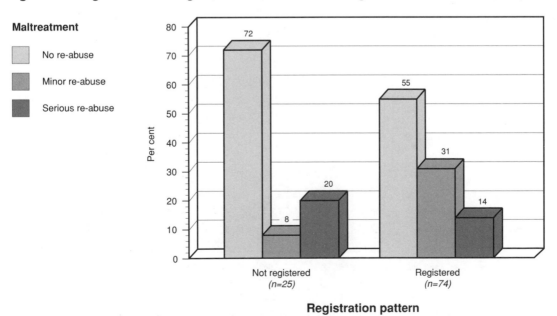

¹ Missing data=4; not statistically significant

The researchers considered registration unnecessary in respect of 59% of the sample (43% of those actually registered). Ten of the seriously re-abused children were among these 59 cases, which might lead to the conclusion that the framework for considering whether registration was necessary (see Appendix 2) was seriously flawed. However, in each of these ten cases this rating was based, not on the vulnerability of the child, but on a judgement that registration would not help the protection plan and might be counter-productive. Six of these children were aged 10 or over, the others being six 8-year-olds and two 9-year-olds. Four were registered at the initial conference and six were not, although one of these, a 9-year-old boy, was later registered under the category of emotional abuse and was living with relatives at the end of the study. In these cases, the maltreatment that occurred after the original conference was emotional abuse or neglect in six cases, sexual abuse in two cases, and over-chastisement amounting to physical assault in two cases. Periods away from home were tried in most of these particular cases but the futures of all except one child appeared firmly bound up with their families. One 8-year-old boy was looked after by the local authority and was unlikely to return home and two were away from home with very uncertain futures. Each of these cases was carefully reviewed to see if, in hindsight, registration would have protected them from further episodes of maltreatment, but we could see no indication that it would have done so.

Figure 9.5 *Maltreatment during the 12 months of the study, by local authority*[1]

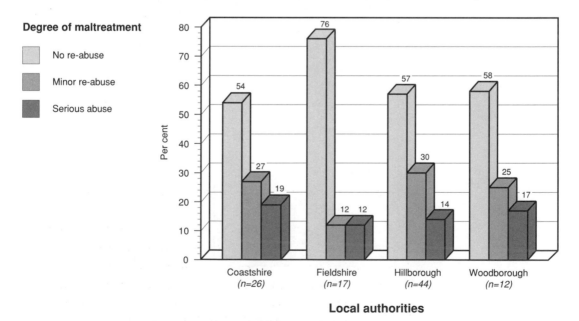

Figure 9.5 shows the percentages of further maltreatment that occurred in the four areas of our study. The differences are small and not statistically significant.

The following case studies show the range of cases in the different outcome groups:

No need/no risk of maltreatment

● ●

Sinead, aged 4 months, was brought to the casualty department at a local hospital with a broken arm, caused by rough handling by her young father. Her basic needs were well catered for and she was meeting all her milestones adequately. The father admitted he had been rough and was very remorseful. The protection plan ensured that the extended family with whom the young couple lived had responsible oversight for Sinead during the next six months and that the parents agreed to work with the social worker to explore their own needs and difficulties. At the review conference Sinead's name was removed from the Register.

● ● ●

Bella's mother had developed a psychotic illness when she was 20 years old and was admitted to a mental hospital where she had lived ever since. Within the last two years, with the use of a new drug, Bella's mother had at last begun to care for herself. It was thought she had become pregnant by another patient; she did not know who the father was. The extended family were unable to offer long-term care for Bella so she was placed for adoption.

● ●

Low need/low risk of maltreatment

● ●

Garfield's mother had been chronically ill over the previous two years and found great difficulty in controlling his boisterous behaviour. He was one of the resilient children in the sample, a large 8-year-old boy with enormous physical energy. Garfield's mother had received consistent and high-quality service from the hospital social worker during her illness. As the case was about to be closed, the family moved house and Garfield's mother became ill again and he became beyond her control. Respite care was arranged, which did not work, and at the child protection conference Garfield's mother asked for his name to be placed on the Register because she believed it would secure her the resources she needed. She continued to see the hospital social worker, and after-school care was arranged for Garfield.

Everything seemed to have resolved itself a year later, with Garfield's name being removed from the Register and his mother's health improved. His mother started a local boys' football team which took part in a park league. This involvement had brought her into contact with other families and provided much by way of reward for her efforts.

● ●

Medium need/low risk of maltreatment

● ●

Ruth was aged 1 year. Her mother's oldest two children, twins, were moved into the care of the local authority seven years previously because of alleged physical abuse. The allegation at the time of the initial child protection conference was that Ruth and her older brothers were being neglected. As a result of the child protection procedures, Ruth's mother took flight and refused to have anything to do with Social Services, even though she had applied for day care for Ruth. After tracking the family via other agencies, finally Social Services were granted an EPO in order to assess the children medically. The children were found to be fine and developing well; the EPO was allowed to lapse. A family group conference was planned at the end of the research year.

● ●

High need/low risk of maltreatment

● ●

Nine-year-old Luke's mother had left home some years ago and then developed Huntington's Chorea. She was reported to have died, although she had not. Luke's father had cared for him but he had joined a religious sect which began to dominate his actions and life to the extent that he was keeping Luke away from school and alone in the house. He refused to allow Luke to see his grandmother and other members of the extended family who were not of the sect. Luke had dialled 999 a number of times and asked to stay with his grandmother or aunt, so his father then isolated him even more, refusing to have anything to do with Social Services. Eventually, an EPO was issued and Luke was removed to foster carers with the agreement of the extended family but not the co-operation of his father, who remained incommunicado through the procedures. Luke was clear that he did not want to return to his father. He developed a close relationship with his social worker and was able to meet his mother just before she died and to work through the consequences of the misinformation about her. He maintained contact with members of his extended family.

● ●

Medium need/high risk of maltreatment

• •

A child protection conference was called because of the health visitor's concern about the care of 5-month-old Jenny. Her mother and father did not live together, although the father spent a great deal of time at the house, as did a lot of other young people. Their relationship was violent. Jenny had been born prematurely and it was known that her mother had not wanted her and had become tearful and depressed soon after her birth. Social Services had already offered a large package of support which included child-minding, with the child-minder collecting Jenny from home and returning her; a family support officer, who came five evenings a week; respite foster care alternate weekends; playgroup for Jenny's 1-year-old sibling, which had been used twice; and counselling for the mother, which she did not take up. Despite this tremendous input, anxieties about Jenny were still high because of the effect of the emotional hostility displayed by her mother. A year later, when Jenny and her mother had moved to a different area to be nearer the maternal grandmother, the new social worker described her as a 'flat child with a frozen watchfulness of her mother'. She said that Jenny was physically well cared for and fed but 'I am still concerned because she [Jenny's mother] could flip and hurt her because she doesn't like her.' Jenny was one of those under 5 at the start of the study whose health and development were still likely to be significantly impaired at the 12-month stage.

• •

High need/medium risk of maltreatment

• •

Ten-year-old Adam was the eldest of a family of four children. His next youngest sister was in foster care following an allegation that her father had sexually abused her a year previously. There was no prosecution. Adam was one of a group of children found performing sexual acts after discovering pornographic magazines in the woods. An initial child protection conference led to the offer of family support services but not to registration. During the following year his mother was reported as having unlawful sexual intercourse with young boys in the neighbourhood. Adam's mother had learning difficulties and seemed unable to recognise the gravity of what she was doing.

Another conference was called and the children's names were placed on the Register. Adam returned to his father, who requested accommodation for him, so Adam was placed with foster carers for two months while a full assessment was carried out. In addition, written agreements were made with Adam's father to assume full care of the children by giving up work and attending a family centre for parenting support, with resources from Social Services. Adam was described by the social worker as a difficult child to parent because of his bed-wetting and stealing and because he 'operates like a little adult all the time'.

●●●●●●●●●●●●●●●●●●●●●●●●●●●●●●●●●●●●●●●

High need/high risk of maltreatment

●●●●●●●●●●●●●●●●●●●●●●●●●●●●●●●●●●●●●●●

Vicky was 14 years old and, from an early age, lived with her father after her mother left the violent marriage. Since then Vicky has had many periods of voluntary care when her father was in and out of prison. When his many partnerships broke up, having ended in violence, she would be the one to care for and mother him. There was a very close emotional tie with her father but it was extremely difficult for her to live with him. His last partner was only a little older than Vicky and Vicky was used by the adults to care for their two small children to such an extent that her school work deteriorated badly. Her social worker described her as 'a very bright, able girl'.

A conference was called when Vicky disclosed sexual abuse by a family friend, a Schedule 1 offender. She was accommodated and care proceedings were initiated. Vicky was clear that she wished to go home and the care proceedings were withdrawn. The social worker said, 'Immediately her school work fell off totally. There was a new baby by this time. Her appearance slumped totally as well, very quickly. She lost a lot of weight, and she fell in love with an older man'. She said that she wanted to have someone who cared solely for her.

●●●●●●●●●●●●●●●●●●●●●●●●●●●●●●●●●●●●●

Likelihood of future significant harm

In earlier chapters it has been emphasised that a distinction should be made between the different types of parental behaviour which may be defined as maltreatment and the resultant harm to a child in terms of significant impairment of health or development. Although the risk of future maltreatment had fallen, the fact that many of the children were still in need of a high level of services is explained in part by the continuing poor circumstances in which most of their families were living. Figure 9.6 and Table 9.4 show a substantial minority were still suffering significant harm from a combination of sources, or that their health or development was likely to be significantly impaired unless services continued to be provided. Although assessment and help during the year had been associated with a resolution of difficulties for

Figure 9.6 *Changes in levels of need during the 12 months of the study*[1]

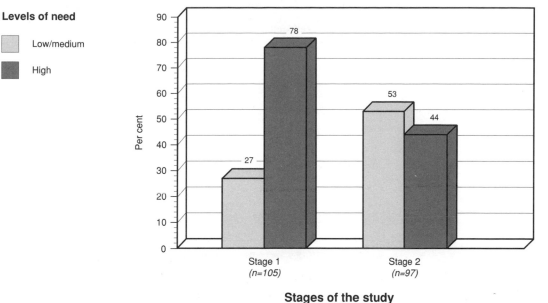

Levels of need

☐ Low/medium

■ High

Stages of the study

[1] x^2:17.636 df:1 p<.0001

Table 9.4 *Harm to the child at Stages 1 and 2*

Significant harm	Stage 1		Stage 2	
	No.	%	No.	%
No significant harm and none likely	2[1]	2[1]	21	20
Actual harm and likely to continue	54	51	50	48
Actual harm not likely to continue	7	7	—	—
No actual harm but likely if protective action not taken	29	28	33	31
Not clear (awaiting further assessment)	13	12	1	1
Total	105	100	105	100

[1] These cases were part of the cohort because it was decided to include all cases if an Emergency Protection Order was made or the child was taken into police protection. These were cases where maltreatment was not likely but need for services was at least moderately high.

20% of the children, and another 32% were being protected from the likelihood of significant harm by the provision of services, 48% were still considered to be suffering or likely to suffer significant harm. Assessment of the needs and problems of one child was still being undertaken.

Putting together the detailed information on the children from all of our sources we arrived at a rating for the well-being of the children after the first

Table 9.5 *Researcher ratings of the children's well-being at Stages 1 and 2*

Interim well-being at Stage 2	Well-being at Stage 1							
	Poor		Some problems		Average		Total	
	No.	%	No.	%	No.	%	No.	%
Poor	15	27	—	—	1	11	16	15
Some problems	32	58	20	61	2	22	54	55
Average	7	13	13	39	7	56	27	28
Good	1	2	—	—	1	11	2	2
Total	55	100	33	100	11	100	99	100

[1] Missing value=6; x^2:35.810 df:9 p<.0001

Figure 9.7 *Improvements in the children's overall well-being by Stage 2*[1]

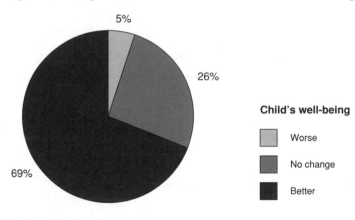

5%

26%

69%

Child's well-being

- Worse
- No change
- Better

[1] n=99; missing data=6

round of interviews (Stage 1) and at the interim Stage 2, 12 months after protective intervention. Table 9.5 shows that, generally, those whose well-being was rated as poor at Stage 1 were still rated as poor or as having some problems 12 months later, at Stage 2. This comes as no surprise given the seriousness of the difficulties which some of these children faced. However, one of the 55 children, whose well-being was rated as poor at the start, was one of the two rated as good a year later; seven were rated as average. In the other direction, one of the 11 rated as average after the first interviews was rated as poor at Stage 2. Overall, the well-being of three children (5% of the 99 about whom we had adequate information) was considered to have deteriorated; there was no change for 42; and it was considered that 54 had moved into a higher well-being group. Some children's well-being improved but they remained within the categories of 'some problems' or average. Figure 9.7 shows that there was evidence of gains in well-being in respect of 69% of the children.

The data were analysed to see if any variables were significantly associated with improvements in the children's well-being during the year (see Table 9.6).

Table 9.6 *Variables associated with improvements in the child's well-being*[1]

Variable	Probability (x^2 test of significance)
Child of minority ethnic origin	p<.01
Harm or likely harm at Stage 1 was sexual or behavioural[2]	p<.05
Improvement was more likely if outcome for parents at Stage 2 was *either* poor[3] *or* good	p<.05
The child was protected from maltreatment during the year	p<.01
The family was in the acute distress, single issue or infiltrating perpetrator groups and not the multiple-problem group[4]	p<.05

[1] Because of overlapping variables and the small cell size in some tables, these data should be interpreted with caution.

[2] If emotional harm, improvement was less likely.

[3] In these cases, a young child was likely to have been placed with substitute parents or with relatives on a long-term basis.

[4] In the multiple-problem group there was more likely to be no change rather than deterioration.

Although there was *improvement* in the well-being of more children in the single issue or acute distress groups, differences in the ratings of *well-being* between children in the different types of family are small and not statistically significant.

As can be seen from Table 9.6 and Figure 9.8, there was more likely to be improvement in the well-being of children of minority ethnic origin than was the case for white British children. This may be the result of the differences in the groups already described, with more of the white British families being in the group with multiple and long-standing problems, where it was harder to achieve change. However, Figure 9.9 shows that, despite these improvements, the well-being of a majority of children in all ethnic groups still gave cause for concern. This is a reminder that, although it may be easier to work with families who are not in the group with multiple and long-standing problems, the children themselves remain vulnerable and are likely to continue to need services even if there is improvement in the overall situation for the family.

Figure 9.8 *Ethnicity of the children and changes in their well-being during the 12 months of the study*[1]

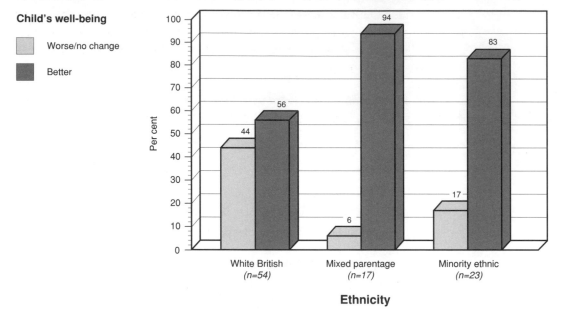

Figure 9.9 *Ethnicity of the children and their well-being at Stage 2*[1]

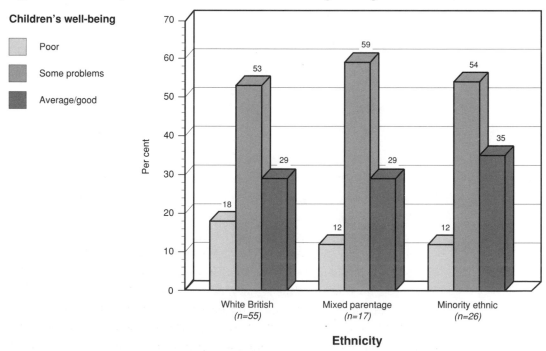

[1] Missing data=7; not statistically significant

Age was not significantly associated with improvements in well-being, although there was a trend towards fewer children in the 5–11 age group at the start of the study having improved well-being. Figure 9.10 shows that the proportion of children in the average well-being group was lower for those who were over 5 at the start of the research. Children over the age of 1 were equally likely to be in the poor well-being group.

Figure 9.10 *The ages of the children at Stage 1, and their well-being by Stage 2*[1]

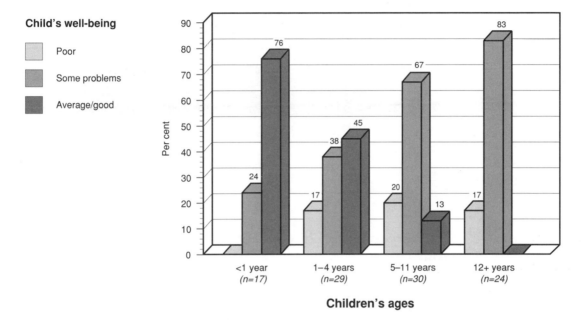

[1] Missing data=6; not statistically significant

There was a trend towards more of the children in Hillborough and Woodborough having improved well-being at Stage 2. Despite this, more in these two areas were still in the group with poor well-being (17% and 25% respectively) than was the case for Fieldshire and Coastshire children (12% and 8% respectively) (see Figure 9.11).

Legal status was not significantly associated with improvements in well-being for the children at this early stage. This is, in part, because those under 1 who were removed early, on Interim or full Care Orders, were of average well-being at both stages. It is also because those aged 11 or older on whom Care Orders were obtained were experiencing even more difficulties at the end of the study, partly because of the negative impact of moves while in care and because of the stress of court proceedings on the parents and their parenting capacities.

Figure 9.11 *The children's well-being at Stage 2, by local authority*[1]

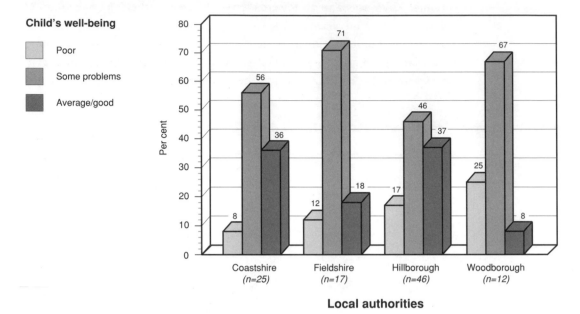

Child's well-being

Poor

Some problems

Average/good

[1] Missing data=6; not statistically significant

The outcomes for 23 children in potentially dangerous situations

In Chapter 4 we described a sub-sample of 23 children who were under the age of 5 at the start of the study and who were living in potentially high-risk situations. A more detailed analysis of the outcomes for those children is presented in terms of the adequacy of parenting, the stability of their placements and their general well-being.

In the light of the recent studies on child protection (Dartington Social Research Unit 1995) the adequacy of the parenting provided to the youngest children was focused upon. The Dartington summary of earlier research identified a group of parents who were 'low on warmth and high on criticism', whose children might be at serious risk of long-term emotional and developmental harm. Table 9.7 gives the conclusions about the parenting received by these children at the beginning and end of our study. Of the seven children who were with their parents (rated as definitely low on warmth and high on criticism at the start) five were no longer with their parents 12 months later. The other two were receiving slightly more adequate parenting although still somewhat 'low on warmth and high on criticism'. Both were receiving intensive support and a range of services and one benefited from shared care arrangements, that is she spent each weekend with her grandparents who provided good parenting and nurturing.

It should be remembered that information for the six children in the intensive sample was far greater than for the 17 children in the background sample, but in many of the background cases there was enough detail about what had happened to the child for a reliable rating to be made. When a child had been placed for adoption, an average rating seemed, on balance, to be appropriate. Whilst research indicates that most children placed early in adoptive families do well, recent studies by Howe (1997) and Gibbons et al. (1995b) suggest that some children, when abused or neglected under the age of 5 and then placed for adoption, do less well in their adoptive families than might be expected.

Table 9.7 Parenting received by children under 5 in the highest risk group at Stages 1 and 2

Child	Stage 1	Stage 2
1	1	1
2	3	1 (with adoptive parents)
3	3	1 (with adoptive parents)
4	0 (removed at birth)	1 (with adoptive parents)
5	0 (removed at birth)	1 (with adoptive parents)
6	2	1
7	0	0
8	3	2 (foster care)
9	1	1
10	0 (removed at birth)	1 (with adoptive parents)
11	2	information not available
12	1	1
13	2	1 (Residence Order, with grandmother)
14	3	1 (with adoptive parents)
15	0	information not available
16	1	2
17	2	1
18	1 (with grandmother)	1 (with grandmother)
19	3	1 (with maternal aunt)
20	0	0
21	3	2
22	0	0
23	3	3

Key:
0 = good parenting   2 = some deficits but generally adequate
1 = adequate parenting   3 = low on warmth and high on criticism

None of the 23 children was in the good well-being group, but 12 were thought to be of average well-being, and eight to have some problems. (There were three cases where it was not possible to make the rating.)

Of the 12 children with average well-being, seven were placed for adoption or with members of the extended family. Three children had improved following intensive social work intervention. The other two children were involved in incidents that looked potentially dangerous but proved to result from an unusual set of circumstances which were not indicative of the general standard of care they received.

Of the eight children with problems in relation to their well-being, two were placed for adoption, but not before their first year of life which had been unstable and erratic. They had been placed in residential units with parents who were low on warmth and limited in their care of the child. Another child already had serious physical and learning disabilities. His parents were seeking to provide the extra care he needed but were still experiencing difficulties. Two children lived in families with multiple and long-standing problems. Social workers and other professionals were closely involved with these families and had made a major investment of time and resources in order to try to improve the parenting received by the children. Their efforts were continuing at the end of the year. Of the three remaining children (two aged 2, and one of 4 years), two were physically well cared for but displaying serious emotional disturbance in their behaviour. The other child suffered neglect as well as sexual abuse by an older brother, who was then placed in care. She was described in the file as 'does not mix, has no social skills, speech delay, appears dirty and unkempt'. A range of practical help was being provided but it appeared to the researchers that this child was not receiving adequate parenting and that accommodation or a Care Order would be in her interest.

Around one-third of the children in this sub-sample were removed from their parents. In all except one case a Care Order was made; and in that case Section 20 accommodation was provided prior to placement for adoption. Only two of the children were removed *before* frequent and serious attempts had been made to engage the parent(s) in work to enable them to keep the child at home or to reunite the family. On the other hand, it is a cause for concern that, when, as in the majority of cases these attempts were made, they appeared to be to the detriment of some of the babies, who remained with their parents receiving erratic and sometimes inadequate care, even in residential family centres, whilst attempts were made to assist in or teach parenting skills. However, the requirement to balance justice with welfare and to ensure that parental responsibilities are not easily overruled would probably have meant that sufficient evidence would not have been available to secure permanent removal of these children early on. Also, with the benefit of hindsight we can see that a policy of earlier court intervention would have meant that seven infants would have been removed before further harm ensued, but two would have been removed unnecessarily.

One of the two cases where the baby was removed at birth was in the intensive sample. The baby's young mother and one other in similar circumstances should also have been included in the sample as children suffering significant harm themselves, but we decided that it would be unnecessarily confusing to have both the parent and child in the sample. We were not entirely satisfied that the needs of these adolescents suffering significant harm were adequately recognised and their support and protection needs met.

● ●

The 16-year-old mother was herself in care at the time of the initial child protection conference. She had 17 placements during her own childhood and adolescence. The young mother did not have a chance to keep her baby because of her recent arson attempts, which precluded all the mother and baby units approached by her social worker from accepting her. In view of a psychiatric assessment on her unpredictability, the initial conference decided that the baby could not be left safely with her alone. Her family was unable to help out and a swift decision was made to remove the baby at birth. The mother said:

> What happened was that I went into hospital and gave birth to Tara and she weighed 8 pounds. I was in hospital one day and I held her twice. I had some visits with Tara. They were for an hour but my last visit didn't go very well. I was a bit upset. It was a bit difficult. She was asleep and I didn't know whether I could pick her up or not and the other social worker said, 'No. She's had her bottle and had her bum changed so leave her.' So I just had to sit there for the visit and not see her. On another visit she started crying and that social worker took her off me because she was crying and then she gave her back to me with her bottle and I gave her a bottle and she stopped crying. That's the only thing I'd done – given her the bottle. At first people kept saying to me to give her up and all, and then I thought, 'Stuff it.' I want her and that's how it's been. I want her and then I think I'll give her up.

● ●

Whether the mother should have been given time to learn baby care and attempt to settle down or whether the baby's need to settle and attach was more important could be the subject of much debate. The balance could be tipped either way, by a range of factors.

One of the five cases where the child was not removed at the start, but a Care Order was made later, was a baby whose mother had learning difficulties.

● ●

Tammy's parents had been cohabiting for a year before she was conceived. Her father was known to hit her mother and consequently, Tammy's mother returned to her parents' home before the birth. Concerns were still high though because of the presence of three potentially savage dogs in the household and due to the frequency of domestic violence among members of the extended family. Tammy was accommodated with both her parents in a self-contained flat in a residential unit but within two weeks the staff were so worried about the lack of care for the baby that they gave notice to the social worker that they were no longer willing to hold any responsibility for the situation. Tammy then went to another unit where it was possible for her to be observed all the time. Despite this provision, Tammy failed to gain weight and there was some violence between her parents. A review conference decided that care proceedings should be initiated and Tammy was quickly placed for adoption.

● ●

Did the well-being of the parents improve?

In Chapter 2 the parents' circumstances are described and details given of their problems and general state of health and well-being at the start of the research and 12 months later. This information about the parents at Stage 2 contributed to an assessment of well-being drawn from all the data available, and a rating of whether there was evidence of improvement in the parents' well-being. There was rarely sufficient information on file about parents who were not living in the household with the child at the start of the study, even though some of them had parental responsibility and played an important part in the lives of their children. (The term 'parents' here refers to the parents or stepparents who were fulfilling the main parenting role at the start of the study. It does not refer to foster or adoptive parents except in the one case, in which a young person already adopted was included in the study.)

Figure 9.12 shows that the well-being of the main parents in just under a quarter of the families was average or good, there being indications that their lives were taking a turn for the better even though the problems of few of them were completely resolved. On the other hand, for a quarter, their well-being and future prospects were poor. Sadly, the prospects were worst for some of the mothers who had themselves been looked after by the local authority, or were still under 18 when their babies were born and therefore, under the terms of the Act, 'children in need' in their own right. Others were vulnerable and in need of support because of mental health problems. Included in this group were most of the parents of the 23 young children who were most at risk of serious mal-treatment in the future and who were looked after by relatives or the local authority on a long-term basis or had been adopted at the end of the study.

At least some of the needs identified at the start of the study had been met in respect of 87% of the parents. There was evidence of at least some improvement in well-being in 68% of cases (see Figure 9.13). There is clearly more scope for improvements if well-being is poor at the start than if it is good.

Figure 9.12 *Researcher ratings of the main parent's well-being at Stage 2*[1]

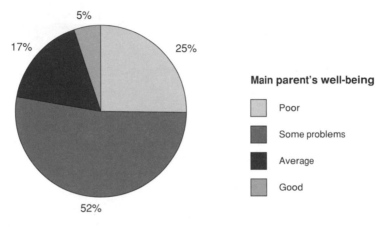

[1] n=92; missing data=13

Figure 9.13 *Changes in the parents' well-being over the 12 months of the study*[1]

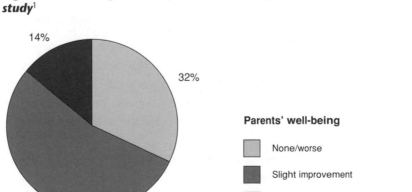

[1] n=91; missing data=14

Figure 9.14 shows a trend (which did not reach statistical significance) towards a higher proportion of the Fieldshire and Woodborough parents having improved well-being at Stage 2 than was the case for Coastshire and Hillborough parents. Table 9.8 lists the child and family variables which were significantly associated with improvements in the well-being of the parents.

Figure 9.14 *Changes in the parents' well-being at Stage 2, by local authority*[1]

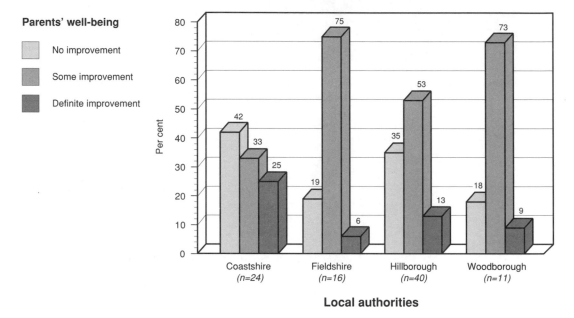

[1] Missing data=14; not statistically significant

Not surprisingly, the well-being of the parents tended to be higher if the child remained at home and the needs of parents and children were met. Improvements in well-being for the parents tended to be associated with their being enabled to continue to care for their children.

Figures 9.15 and 9.16 give a picture in respect of the ethnicity of the children. In neither case is there a statistically significant association. There is a trend towards the parents of minority ethnic origin having poor well-being at Stage 2 despite the fact that the well-being of more of them improved.

Trends in the direction of higher well-being which did not quite reach significance were found when the mother or father alone, rather than both parents together, were believed responsible for the maltreatment; if the maltreatment was physical or negligence, rather than sexual or emotional; if the maltreatment was not categorised as severe; and if the harm at the start was in the likely and not the actual category. More of the single-issue families

Table 9.8 *Variables associated with improvement in the parents'
well-being at Stage 2*[1]

Variable	Probability (x^2 test of significance)
Child aged 1–4 at the start of the study	p<.05
Alleged maltreater was mother or father alone, or other family member, and *not* mother and father jointly or stranger	p<.001
Child lived with parents for most of this period	p<.01
Child's main placement was with person considered to be responsible for maltreatment or likely maltreatment	p<.01
Registration was rated by researchers as probably not necessary	p<.01
Parent had few unmet needs at Stage 2	p<.001
Child was not maltreated during the previous 12 months	p<.05

[1] Because of overlapping variables and the small cell size, these data should be interpreted with some caution.

Figure 9.15 *Ethnicity of the children and the main parent's well-being at Stage 2*[1]

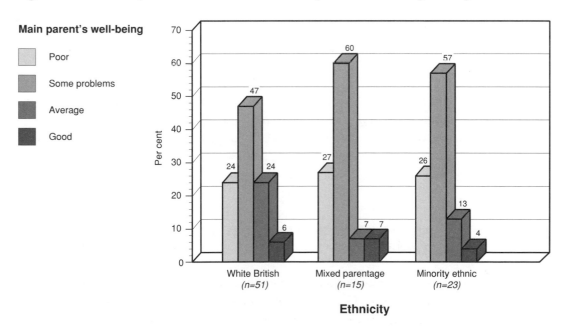

[1] Missing data=16; not statistically significant

Figure 9.16 *Ethnicity of the children and changes in the main parent's well-being by Stage 2*[1]

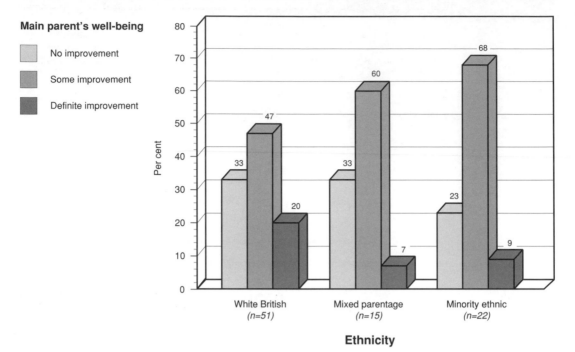

Main parent's well-being

- No improvement
- Some improvement
- Definite improvement

[1] Missing data=17; not statistically significant

were in the higher well-being group. All five parents in the infiltrating perpetrator category were of poor well-being at the end of the study.

There is an overlap between these characteristics and the child being away from home for most or some of the year. The well-being of the parents was rated as poor in the four cases where the child was placed long-term with relatives. Only three of the 22 parents whose children were looked after by the local authority or adopted at the end of the study were of average well-being at this stage.

Social work practice, legal intervention and outcome

Table 9.9 brings together three outcome measures: protection of the child from further maltreatment and improvements in the well-being of the parents and children separately.

Table 9.10 compares the findings with those of Farmer and Owen (1995, p. 291) for a sample of registered cases before the implementation of the

Table 9.9 Outcomes at Stage 2

	%
Child protected?[1]	
No known incidents of abuse	60
Minor re-abuse	25
Serious re-abuse[2]	15
Child's well-being improved?[3]	
Worse	5
No change	26
Better	69
Main parent's well-being improved?[4]	
No improvement	32
Improved to some extent	55
Much improved	14

[1] Inadequate information on six cases

[2] Sexual in three cases; physical in two cases; emotional in seven cases; and severe neglect in three cases

[3] The well-being of 15% of children was rated as poor; 55% had some problems; 28% were average; and 2% were good

[4] Most of the parents' problems were alleviated in 17% of cases, but 29% of them still had serious and debilitating unmet needs.

Children Act. (There are slight differences between the two studies in the parent outcome measures used. In this study, 'parents' well-being improved' is the outcome measure, whereas Farmer and Owen used 'needs of primary carer met'. There were very few cases which would have led to a positive rating in our study had we used this measure, although there was improvement, since most of the parents had substantial unmet needs at Stage 2.) Table 9.10 indicates that it was more likely that the child's well-being would improve than the parents', and that the majority of children were protected during the 12-month period. There were 31 cases where all three outcome measures were positive (a higher proportion than in the pre-Children Act study by Farmer and Owen which used a similar threshold for entry into the research sample), and eight cases where all three outcome measures were negative. In no case did a child suffer permanent physical harm, but there was cause for concern about the emotional well-being of an important minority of children whose emotional health deteriorated over the period of study.

Table 9.10 *Categories of outcome*

	No. (n=85)[1]	%	1989–91 study of registered cases (%)[2]
Child protected Child's well-being improved Parents' well-being improved	31	37	23
Child not protected Child's well-being improved Parents' well-being improved	13	15	7
Child protected Child's well-being improved Parents' well-being not improved	10	12	27
Child not protected Child's well-being improved Parents' well-being not improved	4	5	11
Child protected Child's well-being not improved Parents' well-being improved	9	11	—
Child not protected Child's well-being not improved Parents' well-being improved	8	9	—
Child protected Child's well-being not improved Parents' well-being not improved	2	2	21
Child not protected Child's well-being not improved Parents' well-being not improved	8	9	11

[1] It was not possible to rate on all three variables in 20 cases. Where some, but not all, information was available (18 cases), only one child was re-abused and two children's well-being was not improved.

[2] Farmer and Owen (1995) used a slightly different outcome measure to show that 'the needs of the main parent had been met'. The proportion of parents whose needs had, in the main, been met in our present study was 47%, compared with 30% in the Farmer and Owen study.

Using the information in Table 9.10 as a starting point, a rating was made of cases where there was evidence that the interim outcome was positive. Cases were included in the 'positive outcome' group if the child had been protected and the child's and the parents' well-being had improved. To these were added cases where both child outcomes were positive and the parents' well-being appeared to be no worse than at the start of intervention. However, no child was included in the 'positive' group if, despite improvements, he or she was still considered to be suffering or likely to suffer significant harm. These cases were in a 'middle' (some improvements) group, as were cases where the other two indicators were positive but the child had suffered minor re-abuse, provided that there was evidence that he or she would be protected from mal-treatment in the future. Also included in this 'middle' group were cases where the parents' well-being was worse but there was a positive rating on the two child-focused measures. These tended to be children placed permanently out of the family home.

There was sufficient data to arrive at a rating on 101 cases, each of which was considered by three researchers. From Figure 9.17 it can be seen that there was clear evidence of a positive interim outcome by Stage 2 for 36% of the cases, and in 15% there was no improvement or the outcome was poor.

Figure 9.17 *Cases with a positive interim outcome by Stage 2*[1]

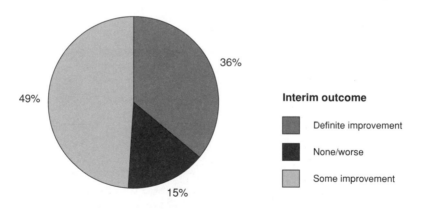

[1] As rated by researchers; n=101; missing data=4

Table 9.11 lists the variables which were significantly associated with the more positive interim outcomes.

It has been noted already that the children of minority ethnic origin were more likely to be in families categorised as 'single issue' or 'acute distress'. These families might have had more personal strengths or perhaps stronger intra-familial relationships to see them through difficult times than was the case with families who had a long history of grappling with multiple environmental, relationship and personal problems. Although not invariably the case, there was also an overlap between the 'acutely distressed' or 'single issue'

Table 9.11 *Variables associated with positive interim outcomes*

	Probability (x^2 test of significance)[1]
Child and family variables	
Child was of minority ethnic origin	$p<.05$
Only one child in the family	$p<.05$
Alleged abuser was the mother *or* the father alone, and not mother and father jointly, relative or non-relative	$p<.05$
Intervention variables	
Child felt supported by social worker	$p<.01$
Social worker thought the work was successful	$p<.05$
Child was not 'looked after' by the local authority	$p<.01$
Child's name was not placed on the Child Protection Register	$p<.05$

[1] Because of overlapping variables and the small cell size in some tables, caution is urged when interpreting these data.

families and whether one of the parents rather than both was believed responsible for the maltreatment or neglect.

Figure 9.18 shows a trend, which did not reach statistical significance, towards more positive overall outcomes for families of children of minority ethnic origin.

Figure 9.19 shows that there was not a statistically significant association between the age of the child and more positive outcomes for the family as a whole. However, only six (13%) of the under-fives (the group for whom, we would argue, intervention, or the lack of it, can have the biggest impact for good or ill) were in the 'little or no improvement' group.

In Chapter 4 we identified a group of 24 children as potentially living in circumstances where there was a risk to life or limb. Figure 9.20 shows a trend towards more of these cases being in the 'some improvement' group but fewer in either the 'definitely successful' or the 'no improvement/worse' group.

Figure 9.21 shows that Fieldshire and Woodborough had more cases in the positive interim outcome group but there were was little difference in the proportions in the 'little or no improvement' group. These differences are not statistically significant and are probably explained by variables about the cases.

Figure 9.18 *Ethnicity of the children and the interim outcomes for the families*[1]

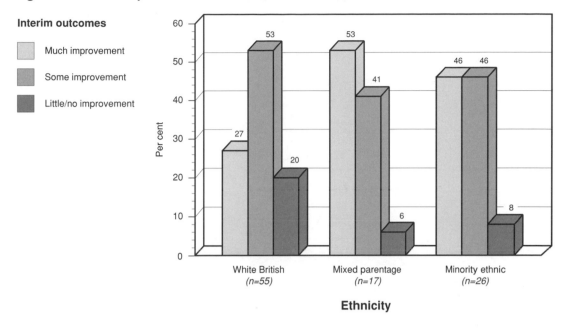

Interim outcomes

- Much improvement
- Some improvement
- Little/no improvement

[1] When two-way analysis is used, combining children who have one or both parents of minority ethnic origin, there is a statistically significant association between positive outcome and the ethnicity of the child: x^2:3.95 df:1 p<.05. Missing data=7

Figure 9.19 *The ages of the children at Stage 1, and the interim outcomes for the families*[1]

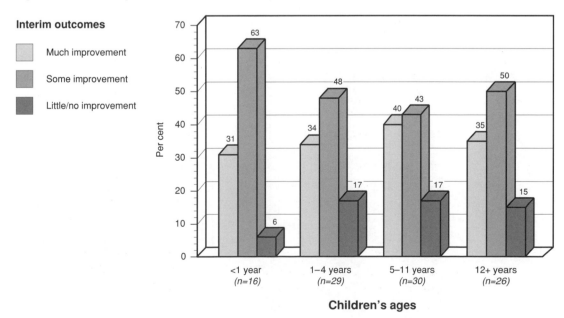

Interim outcomes

- Much improvement
- Some improvement
- Little/no improvement

[1] Missing data=4; not statistically significant

Figure 9.20 *Potential risk of harm at Stage 1, and the interim outcomes for the families*[1]

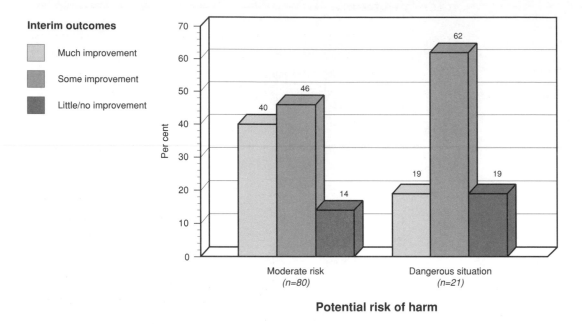

Potential risk of harm

[1] Missing data=4; not statistically significant

Figure 9.21 *Local authorities and the interim outcomes for the families*[1]

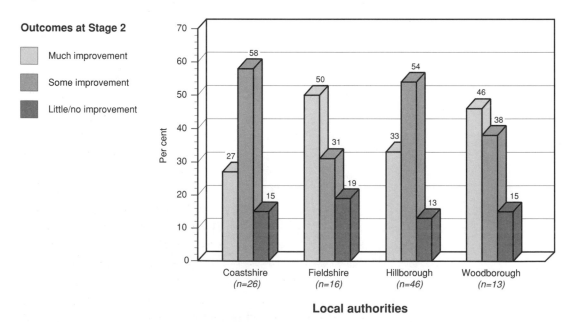

Local authorities

[1] Missing data=4; not statistically significant

The relationship between type of intervention and interim outcome

Given the very different characteristics of the parents and children and the environments and events which shaped their lives, it would be foolhardy to assert a causal link between aspects of social work practice, court intervention and better or worse interim outcomes. Nevertheless, we scrutinised the tables to see if statistically significant associations were to be found between positive outcomes for the children and parents and the different aspects of intervention. The only significant associations are few in number and contain no surprises. They are listed in Table 9.11.

To be allocated to the 'positive' interim outcome group, some improvement (or, in the case of parents, no deterioration) was required for both the child and the parents. Also, because the child being looked after away from home was associated with poorer well-being for most of the parents, it comes as no surprise that there were more cases with a positive interim outcome if the child remained at home. Although not reaching statistical significance, there was a trend towards fewer cases having positive interim outcomes if a Care Order had been obtained. Most of these were in the 'some improvement' group, with only one in the 'no improvement or worse' group. When no order was obtained, more cases were in the positive or negative groups, with fewer in the middle. There were only three cases in which a Supervision Order was made, but two of these were in the 'positive outcome' and none in the 'no improvement' group.

Packman and Hall (1995) have noted that a view persists in the minds of some social workers that Section 20 is another version of 'voluntary care' and is to be avoided rather than seen as one of the family support services. (The use of accommodation is discussed in detail in Chapter 7.) There were signs of this in our study in that, by the time accommodation was provided for some of the older children, the situation for the child and the family had deteriorated to the extent that it would have been unrealistic to expect progress within a 12-month period. Accommodation was also used in some cases as an immediate protective measure, to avoid a too hasty and possibly unnecessary use of the courts. If more decisive action and long-term placement out of the home turned out to be necessary in these cases a Care Order was usually sought. There were few cases in which the social workers managed to counteract the distressing impact that this had on the parents. Some did not even try; some who did try were rejected by angry and distressed parents; but some persisted and there were signs at Stage 2 that they were offering a service that might eventually result in improvements in the parents' health and well-being. As we have pointed out, some of these parents were, in the terms of the Children Act, children themselves and should have been offered a service – both as a child 'in need' and as a parent of a child looked after by the local authority. It was in this area that the principles underpinning the Act (DoH 1989a) were least likely to be in evidence.

In an earlier study of 220 cases considered at initial child protection conferences (Thoburn et al. 1995), associations *were* found between approaches to practice. In particular, there were more cases with positive interim outcomes for the child and the parents when a family casework approach was used, involving the provision of practical help and a supportive relationship. Whatever social work *method* was used, concerted attempts to work in partnership with family members were associated with more positive outcomes. These associations were not found in this present study, for which the threshold for inclusion in the sample was the higher one of evidence of actual or likely significant harm.

The intervention variables listed in Table 9.11 – the child feeling supported, the social worker rating the work as successful, and the Child Protection Register not being used – are likely to be found when partnership-based practice is a feature of the service. There was a trend (which did not reach statistical significance) for more of the parents, who had choices about who

Figure 9.22 *Participation of the parent(s) in the protection process, and the interim outcomes for the families*[1]

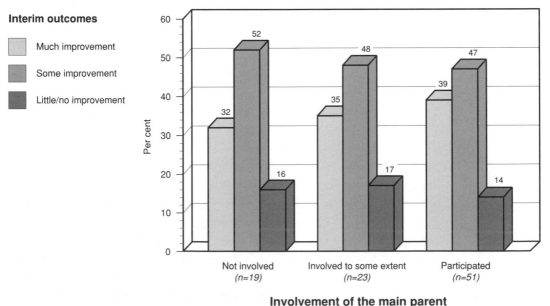

[1] Missing data=12; not statistically significant

Figure 9.23 *Participation of the children in the protection process, and the interim outcomes for the families*[1]

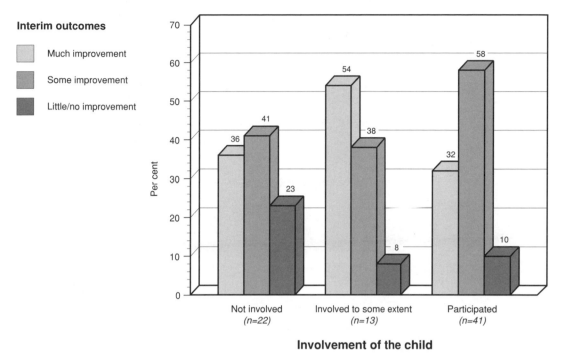

Interim outcomes

- Much improvement
- Some improvement
- Little/no improvement

Involvement of the child

[1] Children under 5 at the 12-month stage omitted; not statitically significant

the social worker should be and what sort of help should be provided, to be in the group with more positive outcomes. However, as Figures 9.22 and 9.23 show, although more of the parents and children participated than was the case in our previous study (55% and 54% respectively, as compared with 17% and 27% in 1990–91; Thoburn et al. 1995), this was not reflected in more positive outcomes for those who *did* participate.

When we look in more detail at the nature of the work (see Figure 9.24), there is a trend (which does not reach statistical significance) towards more positive outcomes when the social work service is characterised as family casework. This was also the case if welfare rights advice or advocacy was part of the service. It was usual for a range of social work methods to be used in parallel or sequentially in these cases so that it was not possible to look for associations between any particular social work method and the interim outcome. Adequate or good supervision was provided for the social workers in the majority of these cases. Forty-five per cent of those families whose social workers had good or adequate supervision, compared with 17% of those in which the social worker had poor supervision, were in the positive outcome group, although this trend is not statistically significant.

Figure 9.24 *Type of social work service provided, and the interim outcomes for the families*[1]

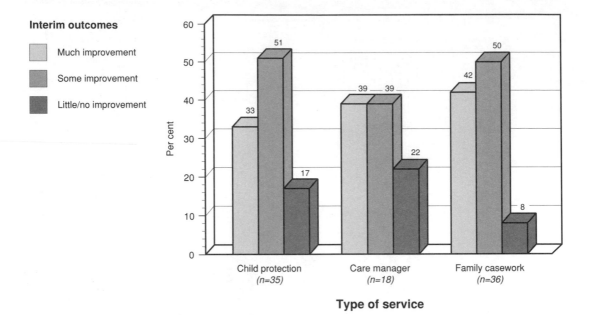

How, then, do we explain the fact that the more positive outcomes were not clearly associated with high levels of service and practice, which fitted text-book or DoH *Guidance* (1991a) about good practice? It may be that, in these difficult cases, 12 months is too short a time to see good practice being rewarded by successful outcomes. Therefore, we have to return to the qualitative data in Chapter 6 to see if it suggests any possible explanations for these findings. There was a trend towards more positive outcomes when the parents were, at least to some extent, satisfied with the help and services offered and considered that they had received support. It may be in the detail of their comments and those of the children that we have to search for clues about the ingredients of practice which, if not able to achieve positive results after 12 months, may pave the way for future improvements. Patterns and characteristics of practice, which parents and children told us they found helpful, have already been noted. In our concluding chapter we draw these threads together.

Summary

In this chapter we describe the interim outcomes found up to 12 months after the identification of actual or likely significant harm for the children and those parents who were principally responsible for their care at the start of the study. Drawing from all the sources of data described in earlier chapters, further incidents of maltreatment are noted, the well-being of the children and the parents is reported upon, and an overall rating is provided of whether the general well-being of the family members had improved or deteriorated over the 12-month period.

Interim outcomes for the children, parents and families

The children

Sixty per cent of the children did not appear to have experienced further maltreatment, 25% had experienced minor abuse or less severe neglect, but 15% had been involved in more serious episodes of mainly emotional ill-treatment or neglect. This latter group of children tended to be older and to have already been recognised as having difficulties or disabilities at the start of the study. Just under a quarter of the children were still considered to be at moderate or high risk of maltreatment at the end of the study.

All except 16 of the 105 children (15%) were still considered to be in moderate or high need of services to avoid their health or development being significantly impaired. Combining harm that might arise from further maltreatment and that which might come from other sources – including poor planning or maltreatment for children looked after – 48% were still suffering harm which could be considered to be significant. They and a further 32% were likely to suffer significant harm in the future unless a high level of services was provided.

Twenty per cent of the children were not suffering nor likely to suffer significant harm, and these were most likely to be cases where the harm at Stage 1 was 'likely' and not 'actual'.

The well-being of 69 children had improved but 55% still had some problems. The well-being of 15% was rated as poor, and for 5% of the 105 it had deteriorated over the year.

The parents

Only 17% of the parents were rated as of at least average well-being at the end of the study but 29% of them still had severe or chronic problems. The well-being of just over half of the parents had improved at least to some extent, but for 14% it had deteriorated over the year.

It was of particular concern that there were parents who were children themselves at the start of the study, some of whom had additional rights to service as young people in care or as care leavers. Others were in need of services as adults with a mental illness or a disability. It was not always clear that their rights to services as individuals were recognised, as opposed to their merely being regarded as parents whose care of children fell short, in the words of the Act, of 'what it would be reasonable to expect' (Section 32 (2)(b)(i)).

The families

A global outcome measure was used to identify a group of 36 cases which could be considered as generally successful for children *and* parents, or were generally successful for the *children,* with the parents at least no worse than at the start of the study. There were 15 cases where there was no improvement or the situation had actually deteriorated for both for parents *and* children. In the middle was a group of 50 cases where there was either little change, or improvements for the child went alongside a serious deterioration in the well-being of the parents.

It could be argued that, since the welfare of the child must be the paramount consideration when children's cases are considered by the courts or a child is looked after, a global rating of success should leave out a consideration of the well-being of the parent. We decided not to take this route since the Children Act 1989 and *Guidance* emphasise the importance of attempting to work in partnership with parents (DoH 1989b). They stress that for the majority of children, including most of those who are placed permanently with substitute parents, their long-term well-being and a positive sense of identity is linked with the well-being of their parents. Additionally, social work ethics – as set out in training regulations (Central Council for Education and Training in Social Work (CCETSW) 1995) and by the British Association of Social Workers (see Thoburn 1992) – require social workers to make concerted efforts to help those in distress irrespective of the reasons for their difficulties or their contribution to society.

Our findings regarding child and family variables or intervention variables being associated with the well-being ratings for parents and children, separately or together, are complex and not easily summarised. They differ from earlier studies in that we did not find an association between different approaches to helping and more positive outcomes. Nor did we find an association between strenuous attempts to involve parents and children in the work and decision-making processes and better outcomes. It may be that, with these complex cases, the willingness to try a range of approaches may be more important. Further, perseverance may be especially at a premium as it may be too soon after only 12 months, to look for changes in some of these entrenched cases.

10

The 1989 Act and protection from significant harm

In this concluding chapter we summarise the research, highlight some themes and issues that have emerged, and present our impressions of how the Children Act 1989 was working in these 105 cases of significant or likely significant harm.

Summary

The research and the areas

The major aim of our research was to provide a detailed picture of the sorts of children who were being considered for support and protective services under the provisions of Section 47 and Part III of the Children Act 1989 and to offer an analysis of the ways in which the agencies and the courts were intervening in the lives of these children and parents. Key themes identified at the start of the research were the:

- relationship between abusive parental acts and 'harm' to the children;

- place of compulsory, negotiated or voluntary services;

- respective roles of the different professional groups;

- way in which assessments were undertaken;

- nature of social work and inter-disciplinary practice with parents and children;

- place of relatives and Section 20 accommodation in providing refuge or respite to parents and children, or longer-term parenting to the children; and

- perceptions of children and parents of the process of protecting and helping, and the extent to which they were enabled to participate in that process.

Following the publication of *Child Protection: Messages from Research* (Dartington Social Research Unit 1995), the appropriate relationship between family support services and court intervention was hotly debated. We interrogated our data with this issue in mind. In particular, we sought to ascertain whether it was possible to identify cases in which there was a danger to life and limb; whether some cases were better dealt with through the mechanisms of the formal child protection procedures, including conferences and registration, rather than planning or network meetings and less formally provided family support services; and whether the necessity for court orders could be predicted.

The provisions of the Children Act 1989 which have a bearing on the identification of, and alternatives for action in cases of significant harm or likely significant harm to children, were considered in our research. The areas in which the children lived and the policies of the agencies charged with providing them with services were explored in detail. The cohort was drawn from eight teams in four authorities. Two of these were parts of rural counties with mixed urban and rural populations, and with pockets of acute material deprivation. The other two areas were in inner cities, both scoring highly on all indices of deprivation and containing above-average numbers of people from minority ethnic groups, including refugee families. Information was collected on the way in which family support and child protection services were organised.

When comparing organisational arrangements with those described in *Child Protection: Messages from Research* (Dartington Social Research Unit 1995), the most obvious difference was that parents were invited routinely to initial and review child protection conferences in all four authorities in our study. In each authority, before the conference started, the chairperson routinely met in private with parents and any children who were going to attend it. Unless there were good reasons to exclude them, family members remained throughout the decision-making parts of the conference, although, in one authority, Area Child Protection Committee guidance required the professionals to meet briefly before the family members joined the conference. Many of the ideas about good practice in *The Challenge of Partnership in Child Protection* (DoH 1995b) were in evidence in each of the authorities.

Although Coastshire and Fieldshire had similar populations and registration rates (around 20 children on the Register per 10,000 children under 18), Hillborough and Woodborough, with similar populations, had very different registration rates (over 80 per 10,000 in Hillborough; fewer than 30 per 10,000 in Woodborough). There were also differences even within the same authorities, where some teams operated higher thresholds for holding conferences.

There were also differences between and within areas on the interpretation of the wording of the guidance on registration. *Working Together* (DoH 1991b, para. 6.39) states that: 'before a child is registered the conference must decide that there is, or is a likelihood of, significant harm leading to the need for a child protection plan', and it refers to registration being linked to 'an inter-agency protection plan'.

Most conference members reached conclusions about significant harm or likely significant harm in broadly similar ways. However, it was noted that, apart from one area, the language used was of abuse, risk, and the narrower criteria for registration listed in paragraph 6.40 of *Working Together*, and not the 'significant harm' of paragraph 6.39. We noted in most conferences what appeared to be an unconscious avoidance of discussion of the nature of 'significant harm' to the child in question, in favour of discussion of specific acts of abuse or neglect and categories of registration. In this respect, there appears to have been little change from the practice reported in the *Child Protection: Messages from Research* studies (Dartington Social Research Unit 1995).

There was considerable variation in the interpretation of 'the need for a child protection plan'. For some conferences, once it was concluded that the child was suffering or likely to suffer significant harm, it followed that there was a need for a formal protection plan and that the child must be registered. For others, a further discussion took place as to whether the child protection plan should be *imposed* under the formal child protection procedures via registration, or whether it would be both possible and preferable to institute a *voluntary* child protection plan as part of services provided under the Part III provisions of the Children Act. In other words, some conferences and some agencies took the view that registration only followed if a *compulsory and formal child protection plan was necessary*, whilst others assumed that formal plans, and therefore, registration were necessary once the significant or likely significant harm threshold had been crossed. These differences were reflected in 41% of conferences resulting in a child being registered in one area and 86% in another. This is partly but not entirely explained by higher thresholds for holding conferences in the first place (the national average is 62%).

The children and their parents

One hundred and fifty-one cases were seriously considered for inclusion in the sample following attendance by a researcher at 110 of 147 consecutive initial child protection conferences or discussions with area team members about those cases where a researcher was not able to attend such a conference. A further four cases were included that appeared to involve significant harm but were not the subject of a formal child protection conference. Some of these were discussed at social services department or multidisciplinary planning meetings.

During a 12-month period, 105 cases were followed after assessments had been made that the children were suffering or likely to suffer significant harm. With the help of parents, children, social workers, other key professionals, and social work records these cases were scrutinised. If more than one child in a family was considered to be suffering or likely to suffer significant harm, the youngest child – who would normally be the most vulnerable to serious consequences in terms of health and development – was identified as the index child. Fifty-three were boys and 52 were girls.

Fifty-nine children (56%) were of white British ethnic origin, 29 (28%) had two parents from a minority racial or cultural background, and 17 children (16%) were of mixed-race parentage. In the areas where material deprivation and environmental hazards were highest, children of minority ethnic origin were over-represented in the sample. However, in the part of Fieldshire which had a substantial population of families of South-Asian descent, these children were *not* over-represented.

It was noteworthy that several of the children had physical or learning disabilities, or emotional or behavioural problems, which often preceded, but were also exacerbated by, the maltreatment. Thus, around six in ten of the cohort of children presented complications and challenges to their parents because of characteristics which would require visits to hospital, special units, special schools, and particularly skilled parenting. Some were already receiving such help but most were not, a point to which we return later in this chapter.

In most respects, the parents in this study are similar to those described in the *Child Protection: Messages from Research* studies. We particularly noted, in common with Farmer and Owen (1995), a high incidence of domestic conflict (a characteristic also emerging in an ongoing study of cases of neglect and emotional abuse (Thoburn et al. 1999); see also Brandon and Lewis 1996 for a fuller discussion of the impact of partner violence on the children in the study). A combination of environmental, emotional and relationship problems contributed to the researchers rating the well-being of 98% of the main parents as poor or giving cause for concern at the time when serious concerns about the child were identified.

Despite their own and the children's difficulties, most of the parents interviewed gave ample evidence that they were committed to the welfare of their children. Over the years, they had sought help for their own and their children's problems. There were only 15 cases where there was no evidence that a parent was committed to the child's welfare, although the problems of many parents and children made it very difficult for them to demonstrate consistently their commitment by competent parenting.

The typology identified by Cleaver and Freeman (1995) was used to give a picture of the sorts of families whose children are identified by the statutory services as suffering or likely to suffer significant harm. All except three of the families could be fitted easily into one or other of these categories. In our study of cases of actual or likely significant harm there are more 'acutely distressed' families than in the Cleaver and Freeman study of cases of 'suspicion'; there was a similar proportion (40%) of families with multiple and long-standing problems. Cleaver and Freeman (1995, p. 52) define 'acutely distressed' families as those where 'problems accumulate, but are not dealt with until one overwhelming incident precipitates child abuse'. The three refugee families in our study came into this group as they struggled with the impact of poverty, loss, and uncertainty about the future in a society with very different laws and expectations.

Maltreatment and harm

The type of maltreatment that was experienced or likely to be experienced by the children was physical assault or persistent punishment in 35% of the cases, sexual abuse in 22%, physical or emotional neglect in 39%, and emotional cruelty in 4%. A major focus of the study was the relationship between *the acts of commission or omission* of the parents (abuse or maltreatment) and the nature of the *significant harm* to the child. We concluded that in many of the cases there was no clear relationship between the *abusive behaviour* which had preceded the conference or planning meeting and the *type of harm* that the child was suffering or likely to suffer. We noted in particular that, whilst emotional cruelty or even emotional neglect occurred fairly infrequently as a major form of maltreatment, emotional harm was almost as likely to be the major cause for concern as physical harm.

This conclusion emphasises an important difference between practice before the Children Act and after it, when the focus of decision-making is on the *harm* suffered or likely to be suffered by the child rather than on the *behaviour* of the adults which may have contributed to it. We noted that, when individual workers and conferences concentrated on the particular incident that had preceded the conference or planning meeting, the resultant protection plan often failed to tackle important problems contributing to the child's distress or likely to contribute to future harm.

In 72% of cases the child was actually suffering harm at the time of the conference or other meeting, which considered future action. Indeed, in most cases, the child had been suffering harm for a considerable period of time. In 28% of cases the child was not actually suffering harm but was considered likely to do so without the provision of services.

The needs of the children and parents were also investigated. Seventy-eight of the 105 children were in high need of services at the time when an abusive incident or accumulating concerns led them to be identified as children suffering or likely to suffer significant harm. All the children crossed the 'in need' threshold as defined by the Children Act, and only eight were considered to be in a low-priority category for the allocation of resources. Not only was the health or development of most of them likely to be significantly impaired without the provision of a high level of services (Section 17(b)), but also it was clear from our interviews that most had been living in seriously harmful circumstances for months or even years, and that a majority of the parents had been seeking help – sometimes successfully, sometimes not – from a range of agencies.

Interim outcomes for children and parents at Stage 2

The children's cases were followed up 12 months later to see whether protective action had been taken and to discover what help, therapy and support had been provided to parents, children and those relatives who were closely involved. Based on data from a range of sources, a rating was made of the well-being of the parents and children at the 12-month stage. Although half of the children in the cohort were no longer suffering significant harm from parental maltreatment or lack of care, nor considered likely to do so, there were still serious concerns about the other half. Forty-four of the children, compared with the original 68, were rated as still in the 'high need' group, but only 11% were still in the 'high risk of maltreatment' group. In contrast, 14% were not rated as being at risk at all and 58% were at low risk, whereas only three were no longer 'in need' and nine were rated as in the 'low need' category. The proportion of the cohort families in the high need *and* high risk of maltreatment group had gone down from 78 to 44 by the 12-month stage.

With these indicators and the standardised schedules as a basis for the 'researcher ratings', a procedure similar to that of Farmer and Owen (1995) was used and each case was rated in terms of three interim outcome measures: was the child protected from further maltreatment?; did the child's well-being improve?; and did the parents' well-being improve? It was more likely that the child's well-being would improve than the parents'. The majority of children were protected during this 12-month period, but 40% suffered some form of maltreatment during the year, and the maltreatment was of a serious nature in 15% of cases. The most frequent form of serious maltreatment was emotional neglect or abuse. In no cases did a child suffer permanent physical harm but there was cause for concern about the emotional well-being of an important minority of children whose emotional health deteriorated over the period of study. A higher proportion of the white children than the black children suffered further abuse during the year, as did more of the older children than the younger ones.

There were 31 cases where all three outcome measures were positive, or where both child-related measures were positive and the parents were no worse. There were eight cases where all three outcome measures were negative. A small number of cases stood out from the rest. These involved children under 1 being placed permanently outside the family. In these cases the well-being of the child was rated as at least average at the 12-month stage, whereas the stress and grief at the loss of a baby usually resulted in a further deterioration of the health and well-being of the parents (some of whom were under 18 and therefore children themselves, as defined by the Children Act). For the others, the well-being of parents and children was inextricably intertwined, leading to the conclusion that a successful outcome was one in which parents *and* children made progress during the year.

The services

The services provided to the families are described in the chapters on social work and multidisciplinary work, the use of accommodation, and the use of the courts. The interviews with parents and children told us a great deal about what had been happening (and what had not been happening) before the events that led to the identification of likely significant harm. It was clear that in a minority of cases help which was offered previously was rejected, and then made available and accepted following the coercion of child protection procedures. However, many services had already been provided before the incident that triggered inclusion in the sample. The main difference, remarked upon by parents and social workers and evidenced in the files, was an increase in the provision of a relationship-based casework service as a context for the provision of practical help and specific therapeutic input to parents or child. This was likely to happen irrespective of whether a formal child protection conference was held or the child's name was placed on the Child Protection Register.

There were more examples of well-planned and co-ordinated multidisciplinary programmes of help and support than was the case in previous studies

(Hallett 1995; Farmer and Owen 1995; Thoburn et al. 1995), although this sort of work was still the exception rather than the rule. There were more cases of co-ordinated work involving partnerships between field social workers and those based in family centres or resource centres. There were also many examples of highly skilled, tenacious and caring practice which give cause for optimism about the ability of properly trained, resourced and supervised social workers to provide an effective helping and protective service based on well-established principles of psycho-social casework (Howe et al. 1999).

In summary, our conclusion is in line with that from the studies reported in *Child Protection: Messages from Research* (Dartington Social Research Unit 1995): a child who is identified as having been maltreated by a parent or carer and continues to be in contact with that parent is likely to receive a service which is at least adequate (though this is not always the case for the parents) especially if the child is removed from their care.

It is clear from the words of the parents and children that they were more likely to become engaged in the work if it fitted the pattern described in *Child Protection: Messages from Research* (p. 55) where efforts are made:

> to work alongside families rather than disempower them, to raise their self-esteem rather than reproach families, to promote family relationships where children have their needs met, rather than leave untreated families with an unsatisfactory parenting style. The focus would be on the overall needs of children rather than a narrow concentration on the alleged incident.

Elsewhere (p. 45) these writers note that:

> the most important condition for success is the quality of the relationship between the child's family and the professionals responsible.

However, even sustained attempts to follow the Department of Health guidance (DoH 1995b) in order to involve family members as much as possible did not, in this study of 'significant harm' cases, result in parents and older children becoming 'partners' in the work or decision-making. This supports the conclusion from an earlier study of working in partnership in child protection cases (Thoburn et al. 1995) that involvement, consultation and keeping family members fully informed may be more realistic goals for the early stages of work when children are already, or highly likely to be, suffering significant harm.

Accommodation and court orders

It was found that the work could be fitted into four patterns based on the two dimensions of negotiation or coercion; and work which was *child and family focused* or *focused on the child alone*. Since the research concerned cases of actual or likely significant harm, it was anticipated that there would be a high level of court intervention. Our original intention had been to study equal numbers of cases where the child was removed by court order and where support and treatment were provided with the child remaining at home or looked after under voluntary arrangements. However, as national statistics demonstrate, the number of court interventions dropped significantly when the Children Act 1989 was introduced, and although numbers were growing in 1993 and 1994 when we started the research, court orders were used in a minority of the cases. Thirty-four children never left home and a further 36 were away for some period of time but back home with their parents for most of the period in question. Thus, only one child in four was living away for most of that period, and six of these were living with relatives. Just over half of the children lived for most of the follow-up period with the person believed to have contributed to the harm or likely harm, and 29% were mainly looked after either by the local authority or at boarding school.

Emergency Protection Orders were used in six cases initially, and in four later, during the year. Ten children were taken into police protection but all except one of these returned home. There were Interim or full Care Orders on 22 children at the 12-month stage, and two children had already been placed for adoption. In seven of these cases the order followed an initial period when the child was accommodated, and in one case a baby was placed for adoption from Section 20 accommodation.

In 65 cases a child was accommodated by a local authority at some stage and there was evidence of Section 20 accommodation being used in the spirit of Section 1(5) of the Children Act to avoid the need for a court order. Packman and Hall (1998) found similarly. In three of the cases an application for a child to be accommodated, which could have been helpful, was turned down. However, in nine cases where accommodation *was* provided, this was (at least to some extent) against the wishes of the parents, and in two cases against the wishes of the child who was old enough to express a view. In a further 29 cases (44% of those where accommodation was used) a parent reluctantly agreed, seeing no alternative and not wishing the case to go to court. A similar number willingly agreed to or requested accommodation. Seventeen children reluctantly agreed to accommodation, but 22 requested it, willingly accepted it, or were too young to express a view.

There were two cases of forced accommodation when parents' rights would have been better respected had the case gone to court. In the other cases where a degree of coercion was used to achieve a Section 20 accommodation placement, there was evidence that information was provided to parents about a court application as an alternative route and that some element of choice was available to them. Our findings in this respect are similar to those of Packman and Hall (1998).

In view of the polarisation of views on this subject at the time of the implementation of the Act, it is interesting to note that there was no case in which a Child Assessment Order was applied for, and only one Family Assistance Order was made (although no assistance was forthcoming under the terms of this order for a grandparent who was desperately in need of it). The Family Assistance Order might have been helpful in this case if more effort had been put into it. These orders could have been useful in other cases in which conflict between *parents* was the major source of harm.

Emerging themes

The importance of difference

The previous chapter notes that a wide range of methods of intervention was used with the families in our study and that no particular methods appeared to be linked with more positive outcomes. This is in part because of the *wide range* of needs in the majority of the cases but also because of the very different family histories which preceded the identification of likely significant harm to one or more of the children. Whilst most analysts of child protection policies and practice note the importance of considering variables such as the age of the child, the type of maltreatment and the identity of the person allegedly responsible, less attention has been paid to the many dimensions and biographies of those involved as *individuals and families* rather than as *abusing families* or *abused children*. In attempting to understand the families, we looked for frameworks which might prove helpful and found that all except three of the intensive study families fitted into the categories used by Cleaver and Freeman (1995). Irrespective of the type of maltreatment or harm to the child, there were discernible differences in the way that social workers and families responded to each other, depending on whether the family had long-lasting and multiple problems or whether a succession of events leading to acute distress, or a single issue, had got in the way of adequate parenting.

This seems an obvious point to make, and indeed is in keeping with widely used social casework approaches such as systems or ecological models.

However, it needs to be re-emphasised in the light of our observation that professionals so often appeared to become mesmerised by abusive acts or symptoms of neglect or maltreatment and failed to understand the complex nature of the events and interactions leading to it. Although much time appears to be given over to assessment of risk, a wider assessment of the families in all their complexity was often lacking. In particular, the complex interplay between a child's disabilities or difficult behaviour and family events such as death, loss, or serious illness too often appeared to be overlooked. Even something so dramatic as having to flee a war-torn country, leaving close family behind, appeared to warrant little attention, a fact which was totally bewildering to the families whose waking (and sleeping) thoughts were dominated by such events. To be in receipt of a letter telling them that their child had been registered, or, for that matter, deregistered, seemed a total irrelevance to some of these acutely distressed families who were looking for understanding and help with their complex practical and emotional needs.

We would argue that frameworks for understanding the biographies of families who maltreat their children could lead to differential patterns of intervention and a more cost-effective service (see Howe et al. 1999). As a first step to such an approach, a broader psycho-social history needs to be compiled with the assistance of all family members, which encompasses the abuse but does not focus so narrowly upon it. Boushel (1994) provides a useful framework. Such a history should include an analysis of whether there has been any involvement with the health and welfare services; the methods of support, intervention or therapy that have been tried and the different family members' reactions to them. Models of assessment that harness the knowledge and energies of all family members, such as family group conferences (Morris and Tunnard 1996; Marsh and Crowe 1998), are an obvious way forward which might lead to a wider range of strategies and protection plans to fit the cultures, family histories, problems and strengths of those in need of protective services.

Risk and danger

'Risk assessment' is a fashionable concept in banking, in assessing environmental hazards, and in child welfare as well. All the children in this study were at risk of significant harm to their long-term emotional development, and those most at risk of such harm were the older children at the end of the study who were looked after away from home. However, in the child protection field, an agency and its staff identify highest risk when it is physical harm to a baby or small child. This view is totally understandable and inevitable when the impact of child abuse inquiries on those whose practice is taken into account. It is also appropriate that risk to life and limb of small and dependent children is given special consideration. Indeed, it is worth remembering that concern for the 'battered baby' led to the development of Child Protection Registers.

With these considerations in mind, the cases were scrutinised to see if it was possible to predict dangerous situations and to establish what proportion of 'significant harm' cases might come into such a category. We stress here *dangerous situations*, not dangerous *families*. Two single mothers might suffer from bouts of illness which prevent them from supervising their toddlers adequately. Neither is more 'dangerous' than the other, but the danger is greater to the child who lives in homeless families' accommodation next door to strangers of dubious reputation, than to the one who lives in a cottage with an enclosed garden and a granny down the lane.

Chapter 4 listed the characteristics of 24 families in which we considered that their situation posed a danger to life and limb. All except one of the index children were under 5. Danger was recognised by the agencies in all the cases, the children received a higher level of service and supervision, and it was more likely than in the other cases in the cohort that a public law order would be made and that the child would be placed away from home. No child in this group was seriously physically harmed during the follow-up period, though there were concerns about emotional harm to two of them at the end of the study. All except these same two children were, at least at the end of the first year, 'false positives', though in most cases there were indications that the support and protective action taken had played a part in keeping the children safe. In six cases this involved the child being placed immediately away from the dangerous situation; in four others, unsuccessful attempts were made to improve the situation and the child was later placed away from home. In nine cases, either the child was initially moved from home or short-term help from relatives helped to contain the situation until a protection plan could be put in place. The early fears in some cases proved insubstantial but parents and children gained from the assistance provided, even though some resented it initially.

Co-operation, negotiation and coercion

Overlapping the issue of risk of long-term harm and dangerous situations is the question of the appropriate use of coercion. This could take the form of child protection conferences and registration, applications for public or private law orders, or the threat of, or actual prosecution in, the criminal courts.

In a minority of cases the parents worked willingly with the social workers and other professionals to secure the help and protective services that they recognised were necessary. In most, coercion and negotiation alternated as a support and protection plan was put in place, with a minority of cases moving in the direction of more coercion and a court order, but most towards more co-operation and partnership.

There were differences between agencies and workers such that apparently similar cases took different routes, but ended the year in similar positions. These differences were apparent both with the group of children who ended the year living permanently away from home as well as with those who lived with their parents at the 12-month stage. There is clearly scope for discretion as to whether the formal child protection procedures, emergency procedures or applications for private or public law orders should be used in similar situations. (The added powers now available under the provisions of the Family Law Act 1988, to exclude a parent from the household in some circumstances, means that there is even more choice.)

Once a case crosses the threshold for the making of an Emergency Protection, Supervision or a Care Order, the 'presumption of no order' principle comes into effect:

> Where a court is considering whether or not to make one or more orders under this Act with respect to a child, it shall not make the order or any of the orders unless it considers that doing so would be better for the child than making no order at all. (Section 1(5))

Until an application to court is made, there is no clear statement of principle (apart from the many places in the *Guidance* where partnership-based practice is recommended) that coercion should not be used unless it is necessary and there is reason to believe that it will be helpful to the plans to protect the child from significant harm. We conclude from our data that such a principle at the different thresholds of intervention would be helpful to parents, children and professionals. The following questions would need to be asked:

♦ Is an initial or incident child protection conference necessary, or would it be equally protective and supportive to invite family members to a multidisciplinary planning meeting or a family group conference?

♦ When a child protection conference has concluded that a child is suffering or is likely to suffer significant harm, is it necessary to place a child's name on the Child Protection Register (or leave it there) or would it be just as safe for the child, and helpful to the parents, to draw up a voluntary agreement about support and protective services, with provision for regular monitoring and review?

♦   Is an application for an Emergency Protection Order or Interim Care Order necessary, or can a placement away from home be negotiated, for the purposes of immediate protection, assessment or securing long-term care or adoption?

Some workers assumed that the guidance to attempt to work in partnership and the sections in the Children Act requiring consultation with parents and children were a *de facto* 'principle of minimum coercion'. They used coercion when necessary but moved back to negotiation as quickly as possible, since coercion, in most cases, slowed down or got in the way of their work with the parents and children.

After the first round of interviews the researchers posed this question in each case: was registration and/or an application for a public law order necessary? For the 23 cases of children under 5 where the situation presented a potential danger to life and limb, we erred on the side of caution and assumed that, even if registration was unhelpful, it was probably necessary to make sure that protection plans were reviewed. For the others, the rating of 'necessary' required that there was some indication that registration would help rather than hinder the difficult task of putting in place the assessment, protection and support which was so clearly needed for all these children.

Had these questions been routinely asked in all the authorities in our study there would probably have been 33 fewer children whose names were placed on the Register (43% of those registered) and 13 fewer applications for a public law order (46% of the 28 applications made). This reduction in workload, costs and stress to all concerned would have been achieved at no cost to the welfare and protection of the children. Using an approach of coercion only when needed would bring to our processes some of the best aspects of European child protection systems (Cooper et al. 1995; Lynch 1992; Marneffe 1992) without losing some of the positive attributes of the UK system, which would still be based on the carefully worked out balances in the Children Act and its *Guidance*.

Section 20 accommodation and placement with relatives

Chapter 7 discusses details of placements away from home, which were arranged without recourse to the courts and often involved relatives. It is important to restate that these placements generally achieved what they set out to achieve. In seven cases which started as accommodation, an application to court was made in order to provide long-term security. The biggest risk in opting for accommodation, rather than applying for a Care Order, is that parents will disappear off the scene, this situation being allowed to get in the way of making long-term plans, as happened in the only case of drift in the cohort. However, it could be argued that parents are even more likely to disappear when court orders are made, and this occurred in two other cases in the sample. Although the disappearance of a parent can be allowed to slow down long-term planning, good practice can ensure that this does not happen, as was the case when a diligent worker tracked down a mother and managed to get her child safely back home.

Another risk of using accommodation in protection cases, which was much discussed when the Children Act Bill was being debated in Parliament, is that parents will remove children precipitately or to situations of danger and thus cause further harm. Ways of counteracting this risk were discussed by Thoburn (1991b). There were no cases in this present study where emergency action was needed to prevent a child from being removed from accommodation, although in the case of one older child, the parents were told that a Care Order would be applied for if they persisted with their plans to resume care of their daughter.

In at least four cases in the intensive sample it was considered that a negotiated placement in accommodation could have been used instead of an immediate application for a Care Order, although the original Emergency Protection Order or police protection might have been necessary. These were cases where a parent had a mental illness or an addiction or alcohol problem. Given the high cost of legal fees, to say nothing of the negative impact on parents and their relationship with the social workers, a policy of applying for a Care Order only when negotiation fails to secure an adequate protection plan would free up resources for family support services to be provided at an earlier stage.

It must be seen as one of the successes of the Children Act that more relatives, especially grandparents, are being drawn into the process of helping and protecting children. This finding is in line with a Social Services Inspectorate report on the use of Residence Orders (SSI 1995b). In all the cases in which they were involved, grandparents' endeavours had a positive impact on the child's welfare. It must be emphasised, though, that their positive influence was gained in many cases, 'on the cheap'. Such penny-pinching may have reduced the long-term stability of some of the placements by causing resentment towards Social Services and by reducing relatives' willingness to seek help in the future.

Conclusion: risk, need and the Children Act 1989

In conclusion we return to the questions discussed in Chapter 1. The picture presented supports the conclusions of the Dartington Social Research Unit (1995, p. 19) that 'in families low on warmth and high on criticism, negative incidents accumulate as if to remind a child that he or she is unloved'. The authors go on to say that:

> putting to one side the severe cases, for those children who suffer from a short period of emotional neglect, the child protection process may not be the best way of meeting their needs. If, however, the family problems endure, some external support will be required, otherwise the health and development of the child will be significantly impaired.

By the time these children came into our cohort concerted action was clearly necessary. What, then, does this research indicate has been the impact of the Children Act on services to children whose health or development is being significantly impaired or who are suffering or likely to suffer significant harm?

First, we saw little to confirm the fears of those who wondered whether the Act, with its message about minimal use of coercion and the importance of attempting to work in partnership with parents and children, would place more children at increased risk of maltreatment. Although the message about working in partnership was taken seriously by all four authorities, the welfare and protection of the children in these cases of significant harm were given the highest priority. The result was that only a minority of the parents we interviewed considered that they had been involved in the work and decisions, although a higher proportion participated at least to some extent than was the case in earlier studies (Farmer and Owen 1995: Thoburn et al. 1995).

The narrow focus on acts of maltreatment or negligence reported by earlier research studies continued to be in evidence in many of these cases and placed obstacles in the way of effective practice to alleviate the conditions leading to significant harm. Although the trigger for registration in *Working Together* (DoH 1991b) is significant harm or its likelihood, most conferences were dominated by the language of abuse or ill-defined risk. It was the exception rather than the rule for the precise nature of the significant harm likely to occur (as opposed to the maltreatment which had already occurred to this or another child of the family) to be spelled out clearly. There was evidence from the case studies that those workers, conference chairpersons and agencies that concentrated on formal procedures to counteract maltreatment tended to produce protection plans which ignored important factors contributing to harm or likely harm to the child. This was most evident when comparing the small proportion of cases where action to reduce the impact of serious marital conflict figured in the protection plan with the large number of cases where it was causing serious harm to the child.

We concluded, along with earlier writers and researchers, that once concerted attention is given to meeting the needs of parents and children, improvements occur in many families that have been known to social services teams to have made no apparent progress in the past, sometimes for periods of years. It is not immediately clear why substantial progress was made in a majority of these cases during the 12 months following heightened awareness of the child protection issues, especially in improving the well-being of children (most of whom had been suffering significant harm before the decisive action was taken). Most of the parents we spoke to, like those in studies by Lindley (1994) and by Hunt et al. (1999), were deeply upset and humiliated by court appearances and, in most cases, by their child's name being placed on the Child Protection Register. Yet there was no obvious difference in the outcome for child or parents in otherwise similar cases, where the formal child protection or court procedures were used, or where negotiation characterised the work and accommodation was chosen (if out-of-home placement was needed).

A previous study (Thoburn et al. 1995) found that partnership-based practice at an earlier stage of the development of problems was associated with more successful interim outcomes for the child and the family. This association was not found in our present study. It appears that once problems are entrenched, even highly skilled workers, making concerted attempts to empower and improve the self-esteem of parents and children, have an uphill struggle. Differences in outcome appear to be explained by a combination of the depth of the problems; the comprehensiveness of the service offered; and the determination of the key social worker and other members of the helping team to break through the hostility, depression or despair of parents and children and to convince them that their situation is not without hope.

There is evidence that protection and support in 33 of the 76 registered cases could have been provided just as successfully, if not more so, outside the formal child protection system. With the benefit of hindsight, in only one case did the researchers consider that a child who was not registered would have gained from having his name entered on the Register. There is scope for developing the innovative practices of some agencies (Sieff Foundation 1995), which are using multidisciplinary planning or network meetings (called in response to Section 27 of the Children Act, which requires agencies to work co-operatively) or family group conferences to bring the benefits of a multi-agency approach to those cases where a Section 47 enquiry is not thought necessary. In making decisions about which course of action to take, major factors to be considered are the willingness of parents to become involved in the protection process, and the degree of danger to the child. (Appendix 2 presents a set of questions, the answers to which allow more coherent and systematic decisions to be taken about the need for coercion.) Once a framework for such meetings is in place, our data suggest that there is scope for reducing the number of child protection conferences held under the *Working Together* guidelines (DoH 1991b). In this, as in earlier studies, there was much evidence of the value of formal, minuted meetings, attended by parents and other professionals, at which the concerns of professionals and family members are clearly stated. Whatever form the meeting takes, the essential elements of a support plan and any necessary protective services must be clearly identified. These should be recorded, together with contingency plans, in case the agreed action does not work and the child is still suffering or likely to suffer significant impairment to health or development. It would be unwise to reduce the number of child protection conferences held because of dangerous situations before guidelines for the appropriate use of multidisciplinary meetings outside the formal child protection system are put in place.

Turning to the 'no order' principle, our analysis suggests that there is no discernible difference in interim outcomes between apparently similar cases where coercion and court action is used and those where it is not, leaving aside a small group of the youngest children where it is abundantly clear from the start that permanent out-of-home placement will be needed. It could be argued that it makes sense to 'play safe' and use the courts and the Child Protection Register to increase control over a larger number of cases where children are suffering significant harm. Indeed, we can well understand why – in the light of these difficult and painful cases, and the knowledge that a misjudgement is likely to lead to personal grief and a blighted professional career – social workers and managers are strongly tempted to reduce the risk of incurring blame for themselves and their agencies by placing the case before the courts. We would not urge this course of action because each case that goes unnecessarily down the route of court or formal registration takes up additional time and resources which are much needed by other children whose health or development is being significantly impaired, either in their own homes or in the care system.

The outcome to the second set of questions posed in our introduction — whether family support services are reaching those who need them if significant impairment to their health or development is to be averted — is less encouraging. There are strong indications that earlier intervention with some of these families, including the provision of Section 20 short-term accommodation or respite care, might have prevented situations of stress leading to significant harm to the children (see Aldgate and Bradley 1999 for a discussion of the benefits of respite care for children whose parents are under stress). This view became apparent when we interviewed the children and their parents for our study.

We see in the majority of these cases, of children suffering significant harm which has been identified three years after the implementation of the Children Act, a pattern of social services involvement reaching back often over a period of years. There were comparatively fewer cases in our study than in *Child Protection: Messages from Research* (Dartington Social Research Unit 1995), where resources were used unnecessarily with families, whose children were placed on the Child Protection Register but the level of need and risk was comparatively low, and where there was no willingness to make use of the various services offered. The threshold for registration appeared to be more carefully guarded than in previous studies, although there was still variation between areas. Mostly, though, the formal child protection conference and registration procedures were being used in the four local authorities studied to help children and families with a high level of need and where the risk of future harm was considerable. It was clear that a minority had been offered an appropriate level of service as children in need before the level of concern increased to the extent that it was considered necessary to use formal procedures. More often, though, the revolving door of one-off or uncoordinated responses to requests for help was in evidence until, as with the work reported in *Child Protection: Messages from Research*, an often comparatively minor event led to a change of gear in the work with these families.

All the evidence from this and other studies points to the conclusion that children coming into the formal child protection systems are 'the tip of the iceberg', representative of many more families struggling with children who have serious problems and whose health or development is being significantly impaired because needed services are not provided. Whilst our study shows that some families received skilled help over many years and that this had little impact on the well-being of either children or parents, it also gives evidence that well-planned services and casework support, made available after consultation with family members, *can* lead to dramatic improvements in the well-being of children and parents. However, the longer the provision of a planned and consistent service is delayed, the more of an uphill struggle it will be to repair the harm or protect the child from future harm.

Our study suggests that more discriminating use of the formal child protection systems and the courts can result in a more cost-effective service to the most vulnerable children, who must continue to be given the highest priority. Such an approach will then free up resources to help more families at an earlier stage, before the harm to the children has already been done.

Research instrument used for decision about inclusion in the cohort

Is the harm significant?

Ill-treatment

1   Is the child being physically ill-treated?
    [No / Suspected / To some extent / Significantly / Don't know]

    Is the child likely to be?
    [No / Suspected / Yes / Awaiting assessment]

2   Is the child being sexually ill-treated?
    [No / Suspected / To some extent / Significantly / Don't know]

    Is the child likely to be?
    [No / Suspected / Yes / Awaiting assessment]

3   Is the child being emotionally ill-treated?
    [No / Suspected / To some extent / Significantly / Don't know]

    Is the child likely to be?
    [No / Suspected / Yes / Awaiting assessment]

Impairment of health

1   Is the child's physical health being impaired?
    [No / Suspected / To some extent / Significantly / Don't know]

    Is it likely to be?
    [No / Suspected / Yes / Awaiting assessment]

2   Is the child's mental health being impaired?
    [No / Suspected / To some extent / Significantly / Don't know]

    Is it likely to be?
    [No / Suspected / Yes / Awaiting assessment]

Impairment of development

1   Is the child's physical development being impaired?
    [No / Suspected / To some extent / Significantly / Don't know]

Is it likely to be?
[No / Suspected / Yes / Awaiting assessment]

2   Is the child's intellectual development being impaired?
[No / Suspected / To some extent / Significantly / Don't know]

Is it likely to be?
[No / Suspected / Yes / Awaiting assessment]

3   Is the child's emotional development being impaired?
[No / Suspected / To some extent / Significantly / Don't know]

Is it likely to be?
[No / Suspected / Yes / Awaiting assessment]

4   Is the child's social development being impaired?
[No / Suspected / To some extent / Significantly / Don't know]

Is it likely to be?
[No / Suspected / Yes / Awaiting assessment]

5   Is the child's behavioural development being impaired?
[No / Suspected / To some extent / Significantly / Don't know]

Is it likely to be?
[No / Suspected / Yes / Awaiting assessment]

Is harm significant and the child in need of protection?

1   Is the child suffering significant harm now (at time of referral)?
[Yes / No / Don't know]

2   Is the child likely to suffer significant harm in the future, but not now?
[Yes / No / Don't know]

3   Will the services meet/address the harm?
[Yes / No / Don't know]

Parental care

1   Is the care given to the child what it would be reasonable for a parent
to give to a similar child?
[Yes / Sometimes / Some aspects / No / Don't know]

2   Is the care likely to be given to the child what it would be reasonable
for a parent to give to a similar child?
[Yes / Sometimes / Some aspects / No / Don't know]

3   Is the child beyond control?
[Yes / No / Don't know]

4   Is significant harm resulting or likely to result from a change of living circumstances – eg. from one parent to another, from foster carer to parent?
[Yes / No / Don't know]

Particular child

1   Is there anything about this particular child which makes her/him hard to care for?
[Yes / No / Don't know]

2   If Yes, please describe:

....

....

....

....

Protocols used for categorisation or rating

Family type, including Cleaver and Freeman's four categories

The categories of family type used by the researchers were adapted from those devised by Cleaver and Freeman (1995) from their survey of 583 child protection cases in one local authority and their detailed study of 30 families over two years in two local authorities.

Multiple problems of long duration

Known to the agencies, these families present an array of problems which could include: chronic ill health, poor housing, long-term unemployment, financial and social problems, petty crime or violence, substance abuse or other addictions, parents having suffered abuse as children, stigmatisation within their communities, maltreatment of children that takes more than one form.

Specific problem (or single issue)

Usually these families are not known to the agencies until a particular incident or suspicion arises, perhaps because a family member discloses abuse or displays symptoms of undiagnosed mental illness. Marital discord or one problem acting as a catalyst to others may trigger behaviour that leads to a child protection referral.

Acutely distressed

These families, who generally cope well enough until one overwhelming incident pushes them into the child protection 'net', are often single or poorly supported parents, or physically ill or disabled. Abuse or neglect may be reported by anxious neighbours or professionals in touch with the family or the child.

Infiltrating perpetrator

There are families where a person, usually a man, gains access to children by pretending to be a caring partner or friend (Schedule 1 offenders). Children's behaviour deteriorates as a result of the change in the family circumstances.

Other

The subject of a conference may be a young perpetrator – a 'beyond control' teenager who may be a parent themself.

Interim outcome for the child

Any assessment of outcome only six months following a child protection conference must of necessity be tentative. However, it was part of our research design that a case should not be seen as satisfactory if there was evidence that the outcome for the child was poorer as a result of the involvement of family members in the process. The researchers allocated cases to the 'good', 'poor', or 'no change' outcome groups according to answers to the following questions:

◆ Do the child's living and parenting arrangements appear to be settled?
◆ Is the child either living with or in contact with parents and other adults who are important to him/her, and is this contact arranged in a way which makes it a positive experience?
◆ Are there any indications that the child is making developmental progress or is slipping backwards?
◆ Are there indications that any emotional or behavioural problems are diminishing or increasing?
◆ Does it appear that the protection plan is offering protection for the child?
◆ Does the protection plan appear to be working as intended for the overall benefit of the child?
◆ Is the professional contact for the child and carers at an appropriate level in view of the problems identified?

The 'no change' category was used only when it was not possible to allocate a case to the 'good' or 'poor' categories. This was usually when a child remained living at home and the child protection process appeared to have had little impact on the child's well-being and circumstances.

Parents' well-being assessed on the Rutter malaise and family problem scales

For the intensive sample, the parents' well-being was based on the responses of the parents to the Rutter 'malaise' scale (Rutter et al. 1981), and the Gibbons family problems checklist (Gibbons et al. 1990). These were supplemented by the interview data. For the background sample, a rating was made if there was adequate information from attendance of conferences, case records and the interview with the social worker. Dimensions used were based on Gibbons' checklist, and comparisons were made with the community and the referred samples in the Gibbons et al. study. The dimensions used were:

♦ health;
♦ finance;
♦ social contact and support;
♦ partner relationships; and
♦ parenting.

Within these categories the rating of well-being was based on answers to the following questions:

♦ Is the parent mostly healthy, with few problems?
♦ Is the parent free from serious mental health, emotional or behavioural problems?
♦ Is the parent settled in permanent long-term housing?
♦ Does the parent have an adequate income; adequate housing; and adequate consumer durables?
♦ Does the parent regard the neighbourhood as safe for him/herself and his/her child?
♦ Does the parent have stability in his/her general relationships, and a supportive network?
♦ Does the parent function adequately as a carer for the child?
♦ Does the parent have access to the help and resources needed to fulfil his/her parenting role?
♦ Are the services that the parent needs in place?
♦ Is the professional support at an appropriate level in view of the problems identified?

The categories and rating for well-being used at Stages 1 and 2 were the following:

♦ Poor (a lot of problems)   =   0
♦ Some concerns (some regular input needed)   =   1
♦ Average/satisfactory/probably a little
  input needed)   =   2
♦ Good (no input needed)   =   3

These were the categories and rating used for comparison:

◆ No improvement	=	0
◆ To some extent	=	1
◆ Improved	=	2

The research rating for potentially dangerous situations

Researches used the following criteria to establish whether a situation was potentially dangerous:

- ◆ the child was under 5 or particularly vulnerable to physical assault because of a disability;

and

- ◆ the child was being, or there was any risk of his/her being, seriously physically injured or sexually assaulted; or
- ◆ the child was being neglected and consequently exposed to the risk of serious injury, assault or life-threatening/life-limiting failure to thrive; or
- ◆ the child's physical health or development was being, or was likely to be, significantly impaired;

or

- ◆ the child was over 5 and not otherwise especially vulnerable, but there was a high probability of life-threatening injury, impairment of development or sexual assault by a parent or other member of the household.

Whether registration was necessary

Researchers questioned whether there was evidence presented to the conference or planning meeting to support or justify the conclusion that:

- ◆ there was, or was a likelihood of, significant harm leading to the need for a child protection plan (*Working Together* (DoH 1991b) 6.39)
- ◆ the abuse, neglect or other harm resulted from acts of parental commission or omission;
- ◆ the child needed a plan to protect him/her and to promote his/her well-being; and
- ◆ the plan needed to be a multidisciplinary plan sanctioned by the . . . ACPC child protection system as defined in *Working Together*.

Risk of maltreatment and need grid

Need	Risk of maltreatment			
	None	Low	Medium	High
None				
Low				
Medium				
High				

Risk of maltreatment: Section 31 of the Children Act =

a that the child concerned is suffering, or is likely to suffer, significant harm; and

b that the harm, or likelihood of harm, is attributable to:

    i the care given to the child, or likely to be given to him if the order were not made, not being what it would be reasonable to expect a parent to give him; or

    ii the child's being beyond parental control

Need: Section 17 of the Children Act =

a that the child is unlikely to achieve or maintain, or to have the opportunity of achieving or maintaining, a reasonable standard of health or development* without the provision for him of services by a local authority under this Part;

b his health or development is likely to be significantly impaired, or further impaired, without the provision for him of such services; or

c he is disabled.

* 'Health' means physical or mental health; 'development' means physical, intellectual, emotional, social or behavioural development.

Research instruments and other methods of data collection

Standardised scales

Rutter behaviour scales A (2) and B (2)

These scales were completed for children of school age by the main parent or carer (scale A) and by teachers (scale B). They provide an indication of emotional problems and conduct disorder in the school setting and at home (see Rutter et al. 1981).

British picture vocabulary scale (BPVs)

This scale, which is based on the well-established Peabody Picture Vocabulary Test: Revised Manual (PPVT-R) (Dunn and Dunn 1981) was used as part of the play-based interview with children aged 3 and above. The scale is a measure of the child's receptive vocabulary and provides a reliable test of one aspect of general intelligence (see Robertson and Eisenberg 1981).

Children's depression inventory (CDI) (Kovacs and Beck 1977)

Depression is commonly noted in some abused children, particularly those who have been sexually abused (Monck and New 1996, Kendall-Tackett et al. 1993). A self-rating instrument, standardised for children aged 8 and above, was used to gauge depression. The 'Kovacs' CDI consists of 27 multiple-choice items that cover overt symptoms of childhood depression such as sadness, sleep and appetite disturbance, and suicidal thoughts. Each item assesses one symptom by presenting three choices graded towards increasing psychopathology.

Post-traumatic stress disorder (PTSD) (not standardised)

An additional three items in the same groups of three sentences were included at the end of the CDI for use with children above 8 years to check whether there were indications that the child might be suffering from post-traumatic stress disorder (Sharland et al. 1996, Wilson and Raphael 1993). This scale has not been standardised and the data should be interpreted with caution.

Assessment and action records

Another non-standardised tool for gaining a clearer picture of these children was an adaptation of the *Looking After Children* materials, the *Assessment and Action Records* (DoH 1995a). The same age bands were retained, namely 0–1 year, 1–2, 3–4, 5–9 and 10–15 years (Parker et al. 1991; Ward 1995). They provided an assessment of the parenting the child received and an indication of difficulties and positive aspects of care across the seven developmental domains of health; education; family and social relationships; identity; self-care and competence; emotional and behavioural development; and social presentation.

Play-based interviews with the children

Pre-school-age children

These interviews were adaptations of the *Griffiths Mental Developmental Scales* (1984) and were a combination of observation of the child playing and responding to family members, and play with the researcher using a box of carefully selected simple toys. An assessment was made about the child's well-being and development in the areas of gross and fine motor skills, communication and language, social skills and relationships, and his/her use of play and cognitive abilities. A clinical psychologist provided consultation on the use of these materials.

School-age children

These interviews provided the vehicle for completing standardised tests (the BPVS and, for children above 8, the CDI) and gaining some rich qualitative material from the children themselves. This ranged from wishes and worries that might or might not be related to any abuse, to views about services and professional help they had received. The interview was a combination of questions, discussion and play activities, and was adapted for children of different ages and developmental levels.

Bibliography

Adcock, M., White, R. and Hollows, A. (eds) (1991) *Significant Harm: Its Management and Outcome,* Croydon: Significant Publications

Aldgate, J. and Bradley, M. (1999) *Supporting Families Through Short-term Fostering,* London: The Stationery Office

Aldgate, J. and Tunstill, J. (1994) *Implementing Section 17 of the Children Act: The First 18 months,* Leicester: University of Leicester

Audit Commission, (1994) *Seen But Not Heard,* London: HMSO

Barton, C. and Douglas, G. (1995*) Law and Parenthood,* London: Butterworths

Bingley Miller, L., Fisher, T. and Sinclair I. (1993) 'Decisions to register children as at risk of abuse', *Social Services Review,* 4 (2), pp. 101–18

Boushel, M. (1993) 'Strategies for surviving adversity: the cross-cultural dimension to child protection' in Ferguson, H., Gilligan, R. and Tarode, R. (eds) (1993) *Surviving Childhood Adversity,* Dublin: Social Studies Press

Boushel, M. (1994) 'The Protective Environment of Children: 'Towards a framework for anti-oppressive, cross-cultural and cross-national understanding' in *British Journal of Social Work,* 24, pp. 173–90

Bowlby, J. (1988) *A Secure Base: Clinical Applications of Attachment Theory,* London: Routledge

Bradley M. and Aldgate, J. (1994) 'Short-term family-based care for children in need', *Adoption and Fostering,* 18, 4, pp. 24–9

Brandon, M. and Lewis, A. (1996) 'Significant harm and children's experiences of domestic violence', *Child and Family Social Work,* Vol. 1.1, pp. 33–42

Brandon, M., Lewis, A. and Thoburn, J. (1996) 'The Children Act definition of "significant harm": interpretation in practice', *Health and Social Care in the Community,* 4(1), pp. 11–20

Braye, S. and Preston-Shoot, M. (1994) 'Partners in community care? Rethinking the relationship between the law and social work practice, *Journal of Social Welfare and Family Law,* 16 (2), pp. 163–83

Brown, G. and Harris T. (1978) *Social Origins of Depression: A Study of Psychiatric Disorder in Women,* London: Tavistock Publications

Children Act 1989 England and Wales (1989), London: HMSO

Central Council for Education and Training in Social Work (1995) *Assuring Quality in the Diploma in Social Work,* London: CCETSW

Children Act Advisory Committee (1994) *Annual Report,* London: HMSO

Cleaver, H. and Freeman, P. (1995) *Parental Perspectives in Cases of Suspected Child Abuse,* London: HMSO

Cockett, M. and Tripp, J. (1994) *The Exeter Study: Family Breakdown and its Impact on Children*, Exeter: University of Exeter Press

Colton, M., Drury, C. and Williams, M. (1995) *Children in Need*, Aldershot: Avebury

Cooper, A., Hetherington, R., Baistow, K., Pitts, J. and Spriggs, A. (1995) *Positive Child Protection: A View from Abroad*, Lyme Regis: Russell House Publishing

Cooper, D. (1993) *Child Abuse Revisited: Children, Society and Social Work*, Buckingham: Open University Press

Creighton, S. (1995) 'Patterns and outcomes' in Wilson, K. and James, A. (eds) (1995) *The Child Protection Handbook*, London: Ballière Tindall

Dahl, R. (1984) *Boy: Tales of Childhood*, London: Puffin

Dartington Social Research Unit (1995) *Child Protection: Messages from Research*, London: HMSO

Department of Health (1985) *Review of Child Care Law: Report to Ministers of an Interdepartmental Working Party*, London: HMSO

Department of Health (1988) *Protecting Children: A Guide for Social Workers Undertaking a Comprehensive Assessment*, London: HMSO

Department of Health (1989a) *Introduction to the Act: Principles and Practice in Regulations and Guidance*, London: HMSO

Department of Health (1989b) *The Children Act 1989: Principles and Practice in Regulations and Guidance*, London: HMSO

Department of Health (1991a) *Regulations and Guidance on the Act*, Vols 1–3, London: HMSO

Department of Health (1991b) *Working Together under the Children Act 1989*, London: HMSO

Department of Health and the Welsh Office (1994) *Children Act Report 1993*, London: HMSO

Department of Health (1994) *Children and Young People on Child Protection Register* (Year ending 31 March 1993), London: HMSO

Department of Health (1995a) *Looking After Children: Assessment and Action Records*, London: HMSO

Department of Health (1995b) *The Challenge of Partnership in Child Protection*, London: HMSO

Dickens, J. (1993) 'Assessment of the Control of Social Work: an analysis of reasons for the non-use of the Child Assessment Order, *Journal of Social Welfare and Family Law*, (April) pp. 88–100

Dunn, L. M. and Dunn, L. M. (1981) *Peabody Picture Vocabulary Test: Revised Manual*, Circle Pines, MN: American Guidance Services

Farmer, E. and Owen, M. (1995) *Child Protection Practice: Private Risks and Public Remedies*, London: HMSO

Fisher, M., Marsh, P. Phillips, D. and Sainsbury, E. (1986) *In and Out of Care: The Experiences of Children, Parents and Social Workers*, London: Batsford/BAAF

Fox Harding, L. (1991) *Perspectives in Child Care Policy*, New York: Longman

Freeman, M. D. A. (1992) *Children, their Families and the Law*, Basingstoke: Macmillan

Freeman, P. and Hunt J. (1998) *Parental Perspectives on Care Proceedings:* London: The Stationery Office

Fundudis, T., Bemey, T. P., Kolvin, I., Famuyiwa, L., Barrett, L., Bhate, S. and Tyrer, S. P. (1991) 'Reliability and validity of two self-rating scales in the assessment of childhood depression', *British Journal of Psychiatry,* 159 (suppl. 11), pp. 36–40

Garbarino, J. (1986) *The Psychologically Battered Child: Strategies for Identification, Assessment and Intervention,* San Francisco: Josey Bass

Garbarino, J., Stott, F. and Faculty of Erikson Institute (1992) *What Children Can Tell Us: Eliciting, Interpreting and Evaluating Critical Information from Children,* San Francisco: Josey Bass

Gibbons, J. (ed) (1992) *The Children Act 1989 and Family Support: Principles into Practice,* London: HMSO

Gibbons, J., Thorpe, S. and Wilkinson, P. (1990) *Family Support and Prevention: Studies in Local Areas,* London: HMSO

Gibbons, J., Conroy, S. and Bell, C. (1995a) *Operating the Child Protection System,* London: HMSO

Gibbons, J., Gallagher, B., Bell, C. and Gordon, D. (1995b) *Development after Physical Abuse in Early Childhood,* London: HMSO

Giller, H. (1993) *Children in Need: Definition Management and Monitoring,* London: Department of Health

Griffiths Mental Development Scales: Record Book 1984, Buckingham: The Test Agency

Hallett, C. (1995) *Interagency Co-ordination and Child Protection,* London: HMSO

Hallett, C. (1993) in Waterhouse, L. (ed) *Child Abuse and Child Abusers: Protection and Prevention,* London: Jessica Kingsley

Hardiker, P., Exton, K. and Barker, M. (1991) *Policies and Practices in Preventive Child Care,* Aldershot: Avebury

Harter, S. (1993) 'Developmental perspectives on the self-system' in Mussen, P. (ed.) *Handbook of Child Psychology,* 4th edn, Chichester: Wiley

Hayes, M. (1995) Care by the family or care by the state?', *Modem Law Review,* Vol. 58, No. 6, November, pp. 878–87

Hoggett, B. (1993) *Parents and Children,* 4th edn, London: Sweet and Maxwell

Howe, D. (1992) 'Theories of helping, empowerment and participation' in Thoburn J. (ed.) *Participation in Practice: Involving Families in Child Protection. A Reader,* Norwich: University of East Anglia

Howe, D. (1995) *Attachment Theory for Social Work Practice,* Basingstoke: Macmillan

Howe, D. (1997) *Patterns of Adoption,* Oxford: Blackwell Science

Howe, D., Brandon, M., Hinings, D. and Schofield, G. (1999) *Attachment Theory, Child Maltreatment and Family Support: A Practice and Assessment Model,* Basingstoke: Macmillan

Hunt, J., Macleod A. and Thomas, C. (1999) *The Last Resort: Child Protection, the Courts and the 1989 Children Act,* London: The Stationery Office

Hunter Johnson, E. (1995) 'Working together for family support', *Family Support Newsletter,* No. 3, Norwich: Family Support Network

James, G. (1994) *Study of Working Together 'Part 8' Reports,* London: Department of Health

Jones, M. (1985) *A Second Chance for Families: Five Years Later. Follow-up of a Program to Prevent Foster Care,* New York: Child Welfare League of America

Kaganas, F. (1995) 'Partnership under the Children Act 1989: an overview' in Kaganas, F., King, M. and Piper, C., *Legislating for Harmony,* London: Jessica Kingsley

Kendall-Tackett K. A., Williams, L. M. and Finkelhor, D. (1993) 'Impact of sexual abuse on children: a review and synthesis of recent empirical studies' *Psychological Bulletin,* 113, pp. 164–80

Kovacs, M. and Beck, A. T. (1977) 'An empirical approach towards a definition of childhood depression' in Schulterbrand, J. G. and Raskin, A. (ed.) *Depression in Children: Diagnosis, Treatment and Conceptual Models,* New York: Raven Press

Kovacs, M. and Devlin, B. (1998) 'Internalising disorders in childhood', *Journal of Child Psychology and Psychiatry,* Vol. 39, No. 1, pp. 47–63

Lindley, B. (1994) *On the Receiving End: Families' Experiences of the Court Process in Care and Supervision Proceedings under the Children Act 1989,* London: Family Rights Group

Lynch, M. (1992) 'Child protection – have we lost our way?', *Adoption and Fostering,* Vol. 16, No. 4, pp. 15–22

Lynch, M. and Roberts, J. (1982) *Consequences of Child Abuse,* London: Academic Press

Marneffe, C. (1992) 'The Confidential Doctor Centre: a new approach to child protection work', *Adoption and Fostering,* Vol. 16, No. 4, pp. 23–8

Marris, P. (1986) *Loss and Change,* London: Routledge Kegan Paul

Marsh, P. and Crowe, G. (1998) *Family Group Conferences,* Oxford: Blackwell Science

Masson, J. (1994) 'Social engineering in the House of Lords: Re M', *Journal of Child Law,* Vol. 6, No. 4, pp. 145–92

Masson, J. and Morris, M. (1992) *The Children Act Manual,* London: Sweet and Maxwell

Millham, S., Bullock, R., Hosie, K. and Little, M. (1986) *Lost in Care,* Aldershot: Gower

Millham, S., Bullock, R., Hosie, K. and Little, M. (1989) *Access Disputes in Child Care,* Aldershot: Gower

Monck, E. and New, M. (1996) *Report of a Study of Sexually Abused Children and Adolescents, and of Young Perpetrators of Sexual Abuse who were Treated in Voluntary Agency Community Facilities,* London: Institute of Child Health

Morris, J. and Tunnard, J. (eds) (1996) *Family Group Conferences: Messages from UK Practice and Research,* London: Family Rights Group

National Children's Home (1994) *Factfile,* London: National Children's Home

NSPCC (1974) *Yo Yo Children,* London: NSPCC Publications

O'Hagan, K. (1993) *Emotional and Psychological Abuse of Children,* Buckingham: Open University Press

O'Hagan, K. and Dillenburger, K. (1995) *Abuse of Women within Child Care Work,* Buckingham: Open University Press

Okely, J. (1993) *The Traveller Gypsies,* Cambridge: Cambridge University Press

Owen, M. (1992) *Social Justice and Children in Care,* Aldershot: Avebury

Packman, J., Randall, J. and Jacques, N. (1986) *Who Needs Care? Social Work Decisions about Children*, Oxford: Basil Blackwell

Packman, J. and Hall, C. (1995) *The Implementation of Section 20 of the Children Act 1989: Report to the Department of Health*, Dartington: Dartington Social Research Unit

Packman, J. and Hall, C. (1998) *From Care to Accommodation: Support, Protection and Control in Child Care Services*, London: The Stationery Office

Parker, R. A., Ward, H., Jackson, S., Aldgate, J. and Wedge, P. (eds) (1991) *Looking after Children: Assessing Outcomes in Child Care*, London: HMSO

Parton, N. (1991) *Governing the Family: Child Care, Child Protection and the State*, Basingstoke: Macmillan

Parton, N. (1995a) 'Neglect as child protection: the political contest and the practical outcomes', *Children and Society*, Vol. 9:1, pp. 67–89

Parton, N. (1995b) 'Child welfare and child protection: the need for a radical rethink', Conference Paper from *Child and Family Support and Protection: A Practical Approach*, London: National Children's Bureau

Phillips, M. and Dutt, R. (1990) *Towards a Black Perspective in Child Protection*, London: London Race Equality Unit

Robinson, C. (1987) 'Key issues for social workers placing children for family-based respite care', *British Journal of Social Work*, 17:2 pp. 257–84

Robertson, J. R. and Eisenberg, J. L. (1981) *Technical Supplement to the Peabody Picture Vocabulary Test-Revised*, Circle Mines, MN: American Guidance Service

Rose, W. (1994) *Report of the Proceedings of the Annual Sieff Conference on Child Protection*, London: Sieff Foundation

Rutter, M., Tizard, J. and Whitmore, K. (eds) (1981) *Education, Health and Behaviour*, London: Longman

Rutter, M., Quinton, D. and Hill, J. (1990a) 'Adult outcomes of institution-reared children: males and females compared' in Howe, D. (1995) *Attachment Theory for Social Work Practice*, Basingstoke: Macmillan

Rutter, M., Quinton, D. and Hill, J. (1990b) 'Adult outcomes of institution-reared children: males and females compared' in Robins, L. N. and Rutter, M. (eds) *Straight and Devious Pathways from Childhood to Adulthood*, Cambridge: Cambridge University Press, pp. 135–57

Rutter, M. (1995) 'Psychosocial adversity: risk, resiliance and recovery', *Southern African Journal of Child and Adolescent Psychiatry*, Vol. 7 (2), pp. 75–88

Saifullah Kahn, V. (ed) (1979) *Minority Families in Britain: Support and Stress*, London: Macmillan

Sharland, E., Jones, D., Aldgate, J., Seal, H. and Croucher, M. (1996) *Professional Intervention in Child Sexual Abuse*, London: HMSO

Sieff Foundation (1994) *Family Support in Protecting the Child*, Surbiton: Michael Sieff Foundation

Sieff Foundation (1995) *Children in the Crossfire*, Surbiton: Michael Sieff Foundation

Social Services Inspectorate (1992) *The Children Act 1989. Court Order Study: A Study of Local Authority Decision-making about Public Law Court Applications*, London: HMSO

Social Services Inspectorate (1994) *The Children Act 1989. Contact Orders Study: A Study of Local Authority Decision-making around Contact Applications under Section 34*, London: HMSO

Social Services Inspectorate (1995a) *Children in Need*, London: HMSO

Social Services Inspectorate (1995b) *The Children Act 1989: Residence Orders Study*, London: HMSO

Stalker, K. (1990) *Share the Care: An Evaluation of a Family-based Respite Care Service*, London: Jessica Kingsley

Stevenson, O. (1996) 'Emotional abuse and neglect: a time for reappraisal', *Child and Family Social Work*, Vol. 1 (1), 13–18

Stevenson, O. (1998) *Neglected Children: Issues and Dilemmas*, Oxford: Blackwell Science

Thoburn, J. (1991a) 'The Children Act 1989: Balancing child welfare with the concept of partnership with parents', *Journal of Social Welfare and Family Law*, No. 5

Thoburn, J. (1991b) 'Permanent family placement and the Children Act 1989: implications for foster carers and social workers', *Adoption and Fostering*, 15, 3

Thoburn, J. (1992) 'Professional ethics and participation' in Thoburn, J. (ed.) *Participation in Practice*, Norwich: University of East Anglia

Thoburn J. (1994) *Child Placement: Principles and Practice*, Aldershot: Arena

Thoburn, J., Lewis, A. and Shemmings, D. (1995) *Paternalism or Partnership? Family Involvement in the Child Protection Process*, London: HMSO

Thoburn, J., Wilding, J. and Watson, J. (1999) *Family Support in Cases of Emotional Maltreatment and Neglect*, London: The Stationery Office

Thorpe, D. (1994) *Evaluating Child Protection*, Buckingham: Open University Press

US Department of Health and Human Services (1988) *Study Findings: National Incidence and Prevalence of Child Abuse and Neglect*, Washington: Department of Health and Human Services

United Nations Convention on the Rights of the Child (1989), Geneva: United Nations

Ward, H. (ed) (1995) *Looking After Children: Research into Practice*, London: HMSO

Waterhouse, L. (1993) (ed) *Child Abuse and Child Abusers*, London: Jessica Kingsley

White, R. (1996) 'Proof in care proceedings, *NLJ Practitioner*, January, pp. 51–4

Wilson, A. (1978) *Finding a Voice: Asian Women in Britain*, London: Virago

Wilson, J. and Raphael, B. (eds) (1993) *Handbook of Traumatic Stress Disorders*, New York: Plenum Press

Wilson, K. and James, A. (eds) (1995) *The Child Protection Handbook*, London: Ballière Tindall

Index

Index by Mary Norris